PRESERVING

PRESERVING

ODED SCHWARTZ

Photography by
IAN O'LEARY

Food Styling by
ODED SCHWARTZ

A DK Publishing Book

Project Editors: Jane Middleton, Kate Scott
Senior Editors: Carolyn Ryden, Nicky Graimes
Art Editor: Jane Bull
DTP Designer: Karen Ruane
Managing Editor: Susannah Marriott
Managing Art Editor: Toni Kay
Production Manager: Maryann Rogers
US Editor: Laaren Brown
US Consultants: Joan Whitman,
Rachel Carey Harper
Assistant Food Stylist: Alison Austin

*This book is dedicated to my mother,
Pnina Schwartz, the ultimate pickler: her
culinary creativeness is the inspiration
for my work*

First American Edition, 1996
2 4 6 8 10 9 7 5 3 1
Published in the United States by
DK Publishing Inc.
95 Madison Avenue
New York, New York 10016

Visit us on the World Wide Web at
http://www.dk.com

Library of Congress Cataloging-in-Publication Data
Schwartz, Oded.
Preserving / Oded Schwartz. --
1st American ed.
p.   cm.
ISBN 0-7894-1053-2
1. Food--Preservation.   I. Title.
TX601.S36 1996   96-10833
641.4--dc20   CIP

Reproduced in Italy by GRB Editrice, Verona
Printed and bound in Great Britain
by Butler & Tanner Ltd.

NOTE
Preserving and canning are not without their risks.
The procedures described in this book should be
taken only as general guidelines; for more specific
information, contact your agricultural extension
agent. For canning, use USDA-approved jars, and
sealants only; many of the jars shown here are
intended for illustration purposes only and are not
appropriate for heat processing or long-term storage.
DK Publishing assumes no responsibility for illness or
injury resulting from the use of this book.

Follow the same units of measurement throughout a
recipe; use either imperial or metric, but never
a mixture of the two.

CONTENTS

INTRODUCTION

BEING AN ISRAELI, I feel that pickling is in my blood. In the Middle East, the love of preserved food crosses all cultural and religious boundaries and is shared by Jews and Arabs, Muslims and Christians alike. Walk into any Middle Eastern food market and you will be amazed by the variety of pickles and preserves available: in the cool, dark interiors you will find a gastronomic Aladdin's cave, stuffed to the brim with exotic spices, oils, fish, and meats.

When I moved to England in the 1970s, I was disappointed by the lack of variety and availability of preserves that I had grown up to believe were everywhere. But the raw ingredients were all there — wonderful fresh fruit and vegetables, and different types of meat and fish. Armed with an extensive knowledge gleaned from my youth, I set out to develop and modify ancient recipes that would work better in the modern international market and appeal to a Western palate.
The culmination of my endeavors can be seen in this book, which covers a variety of preserving techniques, both sweet and sour. My aim has been to give these recipes a truly contemporary feel so that preserving can become as much a part of your life as it is of mine. They are easy to follow and practical, and take into account the constraints and pressures that exist in today's society.

There is a natural and continuous rhythm to the preserving year. Winter is a quiet period when fresh ingredients are often expensive and less readily available. It is the best time to make marmalades, clean out the pantry, and plan the year ahead. The onset of spring brings young shoots and tender vegetables, and when summer finally arrives the pace quickens as soft fruits come into season and markets are laden with ripened fruit and berries. Now is the time to make clear, fragrant jellies, jams, and sweet preserves. During late summer and fall, your kitchen should exude the delicious, sweet aroma of luscious fruit, spices, and drying herbs. It is also the traditional and most suitable time to cure meats and sausages, smoke fish, and make pâtés.

I sincerely hope that *Preserving* will encourage you to experience the pleasure and immense satisfaction of preserving your own food. Believe me, there are few things in life more enjoyable than producing your own pickles, relishes, and sauces, and consuming the fruit of your labor together with family and friends. Try it for yourself!

Oded.

7

PRESERVED GOODS in the author's pantry.

THE HISTORY OF PRESERVING

Today you can walk into any supermarket or delicatessen and be faced with a profusion of foods preserved in exciting and exotic ways. Even with the advent of modern preserving methods such as freezing and canning, many people still yearn for traditionally preserved goods. Ancient techniques, including pickling, smoking, and curing, add a distinctive and delicious flavor to fresh produce.

Moreover, preserves offer a comforting alternative to our usual ephemeral foods. In this age of microwave cookery and instant fast food, the art of preserving reminds us to observe the seasons and the changes that occur throughout the year. It also helps to revive our jaded senses and, especially for those of us living in an urban environment, can bring us closer to nature. In order to master this wonderful culinary art, we need to know something of its history and the evolution of the technical processes that are used today.

Why Food Spoils

Spoilage is caused by the natural deterioration of organic matter as a result of enzyme activity and the growth of yeasts, molds, and bacteria. These processes need certain conditions: a warm, moist, balanced pH environment and a supply of oxygen. Eliminate one or more of these factors and deterioration will be greatly slowed or will cease. Throughout history, people have discovered many ingenious and inventive ways to prevent spoilage: thus, the art of preserving has become of fundamental and lasting importance.

Sun, Wind, and Fire

It is safe to assume that drying was the first method of preservation to be discovered – a piece of meat left out and dried by the sun was found to have an appetizing smell, lasted longer than fresh meat, and was lighter and easier to transport. This discovery meant that there was no need to consume the meat at the site of a kill. It could be dried and transported to a safe, permanent settlement, and stored. This enabled our ancestors to begin to settle down; to organize their food supplies for the community; and to start to plan their lives. They were able to

PREPARED FISH hanging on poles in a nineteenth-century smokehouse.

SALT HAS ALWAYS been a valuable commodity: this illustration from a French manuscript, dated 1528, shows the measuring of salt according to royal regulation.

travel farther and explore more congenial environments, where food could be grown and animals reared. Slowly, the first primitive settlements gave way to more permanent hamlets and villages, laying down roots from which grew our present-day towns and cities.

Sun- and wind-drying were fine in hot, dry climates but not very practical in cold, damp environments. In areas where wood was abundant, fire and smoke were used to hasten the drying process. Smoked fish and meat were found to have a more savory smell and to last even longer, partly because the smoky coating deterred insects.

Salt of the Earth

Ancient peoples discovered the preserving qualities of salt. They found it to be a strong dehydrator, extracting moisture from tissues, drying them and creating an environment that inhibited the growth of harmful bacteria.

For our ancestors, salt became an essential commodity, highly prized and fiercely guarded: the first biblically recorded war was fought over the rights to control salt pans (Genesis 14:10). In ancient Egypt, large quantities of salt, together with vinegar and honey, were used in the process of mummifying. Salted meat and fish played an essential role in the medieval European diet – especially during Lent when salted fish was the only available source of protein. Salt reached a price that was sometimes higher than the value of the flesh preserved – "not worth its salt" indeed! Salted meat and fish were also convenient foodstuffs to take on board ship for long voyages, allowing sixteenth-century Europeans to explore and colonize, and change the course of world history.

Sweet and Deadly

Like salt, sugar is one of nature's most powerful poisons – in high concentrations it creates an environment that cannot support any living organism. In a historical context, sugar is a rather late arrival. It was unknown to the ancient Egyptians and Hebrews and is not mentioned in early Greek or Roman writings – their sweetener was honey from bees or fruit (concentrated nectar).

Originally, most sugar was refined from the sweet sap of the sugarcane, which is indigenous to the Indus Valley. A variety of wild grass, sugarcane was considered to be a gift from the gods and symbolized everything that was good on earth. The complicated technique of sugar refining was perfected at the courts of the emerging Arab Empire, which at one stage ruled almost all the known world. While Europe was in the depths of the "medieval winter," the

THE ROMANS used honey in the preservation of meat.

SUGAR being extracted and made into cones, illustrated in the fifteenth century.

VINEGAR IS PRODUCED from different types of alcohol, each one having its own distinctive color and flavor.

conquering Arab tribes were establishing a creative, indulgent, and luxurious way of life. Trading caravans from all corners of the ancient world brought rare and mysterious new culinary ingredients, spices and cooking techniques. In the kitchen, sugar was combined with fruit and spices and turned into fragrant syrups, halvas, marzipan, and candy.

In the twelfth century, Arab merchants and returning Crusaders brought sugar into Europe. Refined sugar soon became an essential ingredient in the laboratories of alchemists and apothecaries where it was used, literally, to sweeten bitter pills and potions. Sugar craft reached its peak in the wealthy kitchens of Renaissance Italy, where it was used to produce elaborate centerpieces made of sugar paste and lifelike candied fruit. But it was not until the sixteenth century, when sugar was introduced to Europe from the West Indies, that it became an indispensable ingredient, included in everything from candy and cakes to stews. It was later discovered that sugar plays an important role in curing meat, as it counteracts the toughening effect of salt. The Europeans' insatiable appetite for sugar had a devastating and everlasting effect on history, changing our palate and health forever, and encouraging the rise of colonialism and the slave trade.

Vinegar — the Acidic Element

Vinegar, the third essential preserving ingredient, works by creating an acidic environment in which contaminating bacteria cannot thrive. In grape-growing countries, vinegar is made from grapes; in brewing countries, from wheat and other grains. In the East, vinegar is made from rice and fruit. Vinegar is formed by an organic process: when wine or any other fruit-based or grain-based alcoholic brew is exposed to air, a bacterial reaction turns the alcohol into acetic acid.

Vinegar was the most important flavoring agent in the diets of our ancestors. It was used as a dip to add flavor and moisture to otherwise bland or strong-tasting ingredients — bread and bitter vegetables were always dipped in vinegar before eating — a habit that probably led to the development of our modern-day salads and salad dressings.

Oils and Fats

Our ancestors also discovered that food can be preserved by the exclusion of air. This technique is mentioned in the works of Apicius, who wrote the only surviving Roman cookbook. Honey and oil, ingredients through which air cannot pass, were routinely used in meat preservation. In the colder north, where oil was not available, animal fat was used in the same way. This technique is applied when making pâtés,

PRESERVING the summer's bounty.
Photograph from 1920.

HOMEMADE PRESERVES make a
colorful display in the kitchen.

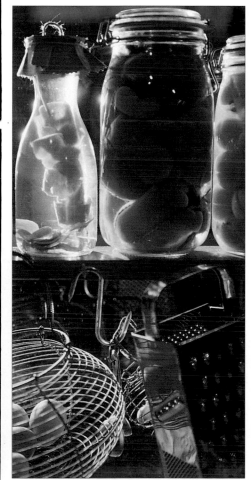

pies, rillettes, and confits. The same principle of preserving (preventing food from coming into contact with air) is behind modern practices such as vacuum-packing, bottling, and canning.

The Global Larder

The most interesting chapter in food preservation started with the European discovery of the "New World" and the sea route to India. This brought a flood of new and exciting ingredients and recipes. Eventually exotic pickles, cured meats, and jams and marmalades started to appear in many European cookbooks and began to influence our palates. By the end of the nineteenth century, the availability of cheap sugar, salt, and spices meant that eating preserves was no longer the privilege of the rich. The art of preserving food blossomed, and homemade jams, chutneys, and sauces appeared on even the most humble table.

For European colonists abroad, food preservation was essential — it meant survival. Living in isolation, surrounded by different cultures, these colonists also discovered that preserving was a way of remembering home. Yet the food these settlers cooked was often adapted, a combination of local ingredients and traditional know-how. Recipes from this time make fascinating reading — specialties from all parts of the world are amalgamated with indigenous ingredients and techniques, creating unique and delicious dishes. This is particularly evident in North America: where else can one find pastrami and salt herring, ketchup and piccalilli living in harmony with salsa, jerky, and chili sauce?

With the advantage of hindsight, we can see how ancient techniques have evolved to suit our hectic lifestyle, and how the art of preserving has had a fundamental impact on our development and survival. Food preservation not only makes sense economically, utilizing gluts of fresh fruit and vegetables and prolonging shelf life, it also provides an opportunity to improve the flavor of bland ingredients and create a *fond de cuisine* of ready-made sauces, relishes, and condiments upon which all creative cooking is based.

SAFETY PRECAUTIONS FOR PRESERVING

• Care should be taken at all times when making preserves. Many factors affect the end result: correct hygiene, temperature control, timing, acidity, and sugar levels, storage conditions, and shelf life are all vital. Refrigeration or heat processing lengthens shelf life and discourages bacteria.
• Study the text on safety and hygiene, sealing and heat processing (see pages 42–45) and the relevant technique before starting a recipe.

• Follow the instructions given in each recipe and do not consume anything that seems questionable (see page 186).
• Extra care should always be taken with foods for vulnerable groups, including pregnant women, young children, and the elderly. Current health guidelines recommend that those in such groups do not consume unpasteurized foods, and therefore they should not eat home-preserved products.

A GALLERY *of* PRESERVES

THIS INSPIRING gallery of fresh produce
shows how diverse preserving can be. It
illustrates the remarkable range of fresh
ingredients — both familiar and exotic —
that can be made into an array of visually
exciting and delicious preserves. Creative
serving suggestions enable you to turn these
convenient products into original and
appetizing dishes.

TOMATOES

FOR MANY COOKS the tomato is indispensable, yet its popularity is relatively recent. It was introduced to Europe from South America in the sixteenth century, but it was only when the Italians embraced it with enthusiasm in the nineteenth century that the tomato became widely known. In preserving, tomatoes can be used at all stages of maturity. Choose firm, vine-ripened, unblemished specimens with a good flavor; avoid greenhouse tomatoes because they have little flavor. Tomatoes are a very good source of vitamin C, which prevents oxidization and so helps maintain color.

TYPES OF TOMATO

There are many varieties of tomato to choose from: familiar red ones, like the flavorful plum tomato and enormous beefsteak tomato; green tomatoes, which are unripe red varieties rather than a separate strain; and more novel kinds such as tiny, sweet-fleshed yellow and red cherry tomatoes.

Yellow cherry tomatoes

Plum tomato

Red cherry tomatoes

Beefsteak tomato

Green tomato

Vine-ripened tomatoes

Round tomato

SERVING SUGGESTIONS

PEAR AND TOMATO CHEESE is *delicious on its own or with roast poultry. (See page 174 for recipe.)*

COOKED TOMATO AND PEPPER SALSA, *a Mexican-style relish, complements grilled foods. (See page 115 for recipe.)*

OVEN-DRIED TOMATOES PRESERVED IN OIL, *tasty with crème fraîche and basil. (See page 108 for recipe.)*

YELLOW TOMATO PRESERVE, essentially a sweet mixture, is enlivened with lemon zest. (See page 163 for recipe.)

SPICED CHERRY TOMATOES provide an evocative taste of summer. (See page 93 for recipe.)

PICKLED GREEN TOMATOES is an excellent way to use up a glut of unripe produce. (See page 92 for recipe.)

FERMENTED TOMATOES is a spicy variation on Brined Cucumbers. (See page 93 for recipe.)

RED TOMATO MARMALADE contains coriander seeds and lemon for a tangy taste. (See page 164 for recipe.)

TOMATO SAUCE is the indispensable topping for pizzas and pasta. (See page 112 for recipe.)

GREEN TOMATO CHUTNEY, a mild, fruity relish, is good with curries. (See page 120 for recipe.)

THE PEPPER FAMILY

LIKE TOMATOES, peppers were introduced to Europe from the New World, where they grow wild. The chili pepper quickly replaced peppercorns as the world's favorite hot seasoning, while its larger, milder cousins became indispensable ingredients in Mediterranean cooking. Large sweet peppers can be preserved in oil or vinegar and are often included in mixed vegetable pickles for their bright color. Fresh and dried chilies are an essential ingredient in savory preserves, from judiciously spiced traditional British chutneys to searingly hot chili pastes from Africa and the Middle East.

TYPES OF PEPPER

The *Capsicum* family includes dozens of chili peppers as well as mild peppers, ranging in color from the common red and green to purple and black. All are rich in vitamin C. Chilies tend to be smaller and slimmer than sweet peppers and, usually, elongated in shape.

Kenyan chili

Red pepper

Serrano chilies

Jalapeño chili

Guero chili

Orange pepper

Green pepper

Purple pepper

Light green pepper

Yellow pepper

"Tomato" pepper

Westland chilies

Anaheim chilies

Thai chilies

Habanero chilies

Caribe chili

Fresno chili

Dried bird's eye chilies

Dried chipotle chilies

Dried guajillo chilies

Dried red chilies

Dried ancho chili

SERVING SUGGESTIONS

SCHUG makes a superb topping for hummus, served with olive oil and a dusting of paprika. (See page 116 for recipe.)

CORN AND PEPPER RELISH is a tasty accompaniment to hamburgers. (See page 112 for recipe.)

HARISSA, layered with lemon slices, is served as a fiery side dish in North Africa. (See page 115 for recipe.)

THE PEPPER FAMILY

SCHUG, a Yemenite spice paste made with cilantro and green chilies. (See page 116 for recipe.)

HOT CRAB APPLE JELLY is spiced up with fresh red chilies. (See page 166 for recipe.)

HARISSA, a ferociously hot paste, is strictly for chili fans. (See page 115 for recipe.)

HUNGARIAN PICKLED PEPPERS are especially good made with fleshy "tomato" peppers. (See page 99 for recipe.)

CORN AND PEPPER RELISH is a traditional classic. (See page 112 for recipe.)

PEPPERS IN OIL, a variation on Charbroiled Vegetables in Oil, make an instant snack. (See page 106 for recipe.)

THE ONION FAMILY

SINCE ANTIQUITY, onions, shallots, and garlic have been almost essential items in every kitchen. They play an invaluable role in preserving — on their own they make delicious crunchy pickles and chutneys, and when combined with other ingredients, they add texture, flavor, and sweetness. If used raw in preserves, they should be salted, brined, or blanched. Onions and garlic do not keep well as they have a tendency to ferment easily, or to sprout and become bitter. It is best to buy them in small quantities and store by hanging in net bags or in a cool, dry, dark place.

TYPES OF ONION

Onions vary in size, flavor, and color and range from the mild, sweet Spanish variety to strong cooking onions. Shallots are interchangeable with onions, though they have a milder, more distinct flavor. Garlic can have white or purple skin, but both types taste the same.

Small pickling onions

Large pickling onion

White garlic

Purple garlic

Cooking onion

Silverskin onions

Yellow onion

Red Chinese shallots

Sweet Spanish onion

Red onion

White onion

Italian borretane onion

Long French shallot

Shallot

SERVING SUGGESTIONS

SHALLOT CONFITURE, a sweet but piquant Middle Eastern-style confection, turns lamb cutlets into a luxurious treat. (See page 161 for recipe.)

ONION MARMALADE makes a delicious filling for little pastry cases, served warm as canapés. (See page 164 for recipe.)

FRESH ONION CHUTNEY is an Indian appetizer, served with pappadoms and a dusting of cayenne pepper. (See page 121 for recipe.)

PICKLED SHALLOTS are prepared in exactly the same way as Pickled Onions. (See page 92 for recipe.)

PICKLED GARLIC, an ancient Persian recipe, has a mild, mellow flavor. (See page 92 for recipe.)

SHALLOT CONFITURE owes its rich, succulent texture to long, slow cooking over several days. (See page 161 for recipe.)

ONION MARMALADE has an affinity with sour-sweet flavors. (See page 164 for recipe.)

SHALLOT VINEGAR is a fragrant variation of Salad Vinegar. (See page 127 for recipe.)

ONION AND PEPPER PICKLE benefits from the refreshing flavor of mint. (See page 96 for recipe.)

PICKLED VEGETABLES, a two-color version made with onions and carrots. (See page 98 for recipe.)

THE SQUASH FAMILY

THIS DIVERSE FAMILY — made up of squashes, gourds, pumpkins, cucumbers, and melons — includes some of the first plants to be cultivated by ancient man. They come in a staggering variety of shapes, sizes, and colors, ranging from the huge Cinderella's carriage-type pumpkin to the petite cornichon. The group is divided into short-life, perishable summer squash, now available year-round, and long-lasting winter squash, in season from late summer to winter. All squash are very versatile — since they have a delicate flavor they can be used in both sweet and savory preserves.

TYPES OF SQUASH

Cucumbers, gherkins (a variety of cucumber especially suited to preserving), zucchini, white squash, Galia melons, and cantaloupes are all types of summer squash. Red kuri squash, butternut squash and pumpkins are all winter varieties.

Mini cucumber

Crookneck

Gherkin

White squash

Kabocha squash

Butternut squash

Galia melon

English cucumber

Summer squash

Green zucchini

Custard squash

Red kuri squash

Piel di sapo melon

Honeydew melon

Cantaloupe

Golden zucchini

Pumpkin

SERVING SUGGESTIONS

BREAD AND BUTTER PICKLE *turns a simple ham sandwich into a feast. (See page 97 for recipe.)*

MELON PICKLED LIKE MANGO *is a spectacular centerpiece for a cold buffet. (See page 101 for recipe.)*

PUMPKIN MARMALADE *makes a deliciously tangy filling for a sweet tart. (See page 164 for recipe.)*

THE SQUASH FAMILY

TOBY'S PICKLED CUCUMBERS
are a zesty sweet-and-sour relish.
(See page 98 for recipe.)

MELON BUTTER *has a subtle
fruity taste, enlivened by lemongrass.
(See page 172 for recipe.)*

BRINED CUCUMBERS
(**GHERKINS**) *contain
dill and chilies for
a flavorful pickle.
(See page 93 for recipe.)*

PUMPKIN MARMALADE *makes
an unusual contribution to breakfast.
(See page 164 for recipe.)*

MELON KONFYT *is a variation
on Fig Konfyt, a South African
specialty. (See page 160 for recipe.)*

OLIVE OIL PICKLE *has a mild
and refreshing flavor. (See page
97 for recipe.)*

**BREAD AND BUTTER
PICKLE** *goes well with mature
cheese. (See page 97 for recipe.)*

ROOT VEGETABLES

FOR CENTURIES NOW, root vegetables have formed the basis of winter fare; they keep well, supplying nourishment when little else is available. Traditionally, root vegetables are cooked before pickling, but I like to use mine raw to maintain their crunchiness and vitamin content. A lot of vitamins and trace elements are also found in the skin and, other than for aesthetic reasons (the peel tends to brown and wrinkle during preserving), there is no need to peel them unless they are old and thick-skinned. Root vegetables also make good jams as they have a high sugar content.

TYPES OF ROOT VEGETABLE

All root vegetables add good texture to preserves, while vibrant types, such as beets and carrots, add color as well. The oddball is kohlrabi – strictly speaking it is not a root but a swollen stem; it grows above ground.

Beet

Baby beet

Daikon radish (mooli)

Kohlrabi

Radishes

Turnips

Celeriac

European radish

Jerusalem artichoke

Parsnips

Carrots

SERVING SUGGESTIONS

CARROT AND ALMOND CHUTNEY *has a sour-sweet flavor that adds zest to a simple meat dish and salad. (See page 121 for recipe.)*

PICKLED TURNIPS *are served with Pickled Eggplants and Beets as an appetizer in the Middle East. (See pages 94 and 91 for recipes.)*

FERMENTED BEET *juice doubles as a light, refreshing borscht. Serve hot or cold, with sour cream and dill. (See Brined Cucumbers, page 93.)*

CARROT JAM, a Middle Eastern-style preserve, contains golden raisins and ginger. (See page 159 for recipe.)

PICKLED CELERIAC AND CARROT SALAD is flavored with dill seeds and orange. (See page 94 for recipe.)

PICKLED EGGPLANTS AND BEETS is a variation on Stuffed Pickled Eggplants. (See page 91 for recipe.)

TURNIP PRESERVE offers an unusual twist on Squash and Ginger Preserve. (See page 162 for recipe.)

PICKLED TURNIPS are given a vivid purple tint by the addition of a few beets. (See page 94 for recipe.)

CARROT AND ALMOND CHUTNEY has a delicate texture and bright color. (See page 121 for recipe.)

PICKLED BEETS are a popular variation of Pickled Onions. (See page 92 for recipe.)

MEAT

WHEN MAN DISCOVERED how to preserve meat, a new chapter in human development opened. The ability to transport long-lasting, protein-rich food over great distances enabled humans to create permanent settlements and start the slow process of land cultivation. For the recipes in this book, find a reliable butcher who can supply you with the best-quality meat that has been properly aged. Organically reared, free-range animals, which have matured naturally, give the best flavor. When preserving meat, always adhere to a very high standard of hygiene (see page 42).

TYPES OF MEAT

Lean cuts, such as beef and venison leg meat, are excellent for drying and curing. Fattier meat portions, including duck, goose, and pork, can be made into pâté. The latter also provide large quantities of fat, which is essential for potted goods.

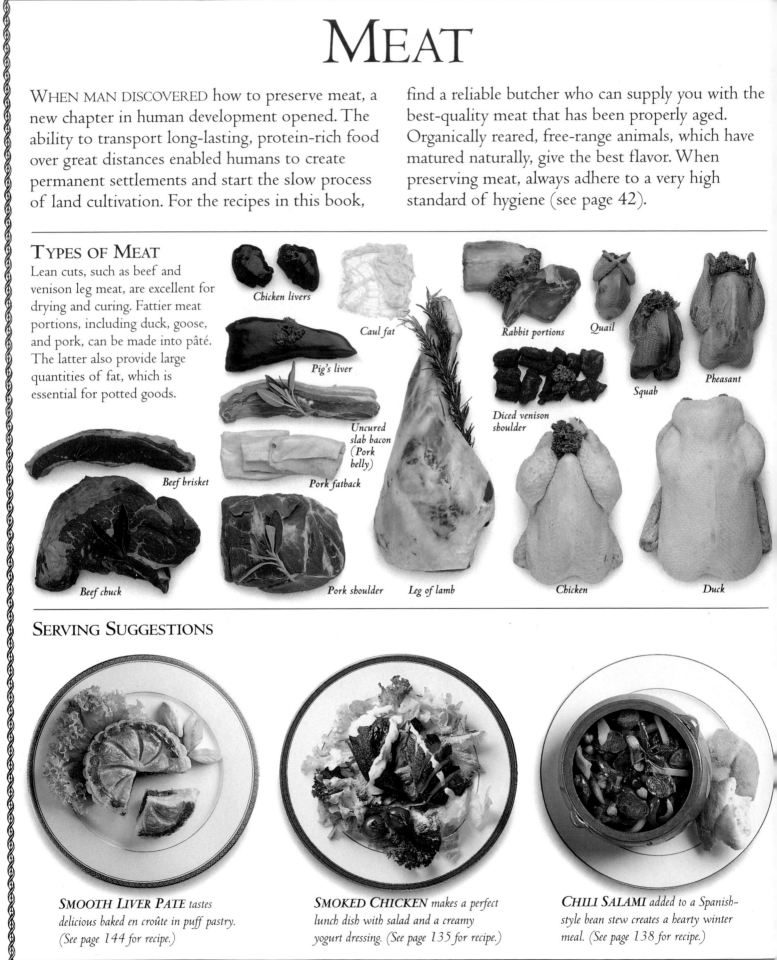

Chicken livers

Caul fat

Rabbit portions

Quail

Squab

Pheasant

Pig's liver

Diced venison shoulder

Uncured slab bacon (Pork belly)

Beef brisket

Pork fatback

Beef chuck

Pork shoulder

Leg of lamb

Chicken

Duck

SERVING SUGGESTIONS

SMOOTH LIVER PATE *tastes delicious baked en croûte in puff pastry.* (See page 144 for recipe.)

SMOKED CHICKEN *makes a perfect lunch dish with salad and a creamy yogurt dressing.* (See page 135 for recipe.)

CHILI SALAMI *added to a Spanish-style bean stew creates a hearty winter meal.* (See page 138 for recipe.)

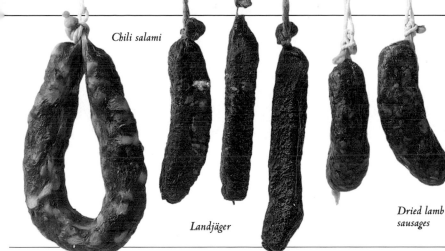

Chili salami

Landjäger

Dried lamb sausages

Garlic and herb salami

Wind-dried duck sausages

CHILI SALAMI, *similar to Spanish chorizo, is spiced with red chilies. (See page 138 for recipe.)*

LANDJAGER *are well-flavored dried sausages, made from beef and bacon. (See page 137 for recipe.)*

RILLETTES *is a coarse-textured, potted pork dish that makes excellent picnic fare. (See page 146 for recipe.)*

Preserved Toulouse sausages

DRIED LAMB SAUSAGES *are aromatic with fennel, paprika, and mint. (See page 136 for recipe.)*

GARLIC AND HERB SALAMI *can be thinly sliced and served with an aperitif. (See page 138 for recipe.)*

PRESERVED TOULOUSE SAUSAGES *are a versatile stand-by. (See page 136 for recipe.)*

RABBIT PATE *(above), a low-fat version of a traditional French recipe, includes carrots, shallots, and fresh herbs to keep it moist. Serve as a light lunch or appetizer. (See page 142 for recipe.)*

QUAIL AND PHEASANT PATE *(below) contains boned quail stuffed with baby spinach and fresh parsley. (See page 143 for recipe.)*

WIND-DRIED DUCK SAUSAGES *taste sweet and spicy. (See page 137 for recipe.)*

FISH & SEAFOOD

FOR PAST GENERATIONS, preserved fish — salted, cured, or smoked — was a staple food; today it is considered more of a delicacy. Fish and shellfish are a good source of essential fatty acids, vitamins, minerals, and trace elements. Preserved seafood develops a strong, distinctive aroma and flavor and, as in the case of anchovy paste or oyster sauce, can be used as a condiment to add instant piquancy to many dishes. Use only the freshest seafood that smells pleasantly of the sea. Fish should be bright, shiny, and firm to the touch; live mussels and clams should have tightly shut shells.

TYPES OF SEAFOOD

Use mussels, scallops, and oily fish — herring, salmon, mackerel, and tuna — for curing and smoking as they retain their moisture; white fish, such as cod, are more suited to drying and salting.

Scallops

Sardine

Squid rings

Baby squid

Mussels

Clams

Rainbow trout

Sprat

Octopus

Raw jumbo shrimp

Cooked jumbo shrimp

Large shrimp

Shrimp

Salmon

Herring

Tuna steak

Monkfish tail

SERVING SUGGESTIONS

ANCHOVIES IN OIL *form a tasty topping and a quick decoration for pizza.* (*See Salt-cured Sprats, page 153.*)

HERRINGS IN MUSTARD SAUCE & **HERRINGS IN CREAM SAUCE** *make a tasty lunch.* (*See page 151 for recipes.*)

GRAVLAX *is best eaten with a simple accompaniment such as dill and mustard sauce.* (*See page 153 for recipe.*)

ROLLMOPS *are a German delicacy that are traditionally served as an appetizer. (See page 150 for recipe.)*

ANCHOVIES IN OIL, *a tasty variation on Salt-cured Sprats. (See page 153 for recipe.)*

SEAFOOD IN OIL *is prepared with a variety of ingredients to make an attractive preserve. (See page 109 for recipe.)*

SMOKED TROUT *can be served like salmon. (See page 152 for recipe.)*

SALT-CURED SPRATS *just need soaking in water before using. (See page 153 for recipe.)*

PICKLED SALMON *(left) is a delicious preserve based on an old Canadian recipe. (See page 150 for recipe.)*

HERRINGS IN SPICED OIL *(above) are flavored with dried red chilies to make a piquant appetizer. (See page 109 for recipe.)*

CITRUS FRUIT

CITRUS FRUITS make delicious conserves and marmalades, yet they also play an essential role in preserving other types of fruit. Rich in pectin and acid, they are added to jams and jellies to help them jell. Do not discard the seeds as they contain the highest amount of pectin: tie them in a piece of cheesecloth and add to the boiling fruit. Citrus fruits are also a good source of vitamin C, a natural antioxidant that prevents the discoloration of fruit and vegetables. Most of the citrus fruits available have been waxed to prevent deterioration; remove the wax by scrubbing the fruit in warm, soapy water.

TYPES OF CITRUS FRUIT

Ranging from the small, sour-sweet kumquat to the large green pomelo, citrus fruits are very versatile and can be used to make pickles as well as the traditional marmalade. They can also be candied, dried, or preserved in alcohol.

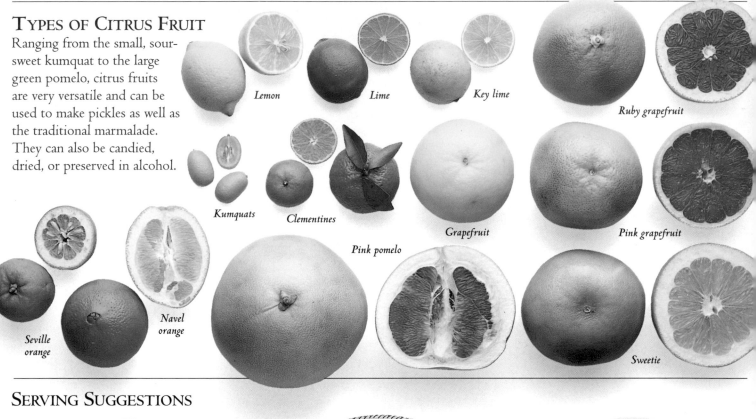

Lemon

Lime

Key lime

Ruby grapefruit

Kumquats

Clementines

Grapefruit

Pink grapefruit

Pink pomelo

Seville orange

Navel orange

Sweetie

SERVING SUGGESTIONS

LEMON CURD *makes a quick and refreshing filling for tarts. (See page 173 for recipe.)*

PRESERVED LEMONS *add piquancy to Moroccan-style chicken. (See page 102 for recipe.)*

FRESH CRANBERRY AND ORANGE RELISH *is perfect with roast turkey. (See page 112 for recipe.)*

DRIED ORANGE PEEL *gives stewed fruit and pies an instant citrus note. (See Oven-drying Chart, page 185.)*

PICKLED LIMES *add zest to hot and spicy foods. (See page 100 for recipe.)*

CITRUS VINEGAR *is Salad Vinegar with a skewer of orange peel added, to impart an intense flavor. (See page 127 for recipe.)*

LEMON CURD *has a rich and creamy taste — delicious on scones. (See page 173 for recipe.)*

SPICED WHOLE ORANGES *are studded with cloves to make a Christmas delicacy. (See page 100 for recipe.)*

PRESERVED LEMONS, *salted and steeped in lemon juice, have a sharp, tangy flavor. (See page 102 for recipe.)*

ORANGE MARMALADE WITH CORIANDER *is enhanced with an orange-based liqueur. (See page 163 for recipe.)*

29

ORCHARD FRUIT

IN ART AND LITERATURE, orchard fruits have long been used to symbolize everything that is good and luscious. Most orchard fruits, especially apples, are high in pectin and therefore play an important role in jam- and jelly-making. Although you can use apples on their own, they lose their flavor in cooking and are mainly added to boost the pectin content of other fruit. The peel and cores can be made into a pectin "stock" (see page 47), as the highest level of pectin is found in the skin and seeds or pits of fruit. Today, different varieties of most orchard fruits are readily available year-round.

TYPES OF ORCHARD FRUIT

Orchard fruit comes in hundreds of different varieties, colors, and flavors. Usually the cooking varieties are more acid and have a solid, compact flesh that will withstand the cooking process.

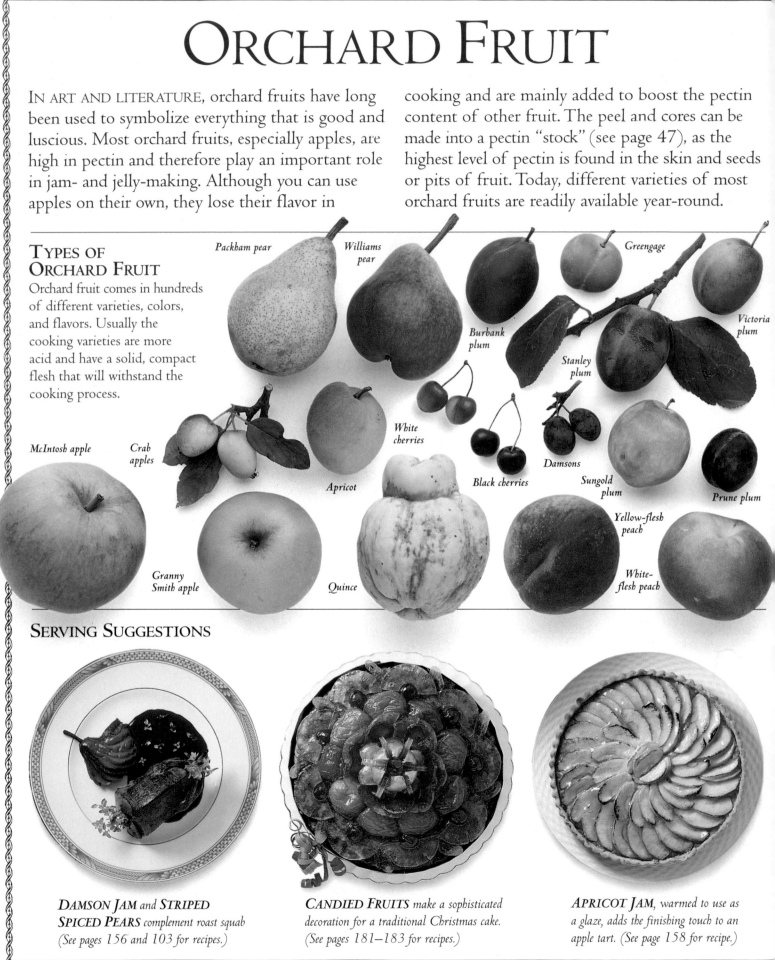

Packham pear
Williams pear
Greengage
Burbank plum
Victoria plum
Stanley plum
White cherries
McIntosh apple
Crab apples
Apricot
Black cherries
Damsons
Sungold plum
Prune plum
Yellow-flesh peach
Granny Smith apple
Quince
White-flesh peach

SERVING SUGGESTIONS

DAMSON JAM and **STRIPED SPICED PEARS** complement roast squab (See pages 156 and 103 for recipes.)

CANDIED FRUITS make a sophisticated decoration for a traditional Christmas cake. (See pages 181–183 for recipes.)

APRICOT JAM, warmed to use as a glaze, adds the finishing touch to an apple tart. (See page 158 for recipe.)

GREENGAGE JAM, a variation on Plum Jam, is a traditional French country preserve. (See page 156 for recipe.)

PEARS IN EAU DE VIE (right) are subtly spiced with a vanilla pod. (See page 179 for recipe.)

PLUM JAM (left) can be made with any variety of plum; here, mirabelle plums give an orange hue. (See page 156 for recipe.)

DAMSON JAM (right), based on Plum Jam, has a sharp flavor that goes with savory and sweet dishes. (See page 156 for recipe.)

MINTED APPLE JELLY is an ideal way to use windfall apples and fresh garden mint. (See page 167 for recipe.)

APRICOT JAM develops a mild almond flavor if a few apricot kernels are added. (See page 158 for recipe.)

PEACH CHUTNEY, a light and fragrant preserve, is good for cooling down hot curries. (See page 125 for recipe.)

SOFT FRUIT

IN MIDSUMMER fresh berries flood the markets; high in pectin and acid, they make wonderful jams, jellies, and sweet preserves. Choose baskets of firm, unblemished fruit with no bruises or mold. Check the bottom of each container for any leakage of juice – a sign of squashed fruit. Soft fruits do not keep well as they contain large amounts of water and should be used as soon as possible. For jellies and jams, the fruit should be slightly underripe, so the pectin content is at its highest; fully ripe fruits are best suited to drying or for making brightly colored, crystal-clear vinegars.

TYPES OF SOFT FRUIT

Fresh, soft summer fruits appear in a large variety of colors, from festive, rich blackberries, through the cool and elegant green of gooseberries, to the dark blue, almost purple, blueberries. Pretty and full of flavor, they make excellent preserves.

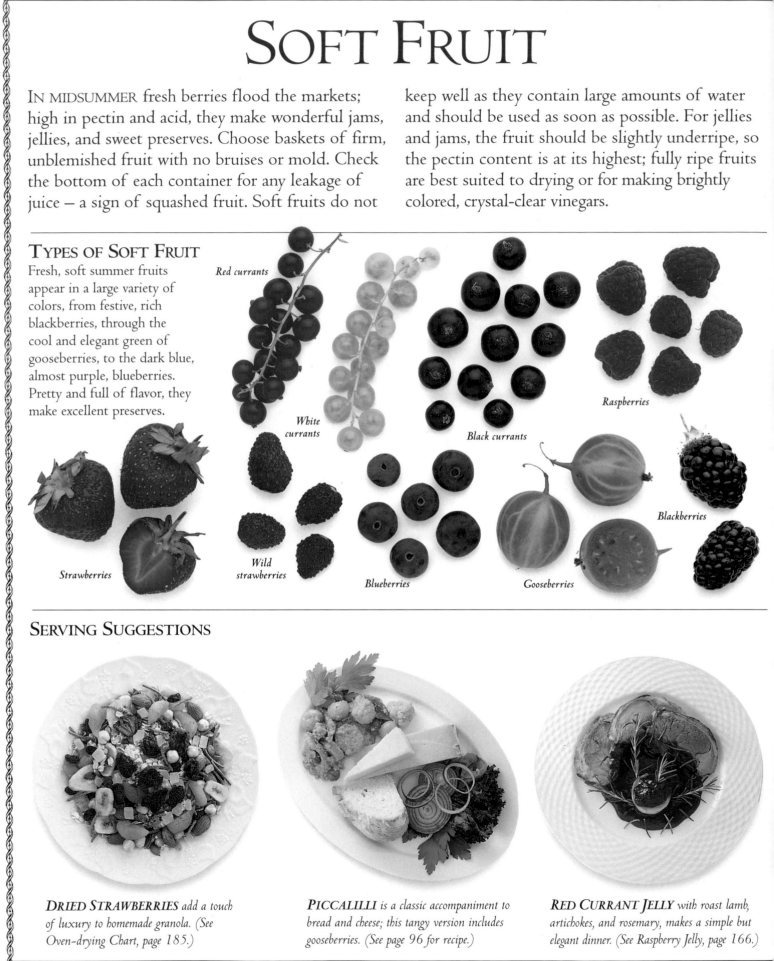

Red currants

White currants

Black currants

Raspberries

Strawberries

Wild strawberries

Blueberries

Gooseberries

Blackberries

SERVING SUGGESTIONS

DRIED STRAWBERRIES add a touch of luxury to homemade granola. (See Oven-drying Chart, page 185.)

PICCALILLI is a classic accompaniment to bread and cheese; this tangy version includes gooseberries. (See page 96 for recipe.)

RED CURRANT JELLY with roast lamb, artichokes, and rosemary, makes a simple but elegant dinner. (See Raspberry Jelly, page 166.)

RASPBERRY JELLY, *a translucent preserve, has a delicate flavor. (See page 166 for recipe.)*

RED CURRANT JELLY, *a variation on Raspberry Jelly, makes a good glaze. (See page 166 for recipe.)*

STRAWBERRY VINEGAR (right) has a skewer of strawberries and basil added to the bottle for a particularly intense flavor. (See page 128 for recipe.)

Gooseberry vinegar

Black currant vinegar

PICCALILLI *contains bite-sized chunks of crisp vegetables and refreshing summer fruit. (See page 96 for recipe.)*

FRUIT VINEGARS (left) subtly enhance sauces, marinades, and salad dressings, and many of them can be diluted to make a refreshing drink. (See page 128 for recipes.)

BLUEBERRY JAM *is the perfect accompaniment to pancakes and waffles. (See page 157 for recipe.)*

RASPBERRY JAM *is densely packed with juicy berries for a year-round taste of summer. (See page 157 for recipe.)*

EXOTIC FRUIT

THERE IS NO ULTIMATE definition of an exotic fruit – what is unusual and foreign in one part of the world may be considered commonplace and humble in another. Most exotic fruits have evocative aromas and vibrant colors, which enhance and flavor other foods; they also make the most wonderful preserves. Buy your fruit from a store that has a fast turnover so you get the freshest produce possible. Look for specimens without any bruising and, when applicable, a good fragrance. Store in a cool, dark place and use quickly while the fruits are still at their best.

TYPES OF EXOTIC FRUIT

The variety of exotic fruits available in the market is ever increasing, so this gallery includes a sampling of some of the fruits from around the world, as well as those grown in the subtropics and tropics.

Prickly pears

Kiwi fruit

Litchis

Fresh dates

Passion fruit

Guavas

Persimmon

Sharon fruit

Mangoes

Pineapple

Baby pineapple

Fresh figs

Dessert banana

Finger bananas

Red bananas

Pomegranates

SERVING SUGGESTIONS

PINEAPPLE CHUTNEY *perfectly complements the flavor of fried chicken. (See Pumpkin Chutney, page 120.)*

MANGO BUTTER *served in a tartlet case with a crème anglaise sauce makes an appealing dessert. (See page 172 for recipe.)*

KIWI FRUIT BUTTER *can be used as an unusual filling for pancakes. (See page 172 for recipe.)*

FIG CHUTNEY *makes an exciting accompaniment to cheese dishes and is excellent with sandwiches. (See page 125 for recipe.)*

PINEAPPLE IN KIRSCH *is delicious served with cream for an indulgent dessert. (See page 179 for recipe.)*

KIWI FRUIT AND RED PEPPER PICKLE *is the perfect partner to cold meat. (See page 102 for recipe.)*

SPICY PRICKLY PEAR JELLY *made with purple fruit has the brightest color. (See page 169 for recipe.)*

POMEGRANATE SYRUP *can be diluted as a drink or used as a sauce for ice cream. (See page 181 for recipe.)*

HOT MANGO CHUTNEY *adds heat and a tangy, fruity flavor to curries. (See page 123 for recipe.)*

DATE BLATJANG (DATE SAUCE) *is a favorite in South Africa. (See page 116 for recipe.)*

PRESERVING EQUIPMENT & TECHNIQUES

LEARN THE BASIC SKILLS of preserving with this photographically illustrated step-by-step guide. Besides the well-known techniques of pickling and jam-making, these easy-to-follow recipes feature the less familiar practices of salting, curing, and sausage-making. In addition, a visual guide to the most useful equipment and the basic ingredients, together with practical advice on safety and hygiene, provides you with all the essentials necessary for successful preserving.

EQUIPMENT

GOOD-QUALITY kitchen equipment is essential for successful and efficient preserving. Most of the equipment shown below can be found in a typical kitchen, but a few items, such as the mechanical shredders and grinders, pots and pans, and other specialized utensils, are required to make preserving easier: you can find most of these in a good kitchen store. Top-quality utensils might be expensive, but they will last you a long time. Some equipment, such as the dehydrator and smoker, can be obtained from specialty stores and suppliers of outdoor equipment.

Large chef's knife

Filleting knife

Boning knife

Kitchen scissors

KNIVES: Sharp knives are essential. Select the best quality you can afford, with solid, well-balanced handles. Sharpen your knives frequently to maintain them.

Mandoline

Hand grater

GRATERS AND MANDOLINES: Ease the task of slicing and shredding vegetables into neat, even slices. Choose a good-quality mandoline with an adjustable blade.

FOOD MILLS: Useful for puréeing fruit and vegetable mixtures.

Paring knife

Hardwood cutting board

GRINDERS: Good for chopping fruit for butters and curds as well as grinding meat.

Food mill

Canelle knife

Zester

Corer

Floating blade peeler

Mortar and pestle

Coffee grinder

PEELERS, CORERS, AND ZESTERS: Make short work of preparing fruit and vegetables.

GRINDERS: The traditional mortar and pestle is ideal for coarsely grinding small quantities of spices. For fine powders use an electric coffee grinder or spice mill.

Hand grinder

Grinding blades

Grinder attachment

Sausage-making nozzle

ELECTRIC GRINDERS: Essential if you frequently make sausages. They are available as an attachment to many food mixers. Many also have a sausage-making device.

HAND-HELD SAUSAGE-MAKERS: These are available from specialty suppliers (see page 192).

Sausage maker

Wooden spoons

Measuring spoons

Measuring cup

Meat thermometer

Candy thermometer

Narrow spatulas

MEASURING EQUIPMENT: Use glass, china, or stainless-steel, and always avoid corrosive metals such as aluminum.

WOODEN SPOONS: Keep a separate set for sweet and savory products.

NARROW SPATULAS: Useful for smoothing surfaces.

Funnel

Jam funnel

Calico

Cheesecloth

Jelly bag

Coffee filter paper

FUNNELS AND STRAINERS: Funnels make filling jars simpler; metal strainers should not be used with acidic fruit as metal can affect colors and flavors.

SKIMMING SPOONS: Skimming is important for a crystal-clear jam or jelly. Use slotted or perforated spoons or special skimmers. Always dip them in cold water before use.

Nylon sieve

JELLY BAGS AND FILTERS: Unbleached cheesecloth or calico are ideal for filtering and straining. Always sterilize before use (see page 42). For filtering small quantities of liquid, use coffee filters.

Meat hooks

Kitchen string

Ladle

Slotted spoon

Skimmer

Colander

39

BOWLS: A variety of sizes is essential. Use large for steeping and mixing, medium-sized for measured ingredients. Avoid bowls made of corrosive materials.

Stainless-steel mixing bowl

Glass mixing bowls

COPPER PANS: A wide preserving pan with a narrow bottom is ideal for making jams and jellies. Always keep scrupulously clean and never use with any acidic foods.

CHOOSE A PAN with a capacity of about 10 quarts (9 liters)

NONCORROSIVE PANS: A stainless-steel preserving pan is essential for making chutney and pickles that contain a high concentration of acid.

A THICK, HEAVY BASE prevents hot spots and keeps the preserve from burning

DEHYDRATORS

Drying can be carried out in a domestic oven, but if you intend to dry large quantities of produce, it is advisable to buy a special dryer. Although relatively expensive, domestic dehydrators are flexible, efficient, consume very little energy, and are easy to use. Always follow the manufacturer's instructions.

THE DESIGN OF these trays allows fast, even drying with no need for rotation and no tainting of flavors

STACKABLE TRAYS enable you to dry different quantities of fruits and vegetables. Drying pressure increases automatically

ADJUSTABLE THERMOSTAT for temperature settings

SMOKERS

A domestic smoker is a wonderful luxury. Choose a model that is easy to operate and clean, and has an automatic temperature and time control. Make sure that your smoker allows you to smoke food at low temperatures — in many models this is an optional extra. Season your smoker before using it for the first time. Always use outdoors.

THE SMOKE BOX controls and directs the flow of smoke. Hardwood chips provide the smoke

VARIABLE TEMPERATURE CONTROL and timer settings, found on some models, allow food to be smoked at just the right temperature and for the correct length of time

THE STEEL DOOR is airtight and should be left ajar when the oven is not in use

CONTAINERS

A SELECTION of containers is required for both visual and practical reasons. For storing moist foods and liquids, always select nonabsorbent materials such as glazed earthenware, enamel, glass, porcelain, or stainless steel. Avoid vessels made of corrosive material, such as aluminum, or plastic, which tends to stain and absorb flavors. Before using a container, check to make sure it has no chips or cracks, then wash it well. Sterilize all storage containers thoroughly before use (see page 42).

HEATPROOF CONTAINERS

Patés, potted goods, and other preserves that are baked in the oven, require glass, earthenware, porcelain, or enameled heatproof containers. Select dishes that complement the color of the finished product. Glass is the ideal material to show bottled preserves at their best and is also noncorrosive. Reused glass jars are only suitable for short-term storage. For long-term preservation, it is advisable to use new canning jars that are suited to high temperatures and have noncorrosive seals.

Porcelain ramekins

Enameled rectangular terrine

Earthenware ramekin

Earthenware bowl

Earthenware oval terrine

Earthenware crock

WIDE-MOUTH JARS are essential for recipes using whole fruits or vegetables

DECORATIVE BOTTLES can be used for flavored oils and vinegars

MAKE SURE stoppers or lids provide an airtight seal

HYGIENE & SAFETY

IT IS CRUCIAL to follow strict hygiene and safety practices. Common sense and diligence about timing, temperature, and cleanliness are essential for preventing food contamination. Make sure that all the ingredients you use are in prime condition, and keep them at the recommended temperatures at all times. Kitchen surfaces and utensils must be kept thoroughly clean. Wipe down surfaces with a sterilizing solution before you start and as you work. Be certain that all preserves are properly sealed (see opposite) before storing, then check them regularly and discard any that show signs of deterioration, or have an unpleasant smell, uneven discoloration, or broken seals (see page 186).

Hygiene and Safety with Meat

Extra care must be taken when preserving meat. If the following hygiene precautions are observed, you should have no difficulty in enjoying the preserved meat products in this book.

• The kitchen must be scrupulously clean. Use a separate set of sterilized utensils for meat and keep them in pristine condition.
• Sterilize equipment in boiling water. Plastic utensils can be cleaned with sterilizing tablets or in the kind of sterilizer used for babies' bottles.
• Warm, moist hands encourage bacterial growth. Wash them frequently with antibacterial soap and always dry them well on a clean towel or paper towel. Keep your nails short and well scrubbed.
• Always work in a cool, but well-ventilated kitchen, ideally between 50–54°F (10–12°C).

• Always buy the best-quality meat you can afford from a reliable butcher, and tell him the purpose of your purchase.
• Never allow meat to become warm: keep it refrigerated at 40°F (4°C). Check the temperature of your refrigerator to ensure it is working efficiently.
• Follow the recipes accurately and always use the recommended quantities of saltpeter, salt, and sugar. Never guess amounts.
• Check your stored products regularly and discard any that develop an unpleasant smell, or show any signs of mold or deterioration (see page 186).

SALTPETER WARNING

There is some controversy about saltpeter (sodium or potassium nitrate). Saltpeter is a naturally occurring substance that, when used in very small quantities, ensures the safety of preserved meats by inhibiting the growth of harmful bacteria. Sodium nitrate (and a similar substance, sodium nitrite) is added to commercially cured meats and I would not recommend drying or curing meat without it.

• Saltpeter is available from drugstores and agricultural supply stores.
• Store it very safely: keep it clearly labeled and out of the reach of all children and pets.
• When using saltpeter, measure it accurately and make sure it is evenly mixed with the other ingredients.
• All the recipes in this book that use saltpeter are marked with this symbol: ✳.

Sterilizing Methods

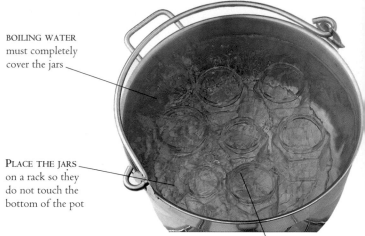

BOILING WATER must completely cover the jars

PLACE THE JARS on a rack so they do not touch the bottom of the pot

MAKE SURE THE JARS do not touch each other or the sides of the pot

BOILING WATER METHOD (preferred)
Sterilize heatproof canning jars (and bottles) before use. Place the washed jars in a deep pot and cover with boiling water. Bring to a boil and boil rapidly for 10 minutes. Drain jars upside down on paper towels, or leave immersed until ready to use. Also sterilize all lids, rubber seals, and corks in boiling water.
Sterilize cheesecloth and **jelly bags** by pouring boiling water through them.

JARS MUST BE without chips or cracks; wash them in hot, soapy water before sterilizing

OVEN METHOD
Place jars on a paper towel-lined tray and place in an oven preheated to 325°F (160°C) for 10 minutes. Allow to cool slightly, then fill with the hot product.

LINE THE TRAY with paper towels to diffuse the heat

FILLING & SEALING

TYPES OF CONTAINER

Always use sterilized containers with the appropriate lids or seals. Use vinegar-proof lids to seal pickles and chutneys, and waxed paper disks and cellophane seals for sweet preserves that will be refrigerated. For long-term storage, canning jars and heat processing are essential (see pages 44–45).

Jam jars

Cellophane seals *Waxed paper disks*

Elastic bands

Corks

Candle wax

Sealing wax

Glass bottle

Filling and Sealing Jars Without Lids

DAMPEN THE CELLOPHANE disk before use

1 Use a ladle and a jam funnel to fill the hot, sterilized jar. Fill the jar to within ½ in (1cm) of the top.

2 Wipe the rim clean with a damp cloth and carefully smooth a waxed paper disk onto the jam (waxed side down).

3 Wipe the cellophane disk with a wet cloth, place over the top, moist side up, and secure with an elastic band. Keep sealed preserves in the refrigerator.

Filling and Sealing Bottles

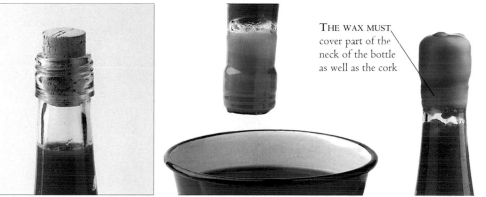

THE WAX MUST cover part of the neck of the bottle as well as the cork

1 Use a ladle and non-corrosive funnel to fill the hot, sterilized bottle to within 1½ in (3.5cm) of the top. Wipe the rim clean.

2 Soak a good-quality cork in hot water for a few minutes. Push it into the bottle as far as it will go, then tap in with a wooden mallet to within ¼ in (5mm) of the top.

3 When the bottle is cold, tap down the cork level with the top using a wooden mallet. Dip the top of the bottle several times into melted candle or sealing wax, allowing the wax to set between applications.

HEAT PROCESSING

Heat processing, also known as boiling-water bath, is essential to keep any bottled or canned preserve without refrigeration, as it greatly reduces the chance of contamination by molds and bacteria. It is especially important for preserves with low acidity, or a low sugar or salt content, which might not be safe after only 3–4 days. The high temperature and exclusion of oxygen produce an environment in which most spoilants cannot survive. The technique is simple: the preserve is packed into sterilized jars or bottles, sealed tightly, and immersed in water. It is then heated to boiling point and boiled for a specific length of time (see box, opposite). On cooling, the contents contract, creating a vacuum. Store in a cool, dry, dark place for no more than two years, checking for any signs of deterioration (see page 186).

TYPES OF CONTAINER

Canning jars come in many shapes and sizes. Select the type that is readily available, for which spare new lids or rubber rings can be found easily. It is always advisable to use new containers that have acid-resistant seals. The two-piece lid and screwband combination is ideal; the lid makes it easier to see that a vacuum has formed or if the seal is broken. In some areas, bail-type jars are no longer recommended for heat processing.

Bail-type jar

Vacuum one-piece lidded canning jar

Vacuum lid and screwband canning jar

Bottles must have a ridge so corks can be secured

Clamp-top bottles must have new rubber seals

Kitchen string

Good-quality corks

One-piece lid

Lid and screwband seal

Rubber seal must be new

Heatproof bottle

Clamp-top bottle

Bail-type Jar

1 Place the new, sterilized rubber ring (see page 42) on the edge of the lid. Grip the lid tightly with one hand and fit the ring over it.

2 Fill the hot, sterilized jar to within ½ in (1 cm) of the top or to the manufacturer's mark. Clamp the lid shut, using a cloth to hold it steady.

Lid and Screwband Jar

1 Fill the hot, sterilized jar (see page 42) to within ½ in (1 cm) of the top. Wipe the rim and cover with the sterilized rubber-edged lid.

2 Hold the jar with a cloth and screw the band until just tight, or according to the manufacturer's instructions. The jar is ready for heat processing.

Sealing Bottles

1 Cork the bottle (see page 43), then make a shallow cut in the top of the cork. Cut a piece of string 20in (50cm) long and, keeping one end 4in (10cm) longer than the other, secure it in the cut, as shown right.

FORM A LOOP with the long end of the string

PLACE THE OTHER END of the string inside the loop

2 Loop the long end of the string around the neck of the bottle, then insert the end of it through the front of the loop.

3 Pull both ends of the string down, to tighten the loop, and tie the loose ends over the cork in a double knot, as shown right.

MAKE SURE the cork is tied securely: it must stand up to the pressure inside the bottle when it is heat processed

Heat Processing

1 Wrap each jar or bottle in a few layers of cloth or folded newspaper to prevent them from bumping against each other. Stand them on a metal rack placed in the bottom of a large lidded pan.

3 Remove from the heat and lift out the jars with tongs. Place on a rack or cloth-covered surface, tighten screwbands immediately, then let cool completely. As the jars cool a partial vacuum is formed.

— TIP —

If a vacuum seal has not formed properly on any preserving jar, refrigerate the product and use within 1 week.

2 Pour in enough hot water to cover the lids or corks by at least 1in (2.5cm). Cover, bring to a boil, and boil for the stated time (see below). Check the water level occasionally and top off, if necessary.

4 To check the seal, gently undo the clamp or screwband and grip the rim of the lid with your fingertips. Carefully lift the jar. If sealed it will support the weight. One-piece lidded jars will dip in the center if a vacuum has formed. If using corked bottles, rest them on their sides to check for any leaks, then seal with melted wax before storing (see Filling and Sealing Bottles, step 3, page 43).

GENERAL HEAT PROCESSING TIMES

The following times are to be used as guidelines. See page 192 for helpful resources.

Jams, Jellies, and Pickled Products (pints, packed hot): process in sterilized jars 5 minutes after returning to a boil.

Tomatoes and other items that are not high in sugar, salt, or vinegar (pints, packed hot): process in sterilized jars 20 minutes after returning to a boil.

Ketchups and Chutneys (pints, packed hot): process in sterilized jars 10 minutes after returning to a boil.

NOTE: For altitudes more than 1,000 feet, boil an additional 1 minute for every 1,000 feet.

BASIC SKILLS

THE VARIOUS SKILLS described on these pages are designed to help ensure that your preserves, from jams and jellies to cured meats and pickles, are successful and trouble-free. They are simple, yet essential techniques, some of which you may be familiar with already. Each one is referred to frequently in the extensive range of preserving recipes that follow on pages 53–182.

Blanching

Blanching plays an important role in preserving as it destroys the enzymes in fruits and vegetables that cause their deterioration and discoloration on exposure to the air (known as oxidation). **Green vegetables** are usually blanched in salted water (1 tablespoon salt to every 1 quart/1 liter water), while **fruits** are blanched in acidulated water (3 tablespoons vinegar or lemon juice or 2 teaspoons citric acid to every 1 quart/1 liter water).

1 Place the ingredients in a wire basket and immerse in a large pan of rapidly boiling water. Return to a boil as quickly as possible and blanch for the required time.

2 Drop the contents of the basket into a bowl of ice water, ensuring that they are submerged. This stops the cooking process and refreshes them. Drain well before use.

Peeling Tomatoes

The simplest way to peel tomatoes is to immerse them in boiling water: this loosens the skin, making it easy to remove. Peaches can be prepared in exactly the same way, while onions are left unscored and steeped in the water until cool enough to handle.

1 Remove any stems and score each base lightly. Place in a bowl and cover with boiling water for a few seconds.

2 Drain off the boiling water and cover with cold water. Peel off the loosened skin with the help of a knife.

Weighting Down

Weighting down keeps the ingredients immersed under liquid, protecting them from the deteriorating effects of oxidation. Use nonporous objects that can be sterilized easily, such as a water-filled glass bottle or jar, or a glazed plate. When using a wide-mouth jar, a mesh made of wooden skewers can be added to the top of the container to keep the contents submerged. After weighting down, check that there is enough liquid to cover the ingredients by at least ½ in (1cm), and add more if necessary.

A BOTTLE OR JAR filled with water makes a useful weight

FOR PATES AND MEAT use smooth, clean pebbles (or cans of food) to weight down a foil-covered piece of cardboard

STERILIZED PEBBLES can be added to jars to keep the ingredients submerged. Do not use with delicate foods that could be crushed

A PLATE PLACED in the top of a bowl will keep soaking fruits and vegetables immersed in the liquid

Pectin Test

A jam or jelly requires pectin to jell. You can test its content in fruits, as shown below, and increase it by adding a third to a half the total volume of fruit pulp in pectin stock. Test again and increase the sugar content in the recipe if necessary (see page 76).

TESTING FOR PECTIN CONTENT

Place 1 tablespoon each of the cooked, unsweetened fruit juice and denatured alcohol in a bowl. Stir together for a few minutes, until it starts to clot. A large lump indicates a high pectin level, while small clots indicate a low pectin level.

PECTIN STOCK
(makes about 1 quart/1 liter)

Core 2lb (1kg) apples, reserving the cores, and chop in a food processor. Place the chopped fruit and the cores in a noncorrosive saucepan with enough water to cover. (Alternatively, use 2lb/1kg of apple cores and peel.) Bring slowly to a boil, then simmer for 25–30 minutes, or until soft. Strain through a sterilized jelly bag (see step 4, page 80) and reserve the juice. Return the pulp to the pan, with water to cover. Bring to a boil, then simmer for 30 minutes. Strain again. Combine both quantities of juice in the pan. Boil rapidly for 10–15 minutes, or until reduced by a quarter. Bottle and seal (see pages 42–43). Refrigerate and use within 1 week. To keep for up to 1 year, heat process (see pages 44–45).

Testing for Jelling

When a jam, or other preserve with a high sugar content, is heated to 220°F (105°C) the sugar reacts with the pectin and starts to jell. Check with a candy thermometer for accuracy or carry out the "spoon" or "plate" test (see page 76 for technique).

Filtering

Sometimes, even carefully prepared liquids become cloudy and need filtering. Pour the liquid through a sterilized jelly bag, or a double layer of sterilized cheesecloth, thin layer of calico, or paper filter (such as a coffee filter or filter for a home-brewing kit).

Filtering through cheesecloth

Filtering through a paper filter

Use a strainer to hold a small piece of cheesecloth or calico, or tie a large piece to the legs of an upturned chair. Support a paper filter with a funnel.

Making Brine

Brine is used when curing and drying meat (see Cured Ham, page 134 for recipe). The meat is steeped in a strong salt solution, that extracts the moisture from the meat. Always use a noncorrosive container when making a brine.

1 Place all the ingredients, except the flavorings, in a pan. Bring slowly to a boil, stirring until the salt has dissolved. Skim well and add the flavorings. Return to a boil, then reduce the heat and simmer for 5 minutes.

2 Remove the pan from the heat and let stand until the brine is completely cold. Lift out the flavorings, then strain the brine through a cheesecloth-lined sieve to remove any remaining froth and impurities. Use as required.

Spice Bags and Herb Bundles

Putting spices in cheesecloth bags and tying herbs in bundles is a convenient way to add flavor. They are easy to remove after cooking.

PLACE THE FLAVORINGS in the center of a small square of cheesecloth, then draw up the corners to enclose the spices and secure with kitchen string

USE A VARIETY of fresh herbs and tie together with kitchen string

PRESERVING INGREDIENTS

SOME SPECIAL ingredients are essential to preserving. Buy the best quality available and do not be afraid to experiment with the basics, such as different vinegars, oils, and sugars. Many ingredients are affected by oxygen and direct sunlight, so store them in airtight containers in a cool, dark place. Whenever possible, use unrefined ingredients: although they can affect the clarity of preserves, the flavor is better.

SUGARS

Many types of sugar are now available – most of them are interchangeable. White refined sugars produce a clear, sparkling, and hard-set preserve, while honey and raw sugars, syrups, and molasses give a softer product with a more pronounced flavor.

Granulated sugar

Preserving sugar

MOLASSES SUGAR: Moist, soft, and dark with a strong flavor.

GRANULATED and **PRESERVING SUGARS:** Refined and interchangeable. For clearest results, use preserving sugar.

MOLASSES: A rich blend of refined syrup and raw dark brown sugar.

HONEY: The natural sweetener; use single flower honey for extra flavor.

LIQUID GLUCOSE: A complex sugar that helps prevent crystallization.

RAW SUGAR: A flavorful sugar with low molasses.

LIGHT BROWN SUGAR: Raw, fragrant, all-round sugar.

DARK BROWN SUGAR: Moist with a pronounced flavor.

PALM SUGAR: From the sap of palms, fragrant and tasty.

JAGGERY: A raw Indian sugar with a distinct taste.

OILS

Mild oils are best for preserving as they do not mask the flavor of the ingredients. For a more robust end result, use unrefined cold-pressed oils to add flavor. Oils should be kept in a cool, dark place.

MUSTARD OIL: Made from mustard seeds, strongly flavored and used extensively in Indian pickles.

PEANUT OIL: An excellent, refined, mild, all-purpose oil.

REFINED OLIVE OIL: Light in flavor and color, excellent for delicate preserves.

OLIVE OIL: A mixture of refined and virgin, is a good all-purpose oil.

EXTRA-VIRGIN OLIVE OIL: Strongly flavored and fragrant.

Mustard oil

Peanut oil

Refined olive oil

Olive oil

Extra-virgin olive oil

FATS

Fats are used extensively to seal and add moisture. They should be a good color and smell sweet. As they are easily affected by changes in temperature, keep them at the bottom of your refrigerator.

CLARIFIED BUTTER: Butter-oil, mild and flavorful, for sealing potted goods.

GOOSE FAT: Has a distinctive taste, use in confits and rillettes.

LARD: Rendered, clarified pork fat, widely used as a sealant.

BUTTER: Adds flavor and enriches meat and sweet preserves alike.

SALTS

Do not use ordinary table salt for preserving. Most brands contain anti-caking agents that will cloud brines and distort flavors. Also avoid sea salt; it is expensive and many types are not pure enough for preserving use.

SALTPETER: Essential for curing meat (see page 42). **TABLE SALT:** Use only for flavoring.

COARSE KOSHER SALT: Large crystal salt, perfect for dry-curing fish.

KOSHER SALT: Crush and use for curing if preserving salt is unobtainable.

PRESERVING SALT: Medium crystal salt, used widely in curing.

ACIDS

Acids are very important as they help jams and jellies to jell, and prevent discoloration. To retain freshness, buy in small quantities and keep in airtight containers.

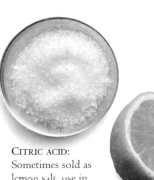

CITRIC ACID: Sometimes sold as lemon salt, use in place of lemon juice.

LEMON: A natural antioxidant; adds pectin and enhances color.

VITAMIN C: An antioxidant; helps preserve a good color.

TAMARIND: The sweet-sour pulp of the tamarind pod.

VINEGARS

Select clear vinegars with a good color and aroma. Dark vinegars are suitable for chutneys and flavoring, while pale and distilled vinegars are used for pickling.

CIDER VINEGAR: A flavorful and fruity, all-purpose vinegar, ideal for chutneys.

WHITE WINE VINEGAR: Mild and mellow, ideal for delicate preserves.

RED WINE VINEGAR: Adds a delicate red color, ideal for spiced fruits.

MALT VINEGAR: An all-purpose vinegar, use in chutneys and dark pickles.

RICE VINEGAR: A delicate and mild, all-purpose clear vinegar.

DISTILLED WHITE VINEGAR: An all-purpose, clear vinegar.

Cider vinegar   *White wine vinegar*   *Red wine vinegar*   *Malt vinegar*   *Rice vinegar*   *Distilled white vinegar*

FLAVORINGS

THE HISTORY OF good cooking began when people discovered that adding fresh herbs and spices to food turned it into a fragrant delicacy. Since then, achieving the correct balance of flavors has been at the heart of all cuisines. Herbs and spices are valued not only for their flavor and aroma, but also because many of them have antiseptic qualities and aid digestion – besides actively helping the preserving process. Remember that flavorings are the cook's equivalent of the artist's palette; it is worth experimenting to find your own favorite combinations and so develop a personal touch.

SPICES

Whenever possible, grind spices just before use. Whole spices will keep for up to two years in an airtight container, while ground ones quickly lose their aroma.

Ground turmeric

TURMERIC: A mild yellow spice used mainly to impart color. It has a warm, earthy flavor.

Turmeric root

Mace

Nutmeg

NUTMEG AND MACE: The kernel and membrane of the same nut.

VANILLA PODS: Have a superior flavor and fragrance to vanilla extract.

PEPPERCORNS: Can be black, white, or green, depending on maturity.

CORIANDER SEED: An essential in curry powder and also used as a pickling spice.

DILL SEED: An essential pickling spice with a fragrant, refreshing taste.

CELERY SEED: A useful means of adding a celery flavor to many pickles and preserves.

CARAWAY SEED: Add a mildly pungent note to many northern European preserves.

ANISEED: Used in sweet and savory preserves in the Middle East and Mediterranean.

Black cumin   *Common cumin*

CUMIN SEED: Comes in two distinct varieties: common and black (*kalajeera*), which has a drier, earthier flavor.

JUNIPER BERRIES: Useful for pâtés, preserved meats, pickles, and liqueurs.

Ginger root

Ground ginger

GINGER: A warm, spicy, aromatic root, invaluable for many sweet and savory preserves.

CLOVES: Dried buds with a distinctive taste and powerful antiseptic qualities.

Chili flakes   *Paprika*

Chili powder

STAR ANISE: An exotic flavor to match its striking appearance and extensively used in Chinese cooking.

CHILI: Ground from whole dried peppers, it is an easy way to spice up preserves.

Black cardamom   *Green cardamom*   *White cardamom*

CARDAMOM PODS: Used for sweet preserves and with meat. The green and white pods are interchangeable, but the black is more pungent.

ALLSPICE BERRIES: Have a complex flavor of cinnamon, cloves, and nutmeg.

GALANGAL: A Southeast Asian spice, it is related to ginger and tastes similar.

Yellow   *Brown*   *Black*   *Mustard powder*

MUSTARD: An ancient, aromatic spice with a warm, pungent flavor and many useful preserving properties. It is widely used in pickles and other preserves.

Cinnamon sticks   *Ground cinnamon*

CINNAMON: The bark of a tree, available in sticks or preground. It enhances sweet and savory preserves.

NIGELLA SEED: Also known as *kalonji*, and popular in India for spice mixes, breads, and preserves.

FENUGREEK SEED: Has a pungent curry flavor. It tastes best if dry roasted before use.

SAFFRON: The stigma of the saffron crocus. It adds a subtle flavor and golden hue to many dishes.

HERBS

Store fresh herbs in a pitcher of water, or in the bottom of the refrigerator with the stems wrapped in damp paper towels. Dried herbs can be substituted for fresh (except delicate varieties such as basil and parsley), but as their flavors are more concentrated, use half the quantity of fresh.

Common sage

Purple sage

SAGE: A large family of aromatic herbs with a real affinity for meat.

Variegated sage

HYSSOP: With its hint of camphor, it should be used sparingly.

TARRAGON: Good for flavoring vinegars or with fish and chicken.

BAY: Added to preserves for its flavor and its decorative qualities.

GERANIUM LEAVES: Subtly flavor jams and jellies.

CILANTRO: With its musky taste, adds pungency to Indian chutneys and Mexican salsas.

LEMONGRASS: A tropical plant from Southeast Asia.

Golden marjoram

Sweet marjoram *Pink-flowering marjoram*

OREGANO: Popular in Italy, where it is added to meat and vegetable preserves.

CELERY LEAF: A favorite in the Mediterranean, it has a strong celery flavor.

MARJORAM: Related in flavor to oregano, and added to meat and vegetable preserves.

Green basil

Purple basil

Common thyme

SAVORY: Has a pungent taste rather like thyme and is often used in sausages.

BASIL: Has a superb perfume and a pleasant, peppery taste. Use to flavor oil or with tomatoes.

Lemon thyme

BORAGE: Has a fresh cucumber flavor. The flowers can be candied or added to drinks.

THYME: A powerful herb with antiseptic properties. Add to bouquets garnis and preserved meats.

ROSEMARY: Good both fresh and dried in marinades and oils or with meat.

Variegated mint

Flat-leaf parsley

Curly parsley

MINT: A vast family of aromatic herbs, with widely differing flavors. Use to add a fresh note to chutneys and sausages.

DILL: Associated with northern Europe, where it is added to cucumber, pickles, and preserves.

PARSLEY: An essential in bouquets garnis, it should always be fresh. The flat-leaf variety has a stronger, more refreshing flavor.

Applemint

Spearmint

PICKLING IN VINEGAR

THERE ARE TWO stages to pickling in vinegar. First the ingredients are salted to draw out excess moisture that would otherwise dilute the vinegar. This is done either by dry-salting or by steeping in a strong saline solution. Vegetables should be soaked for 12–48 hours, depending on size, and kept in a cool place. In hot climates it is advisable to change the salt solution daily as it tends to ferment. The second stage is to cover the vegetables with vinegar, which can be plain, spiced, or sweet (see pages 129 and 130). Flavorings such as dried chilies, peppercorns, and mustard seeds are usually added. If you like crunchy pickles, let the vinegar cool before pouring it in; for a softer pickle, use boiling vinegar. Pickled green vegetables tend to lose their color in time, but blanching them briefly will combat this to some extent. A little baking soda can be added to the water to preserve color (1 teaspoon for every 2 cups/500ml water), but it does destroy vitamins in the vegetables, so is not ideal. Pickled Onions are shown below, but other vegetables can be prepared in the same way.

Pickled Onions (See page 92 for recipe.)

1 For easy peeling, pour boiling water over the onions and let stand until cool enough to handle. Peel off the skins and place the onions in a glass bowl.

2 Make enough strong brine to cover the onions, using ¼ cup (75g) salt for every 4 cups (1 liter) water. Pour this over the onions, weight down (see page 46), and leave in a cool place for 24 hours.

3 The next day, rinse the onions well to remove the salt and arrange in hot, sterilized jars with the mustard seed, bay leaves, and chilies, if desired.

4 To make a flavored vinegar, prepare a spice bag (see page 47) and place in a noncorrosive pan with the vinegar of your choice. Bring to a boil and boil for about 5 minutes. For a fuller flavor, let cool, then discard the spice bag and bring the vinegar to a boil once more.

TIE THE SPICE BAG onto the side of the pan for easy removal

5 Pour the boiling vinegar over the onions, making sure they are completely submerged in the pickling liquid. Weight down (see page 46), seal the jar with appropriate lid (see page 43), and refrigerate. The onions will be ready to eat in 3–4 weeks.

POUR ENOUGH boiling vinegar over the onions to cover them. For crunchier pickles, allow the vinegar to cool first

Shelf life
2 years,
refrigerated

SERVING SUGGESTION

Traditionally, Pickled Onions are eaten with bread and cheese, but they can also be used to garnish a cheese tart.

PRESERVING IN OIL

ALTHOUGH OIL IS NOT technically a preservative, it does act as a sealant, protecting the steeped ingredients from exposure to air and therefore deterioration. Because the food is not fully preserved, it is best to process it first – by salting, cooking, marinating in vinegar, or, as in the case of the recipe below, making it into cheese. Use a good-quality mild oil as a strong-tasting one can be overwhelming. I prefer light olive oil combined with a milder type, such as peanut or corn. Herbs and spices are frequently added to the jar for extra flavor. Any oil left over after the preserved contents have been eaten can be used in salads, stews, or soups, or drizzled over broiled food.

Labna (Soft Cheese) (See page 108 for recipe.)

1 Place the yogurt in a large bowl with the olive oil, lemon rind and juice, and the dried mint and thyme, if desired. Beat well with a wooden spoon until everything is mixed.

2 Line a large bowl with a double layer of cheesecloth, leaving plenty of material overlapping the sides. Pour in the yogurt mixture.

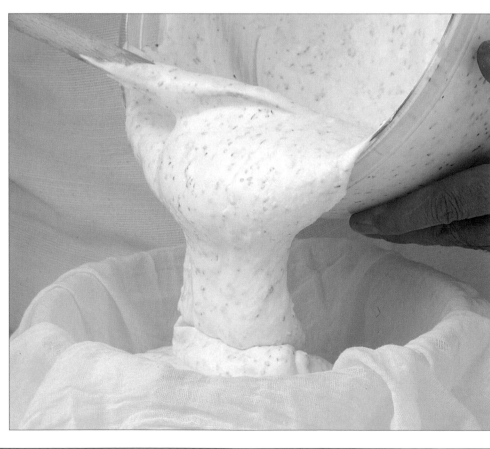

3 Tie the ends of the cheesecloth together and hang it over the bowl. Let drain in a cool place such as a pantry or an unheated room (between 42–46°F/6–8°C) for 2–3 days in winter or 2 days in summer. On hot days, you may need to refrigerate the mixture.

LIGHTLY ROLL the cheese into a ball on the palm of your hand

4 Chill the mixture until firm; this makes it easier to handle. Using your fingers, shape the resulting cheese into 1½ in (4cm) balls.

5 Chill the cheese balls again if necessary, so they keep their shape, then arrange them in the sterilized, wide-necked jar.

6 Top off with olive oil, making sure that there are no air pockets and the cheese is completely covered. The cheese is ready to eat immediately, but it improves with time, soaking up the flavor of the oil.

SERVING SUGGESTION

Serve the Labna drizzled with oil as an appetizer, with raw vegetables and pita bread.

Shelf life
6 months, refrigerated

MAKING KETCHUP

KETCHUP ORIGINALLY came from China, where, many centuries ago, it was the liquid in which fish had been pickled, popular among seafarers for pepping up their boring diet of rice gruel. It was brought to Europe at the beginning of the eighteenth century by merchants returning from the Orient. Ketchup, or rather tomato ketchup in particular, quickly became the most popular condiment in the world. Homemade ketchup is a product altogether superior to the bland, sweet commercial varieties. It can be made from many other fruits and vegetables besides tomatoes; especially good are red peppers (as shown here), mushrooms, peaches, apples, pears, and plums.

Red Pepper Ketchup

(See page 113 for recipe.)

1 Roast the peppers over an open flame or broil them for 5–7 minutes, until evenly charred. Place in a heavy plastic bag for 5 minutes (this makes peeling easier).

2 Remove the peppers from the bag and, with your fingers, rub off the skin under cold running water. Remove the core and seeds and wash the peppers well.

3 Finely chop the pepper flesh, using a knife or a food processor, along with the shallots or onions, apples, and chilies, as desired.

4 Make an herb bundle and a spice bag (see page 47). Place in a noncorrosive saucepan with the chopped vegetables and add enough water to cover. Bring to a boil, then simmer for 25 minutes, or until soft.

5 Let cool, then discard the herbs and spice bag. Pass the mixture through a food mill or strainer.

6 Place the resulting purée in the cleaned saucepan and add the vinegar, sugar, and salt. Bring to a boil, stirring until the sugar has dissolved, then simmer for 1–1½ hours, until it is reduced by half.

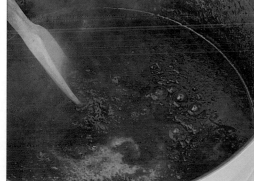

7 Mix the arrowroot or cornstarch to a paste with a little vinegar and stir into the sauce. Boil for 1–2 minutes, until slightly thickened.

8 Pour the ketchup into hot, sterilized bottles, wipe the rims clean, and seal. Heat process (see pages 44–45), then let cool and check the seals.

A FUNNEL is the easiest way to fill the bottles

BOTTLES WITH CORKS need to be sealed with wax to keep them airtight

Shelf life 4–5 months, refrigerated; 1 year, heat processed

MAKING CHUTNEY

IN INDIA the word "chutney" refers to a wide range of products, from slow-cooked preserves that are matured for several weeks before use to simple relishes made from finely chopped raw ingredients that are ready to eat after a few hours' marinating. What they all have in common is the inclusion of acid, spices, and a sweetener. Shown below is the method for making a traditional cooked chutney. It is a very straightforward recipe and can be based on almost any combination of fruit and vegetables; here, pumpkins are used. Although any type of vinegar is suitable, I prefer to use cider vinegar, as its fruity flavor seems particularly appropriate for chutney.

Pumpkin Chutney

(See page 120 for recipe.)

1 Cut the pumpkin into quarters, then peel and remove the seeds and fibers. Cut the flesh into 1in (2.5cm) cubes. (Do not throw away the seeds — they make a delicious healthful snack. Wash them well to remove any fibers, then dry them in the sun or a low oven.)

2 Place the pumpkin in a noncorrosive pan with the chopped apples, fresh ginger, chilies, mustard seed, vinegar, and salt and mix well. If you prefer a hotter chutney, do not remove the seeds from the chilies.

3 Bring to a boil, then simmer gently for 20–25 minutes, or until the pumpkin is just soft but not mushy. Stir occasionally to keep it from sticking. If the mixture seems dry, add a little more vinegar or water.

4 Add the brown sugar and stir until dissolved, then bring the mixture back to a boil. The sugar prevents the pumpkin from softening any further, so if you prefer a softer product, cook the pumpkin for a little longer before adding the sugar.

5 Cook for 50–60 minutes, until the mixture is thick and most of the liquid has evaporated. Stir frequently to keep it from sticking.

Shelf life
2 years, heat processed

6 Ladle through a funnel into the hot, sterilized jars, then seal immediately. The chutney will be ready to eat in about 3 weeks but improves if kept longer. Store in a cool, dark place.

SERVING SUGGESTION

Serve Pumpkin Chutney with lamb curry and steamed basmati rice.

DRYING FRUITS & VEGETABLES

DRIED FRUITS AND VEGETABLES make convenient pantry standbys: they have a prolonged shelf life and are easy to use because they simply require steeping in hot water to rehydrate. Vegetables can be added to casseroles and soups, while fruits are ideal for desserts and baking – and since the drying process concentrates flavors, dried fruits also make a delicious snack on their own. In hot, sunny weather produce can be dried outside in the full sun, over a period of 2–3 days. Lay it out on baking sheets and cover with cheesecloth, bringing the sheets inside at night to protect against dew. Alternatively, hang produce to dry in an airy room (see opposite). If you dry fruits and vegetables completely, until brittle, they will keep indefinitely; however, I prefer to dry fruits until most of the moisture has evaporated, but they are still pliable. In this state they will keep for up to 2 months. In unsuitable weather, drying can be done in an oven, as shown below using peaches (for oven-drying other fruit, see page 185). For drying large quantities of produce on a regular basis, it is best to use a dehydrator (see page 40).

Oven-drying Peaches

1 Blanch some peaches in boiling water for a few seconds (see page 46). Refresh in cold water, then peel off the skin.

2 Halve the peaches, remove the pits, and either leave as they are or slice into quarters or even smaller pieces.

3 As the fruits are prepared, place them in a bowl of acidulated water (see Dips, opposite), then lift out and drain well.

4 Arrange the peaches flat side down on a wire rack set over a foil-lined baking sheet. Place in an oven preheated to 225°F (110°C), leaving the oven door slightly ajar.

5 Peach halves will take 24–36 hours to dry, quarters about 12–16 hours, and smaller pieces 8–12 hours. Turn the peaches over when they are halfway through drying.

6 To store the peaches, arrange them in layers, between pieces of waxed paper, in an airtight container. Store in a cool place and keep in the dark if the container is transparent.

Air-drying Vegetables

String mushrooms and chilies on cotton thread and hang in the sun or in an airy room for 2 weeks, until shriveled and dry.

STORE DRIED VEGETABLES in cloth or paper bags so that any remaining moisture can evaporate

ACIDULATED AND HONEY DIPS

Some fruits discolor during drying (see Drying Chart, page 185). To prevent this, coat with an acidulated dip or a honey dip first.

• For an acidulated dip, add 6 tablespoons lemon juice or 2 tablespoons ascorbic acid crystals or powder to 4 cups (1 liter) warm water and mix thoroughly.

• For a honey dip, blend 1 cup (250g) honey and 1 cup (250g) sugar with 1 cup (250ml) water in a heavy-bottomed saucepan. Stir over low heat to dissolve the sugar, then bring to a boil. Boil for a second or two, then remove from the heat and let cool completely.

TIPS

• Use good-quality fresh fruits that are just ripe and unblemished.

• For oven drying, remember to turn produce over halfway through the drying process, and to change baking sheet positions around.

• Make sure dried produce is completely cold before storing.

• Regularly check stored dried fruit and vegetables to make sure that no moisture has gotten into the container. If there is any sign of mold, the produce should be thrown away.

SERVING SUGGESTION

Dried Mushrooms can be rehydrated and used to make a sauce for pasta.

Shelf life
2 years, fully dried; 2 months, semidried

DRYING MEAT

IN THE DAYS BEFORE refrigeration, dried meat was more convenient than fresh: it kept for much longer and did not need cooking. Now that fresh meat is so readily available, the technique of drying meat is used more to add flavor. In hot, dry climates, meat can be dried outside, although this is not recommended in urban areas — it requires the clean breeze of open spaces. But ideally, for hygiene reasons, the meat should be dried indoors, in the oven if necessary. There are two main types of dried meat: Biltong, a South African speciality; and Jerky, from North America. The drying technique is the same for both, but Jerky, unlike Biltong, is not cured before drying and originally was not flavored either. Ask your butcher to keep the meat in one chunk, then, at home, freeze it for a few hours until it is just firm. This will make slicing a lot easier. Select only lean meat for drying — leg and back are the most suitable. Remove all traces of tendons and pull out loose fat in the meat; fat tends to turn rancid if kept for too long.

IMPORTANT INFORMATION

- The rules of proper hygiene should be strictly followed at all stages of preparation and storage (see page 42).
- The meat should be marinated in a cool place, preferably the bottom of the refrigerator.
- Discard the meat if it develops any off odor during the drying process.
- Check the stored meat regularly; if it turns moldy or develops any off odor, discard it.

Biltong

(See page 139 for recipe.)

1 Using a sharp chef's knife, slice the meat along the grain into long strips about 2in (5cm) thick. Then, if the meat is partially frozen, let it defrost.

2 For the marinade, put the salt, sugar, saltpeter, lightly toasted coriander seed, and crushed black pepper into a glass bowl and mix until evenly blended.

3 Sprinkle an earthenware baking dish with a layer of the salt mix. Add the meat and cover it with the remaining mix, rubbing it in well.

4 Spoon the vinegar evenly over the meat and rub the salt mix into both sides of the meat again. Cover the dish and marinate in the bottom of the refrigerator for 6–8 hours. To ensure even curing, rub the meat again with the marinade after 3–4 hours.

5 After the meat has marinated in the cure, it will have become paler in color and stiffer in texture. Lift the meat out of the cure and brush off any loose salt.

6 Press a meat hook through one end of the meat or make a hole in each piece and tie a loop of string through it. Hang it in a cool, dry, dark, airy place (between 42–46°F/6–8°C) for 1½ weeks. After this time the Biltong will be semidry, so its shelf life will be limited. Wrap in waxed paper, refrigerate, and eat within 3 weeks.

THE MEAT will be much paler when it has finished marinating

WHEN THE BILTONG is dark and bone-dry it is ready to eat

--- TIP ---

• To store the Biltong, wrap it in good-quality waxed paper or baking parchment and keep it in a cool, dry, dark place (between 42–46°F/6–8°C), or in a refrigerator. The Biltong can also be frozen for up to 3 months.

✳ Warning: This recipe contains saltpeter. See page 42.

7 For a longer-lasting product, dry the meat more, until it is fully dry and splinters when bent in two. To speed up the drying process, use an oven to dry the Biltong. First line the bottom of the oven with foil to catch the drips. Place one of the oven racks on the highest position and hang the meat from the bars. Dry the Biltong at the lowest possible oven setting for 8–16 hours, until it is fully dry and dark and splinters when bent in two.

--- TIP ---

• Do not cut off the layer of fat on the edge of the meat, as this acts as a protective layer while the Biltong is drying.

SERVING SUGGESTION

Thinly slice the Biltong and eat on its own as a tasty snack.

Shelf life
3 weeks, semidried;
2 years, fully dried

CURING HAM

ORIGINALLY, MEAT was salted to preserve it for the lean winter months – today, curing is used to give additional flavor to meat. There are two basic methods of curing meat (and fish): dry curing, which preserves the flesh by burying it in salt (see Salt-cured Sprats, page 74); and wet or brine curing, when the meat is totally immersed in a saline solution. A softening agent, usually sugar, is added to the meat as the salt makes it tough, and aromatic herbs and spices are also included to impart their own special flavors. An important ingredient in any cure is saltpeter (see page 42), which inhibits the growth of bacteria and helps maintain the appetizing pink color of cured meats

such as ham and pastrami. The recipe below produces a mild-flavored ham and is also suitable for using with mutton.

IMPORTANT INFORMATION

• Buy the best and freshest meat you can afford from a reliable supplier.
• Do not attempt to cure meat in the summer or if you do not have the proper facilities: all processing and storage must be carried out at low temperatures, below 40°F (5°C).
• Always follow the preparation and storage procedures laid out in the

recipes, and at all times carefully observe the proper hygiene rules (see page 42).
• At all stages of preparation the meat should have a pleasant smell; if any unpleasant odors develop, do not eat it.
• If the brine develops an off odor, changes consistency, or becomes ropy, lift the ham out and rinse it well. Discard the brine and cover the meat with a fresh, cold brine.

Cured Ham

(See page 134 for recipe.)

1 Rub the pork with salt, making sure it is pushed into all the crevices. Place on a thin layer of salt in a dish and cover with the remaining salt. Refrigerate for 24 hours.

2 For the brine cure, place the water in a large pan; add the salt and the rest of the ingredients. Boil steadily for 10 minutes, then turn off the heat and allow the mixture to cool completely.

BE SURE THE BRINE totally covers the meat

3 The next day, brush all the salt from the meat and place it in a large earthenware crock or other noncorrosive container. Strain the cold brine over it, making sure that the meat is fully covered – if necessary, weight the meat down (see page 46).

4 Cover the crock with a lid or plastic wrap. Leave in a cool place, below 40°F (5°C), for 2–2½ weeks. Check the meat every day to be sure the brine is sound (see Important Information, opposite).

AFTER DRYING for 2–3 days, the surface of the ham will dry out

5 Remove the meat from the brine, rinse it well, then dry. Insert a meat hook into the shank end of the leg and hang it in a cool, dry, dark, airy place (between 42–46°F/ 6–8°C) for 2–3 days.

6 After the ham has hung for 2–3 days, it can be cooked and served either hot or cold (see recipe page 134). To give the ham a stronger flavor, continue the hanging process, following step 7, below.

THE COLOR of the skin will darken with time

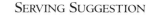

TIPS

• While the ham is drying, it can be covered with sterilized cheesecloth if it is not hanging in an insect-proof place. Do not allow the cheesecloth to touch the meat while it is wet.

• To store the dried ham, wrap it in sterilized fabric and keep in a cool, dry, dark place (between 42–46°F/6–8°C).

✽ Warning: This recipe contains saltpeter. See page 42.

SERVING SUGGESTION

Serve the Cured Ham cold, as the centerpiece of a buffet.

7 Mix the flour, salt, and water together to make a paste, and spread all over the exposed meat, to seal, then hang the ham for 2–2½ weeks longer. If desired, the ham can be smoked before cooking.

Shelf life
2 years, uncooked;
3 weeks, cooked

SMOKING FISH

SMOKING IS ONE of the most ancient preserving techniques: its antibacterial and antifungal properties help inhibit the growth of molds, and it adds its own distinctive flavor to all types of fish and meat. As smoking does not fully preserve foods, the produce needs to be cured first. There are two methods of smoking: cold-smoking, when the smoke does not exceed a temperature of 82°F (28°C), and the final product's texture is not changed as the flesh remains raw; and hot-smoking, carried out at a temperature no lower than 130°F (55°C), when the flesh is partly or totally cooked. Most types of wood can be used for smoking, but resinous woods, such as pine, should be avoided or used sparingly as they impart a strong, bitter taste. Hard fruit woods, like apple, pear, and cherry, as well as oak and hickory and the exotic mesquite, are especially good. Aromatic herbs and spices can be added to the wood to give extra flavor. After mastering the basic technique, experiment to create your own flavor combinations. Smokers are available in several shapes and sizes. Always follow the manufacturer's instructions.

Smoked Salmon

(See page 152 for recipe.)

1 To fillet the salmon, cut around the head on one side, using a sharp filleting knife. Slide the knife between the flesh and the backbone, keeping it as close to the bone as possible, and slice off the fillet in one piece.

2 Turn the salmon over and repeat the filleting procedure on the other side. Run your fingers along each fillet to locate all the remaining bones, then remove them with tweezers. Rinse the fillets and dry well.

3 Sprinkle some of the coarse salt and sugar into a noncorrosive container to form a ¼ in (5mm) layer. Lay one fillet skin side down on top, then sprinkle with another layer, about ½ in (1cm) thick, thinning the mixture toward the tail end.

4 Place the second fillet skin side down on top of the first, and sprinkle with the remaining salt mix. Cover the dish with plastic wrap and let stand for 3–3½ hours in a cool place or refrigerator.

5 Remove the salmon from the salt mix and rinse under running water, to remove the excess salt. Dry well with paper towels. Push a wooden skewer through the back of each fillet at the head end.

6 Brush both sides of each fillet with the whiskey and hang to dry in a cool, dry place for about 24 hours, or until the sides of the fish are almost dry to the touch and have developed a shiny salt glaze.

THE SALMON will have a glaze by the time it is ready to be smoked

7 Place the fillets on a rack in the smoker and either cold-smoke at 82°F (28°C) for 3–4 hours, or hot-smoke at 130°F (55°C) for 2–3 hours. Remove the salmon from the smoker and let cool completely.

LOOP A PIECE of string around the skewer to hang the fish up

WRAP THE SALMON in waxed paper to store

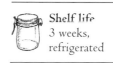

Shelf life
3 weeks, refrigerated

SERVING SUGGESTION

Cold-smoked Salmon and cream cheese make a delicious topping for bagels.

PLACE THE SALMON on a piece of foil-covered cardboard to make it easier to lift

CURING SAUSAGES

DRIED SAUSAGES are probably one of the most ingenious inventions of the charcutier – a tasty way to use up scraps of meat left over after cutting up a carcass. Making dried sausages at home is relatively easy, but should be attempted only if you have the right environment to work in. Your kitchen must be very cool, ideally between 50–54°F (10–12°C), scrupulously clean, and all equipment must be sterilized before use (see page 42). A cool, dry, and dark area (below 40°F/5°C) should be available for drying the sausages – I use a cool pantry, but a clean, dry cellar or unheated room would also be

suitable. Always use the freshest possible ingredients and keep the meat chilled at all times – temperature affects the keeping quality of the sausages and also plays an important part in their final texture (see page 64). Organic, free-range meat gives the best flavor and is drier and firmer to work with. Sausage-making requires some special equipment – a strong grinder and a sausage-stuffer, or grinder and sausage funnel attachments for an electric mixer (see Equipment, page 39) for grinding meat and filling the casings. Sausage casings are available from some butchers or from specialty suppliers.

Garlic and Herb Salami

(See page 138 for recipe.)

1 Place the meat in a large bowl, sprinkle with the salt, saltpeter, and vodka and mix together well with your hands. Cover and refrigerate for 12 hours.

2 Put the meat through the fine blade of a grinder, and the fat through the coarse blade. Mix together well, adding any liquid left in the bowl.

3 Add the garlic, thyme, whole and ground black peppercorns, coriander seed, and allspice. Mix thoroughly but lightly, then chill for at least 2 hours.

4 Meanwhile, prepare the casing. Rinse it to remove the excess salt, then soak in cold water for 30 minutes. Next, rinse the inside of the casing by fitting it over a slow-running cold tap and allowing the water to run through it for a few seconds.

5 Place the casing in a bowl of water, add the vinegar, and soak until needed.

6 Fit one end of the casing on the sausage stuffer, or electric mixer attachment. Stuff with the meat, making sure it is firmly packed. If there are any air pockets, prick with a skewer. Tie into individual sausages or 8in (20cm) links.

FOLD THE END of the casing over and loop kitchen string around

PULL THE STRING tight to secure it, then repeat for the other end

7 Hang the sausages in a cool, dry, dark, airy place (below 40°F/5°C) for 5–6 weeks to dry. Every day check the sausages, which at all stages should have a savory, appetizing smell and be dry to the touch. Discard the sausages if any disagreeable odors develop.

8 After 5–6 weeks the sausages should have lost 50–60 percent of their weight and be perfect for eating raw. To improve their flavor for cooking purposes, they can be hung for up to 3 months.

TWIST THE ENDS of the paper to seal

SERVING SUGGESTION

Serve Garlic and Herb Salami as part of a mixed salami platter with pickles and bread.

Shelf life
4–5 months, refrigerated

✳ Warning: This recipe contains saltpeter. See page 42.

—— HOW TO STORE ——

• To store the sausages, wrap them individually in waxed paper and hang in a cool, dry, dark, airy place (below 40°F/5°C). Alternatively, fill a container with polystyrene beads and bury the sausages in the middle.

• The sausages can also be frozen. Wrap individually in waxed paper, then seal in freezer bags. Use within 3 months.

MAKING PATE

THERE ARE FEW THINGS more delicious than a slice of homemade pâté, a chunk of fresh bread, and a glass of wine. Simple pâtés are a great standby, as well as being inexpensive and easy to make. They are preserved by sealing the surface with fat, which excludes air and moisture and therefore slows down the activity of bacteria. Before the days of refrigeration, pâtés were stored in cold cellars for up to 3 months, but now it is recommended that they be refrigerated and used within 4 weeks. Many pâtés, especially highly flavored ones, should not be kept for more than 3 weeks, as their flavor quickly deteriorates. Always make sure pâtés are visually pleasing, since cooked meat can turn an unattractive shade of gray. The pink color of commercially produced pâté is usually due to the inclusion of nitrates (saltpeter – see page 42). The recipe below uses bacon to lend a pinkish hue.

Pâté de Campagne (See page 144 for recipe.)

1 Mix together the pork, liver, and bacon and put through the fine blade of a grinder. Add the garlic, herbs, spices, seasoning, prunes, white wine, and brandy and mix well. Cover and refrigerate for 3–4 hours to allow the flavors to develop.

2 Line the terrine with caul fat, leaving an overhang of at least 1in (2.5cm) so it can be folded over to cover the pâté. Alternatively, line it with bacon, stretching the slices with the back of a knife blade. Overlap the bacon in the dish and let the ends overhang.

LINING WITH BACON

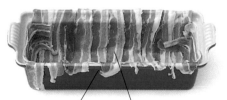

ALLOW THE ENDS of the bacon to hang over the edge of the terrine

OVERLAP the bacon slices to form a seal

3 Fill the dish with the meat, pushing it well into the corners, then rap it on a work surface to release any air pockets. Fold over the flaps of caul or bacon and place the lemon or orange slices and bay leaves on top. Cover with the lid or foil.

4 Place the terrine in a roasting pan filled with enough warm water to come halfway up the sides of the terrine. Cook in an oven preheated to 325°F (160°C) for 1½–2 hours, until the pâté has shrunk from the sides of the dish and is surrounded by liquid fat.

5 Let the pâté cool, then cover with foil-covered cardboard and weight down (see page 46), to make it easier to slice. Refrigerate overnight.

6 The next day, remove the lemon or orange slices and bay leaves, run a hot knife blade around the edge of the terrine, and carefully unmold the pâté. Wipe off all traces of the jelly surrounding the meat with paper towels.

7 Pour melted lard over the bottom of the terrine in a layer about ½ in (1cm) thick. Let set, then place the pâté on top and pour over enough melted lard to cover the pâté by about ½ in (1cm). Cover with the lid or foil and refrigerate. Let mature for 2–3 days before serving.

Shelf life
1 month, refrigerated

GARNISH WITH juniper berries, bay leaves, and cranberries

SERVING SUGGESTION

Serve Pâté de Campagne with fresh country bread, salad, and pickles.

POTTING

THE VICTORIANS used potting as a convenient means of preserving leftover meat, adding flavorings such as pepper, cayenne, nutmeg, or anchovy paste. Potting preserves food by insulating it from the air with a layer of solid fat. In the past this tended to be lard or mutton fat, but now clarified butter is more common. The ingredients to be potted are cooked first and are then usually pounded to a paste with some butter or other fat. If you are potting meat, use only the best cuts and make sure you trim away any tendons and connective tissue. Illustrated below is Potted Venison. Other game, poultry, fish, and cheese can be prepared in the same way.

Potted Venison

(See page 146 for recipe.)

1 Trim the bacon slices (if necessary), tie the rinds together with string, and set aside. Coarsely chop the bacon. Make an herb bundle with the thyme, sage, bay leaf, and lemon rind (see page 47).

2 Put the bacon and rinds in a casserole with cubed venison, diced butter, garlic, juniper berries, pepper, mace, herbs, and red wine. Cover and bake in an oven preheated to 325°F (160°C) for 2½ – 3 hours, until the meat is very tender.

3 Remove the herbs, mace, and the bacon rinds and process the meat to a smooth paste in a food processor.

4 Pack the paste into an earthenware dish or individual ramekins and let cool completely. Chill for 2–3 hours.

5 Pour the clarified butter over the potted venison until it forms a layer about ½ in (1cm) thick. Chill until the butter has set. Garnish with bay leaves and cranberries, if desired.

SERVING SUGGESTION

Serve Potted Venison with watercress and melba toast.

A DECORATIVE GARNISH gives the paste an attractive appearance

HOW TO CLARIFY BUTTER

To clarify butter for the topping, put it in a small saucepan, melt over a very low heat, and let it foam for a few seconds. Skim the froth from the surface and let the butter cool. Pour the cooled butter through a cheesecloth lined strainer, leaving the milky sediment in the pan. Rinse the cheesecloth in cold water and wring it out well before use; this helps catch any remaining froth.

TO BE SURE of a good seal, the butter should cover the meat by about ½ in (1cm)

Shelf life 1 month, refrigerated

SALTING

SALT IS a natural dehydrator. It preserves by drawing moisture out of food, thus inhibiting the growth of bacteria. The technique of salting has played an essential role in the history of how and what we eat. For centuries salted fish, mainly herring, was the staple food of Europe. Demand for this humble, silvery fish started wars and made the fortunes of many nations. A good source of protein and vitamins A, B, and D, salt-cured fish can still make a useful contribution to our diet. The recipe below uses sprats, but works well with herrings and anchovies, too. Choose perfectly fresh fish with a good shiny skin. Leaving the heads on results in a stronger flavor, since they contain a lot of oil.

Salt-cured Sprats ——————————— *(See page 153 for recipe.)*

1 Using a small, sharp pair of scissors, make a little cut in each fish just below the gills.

2 Next, carefully snip right down the belly of each fish from gills to tail and open out the cut slightly.

3 Pull out the stomach contents with your fingers and discard. Rinse the fish under cold running water.

4 Sprinkle a little fine salt in the cavity of each fish and all over the outside, rubbing the salt well into the flesh.

5 Arrange the fish in layers in a shallow dish, adding a thin sprinkling of the fine salt between each layer. Cover and refrigerate for 2–3 hours, until some of the moisture has been drawn off.

• First remove the oil that will have accumulated on top. If not enough brine has developed to cover the fish, top it off with a strong salt solution made with equal quantities of salt and water. Seal the container tightly and store in a cool, dark place.

• When you want to use the sprats, remove them from the brine and soak for a few hours in water or a mixture of milk and water.

SERVING SUGGESTION

Dress Salt-cured Sprats in oil and Black Currant Vinegar (see recipe, page 128) and serve garnished with parsley and finely diced red onion.

6 Lift out the fish and dry thoroughly on paper towels.

Shelf life
2 years, refrigerated

7 Sprinkle a layer of the coarse salt over the bottom of a large container. Arrange some fish on top with a bay leaf and a few peppercorns. Cover with a ¼ in (5mm) layer of coarse salt. Repeat the layers, finishing with a layer of salt.

8 Have a plate that just fits the opening of the container ready. Place it over the fish and weight down – a bottle filled with water is ideal. Cover and refrigerate or leave in a cool, dark place (between 42–46°F/6–8°C) for one week before eating.

MAKING JAM

JAM-MAKING is one of the simplest methods of preserving; almost any fruit can be used, and a surprising number of vegetables. Sugar reacts with pectin and acid to make a jelly, and also works as a preservative since a high sugar concentration in the jam prevents the growth of molds. The crucial factor is to have the perfect balance of acidity and pectin to create a good set. Many fruits naturally have the right balance (see Preserving Chart, page 184), but some need a little help. You can do this by adding lemon juice and pectin-rich fruit, such as apples, or a homemade pectin stock (see recipe, page 47); alternatively, you can buy a commercially prepared pectin. If you have to increase the pectin level by a large amount, it is necessary to raise the sugar content accordingly: for example, if the addition of a pectin stock increases the volume of fruit pulp by a third, then a third more sugar must be added. The amount of sugar in the following jam recipes can be reduced by up to 30 percent, if desired. In many cases this results in a fresher-flavored product, but the jam will be softer and have a much shorter shelf life.

TESTING FOR THE JELL

A jam is ready when it reaches the jelling point. This can be tested in any of the following ways:

Candy thermometer
Warm the candy thermometer in a bowl of hot water before using it, or it could break. Clip it onto the side of the saucepan, making sure the end is not touching the bottom of the pan. Boil the jam at a good rolling boil until the thermometer registers 220°F (105°C).

Flake test
Dip a metal spoon into the jam, then turn it so that the jam runs off the side. The drops should run together and fall from the spoon in flat flakes or sheets.

Wrinkle test
Pour a little hot jam onto a cold saucer and let it cool for a few minutes. Push the jam with a finger; if it wrinkles it has reached the jelling point.

Exotic Fruit Jam

(See page 159 for recipe.)

1 Finely chop the peeled and cored pineapple and apple in a food processor. Transfer to the saucepan and add the canned or fresh litchi halves, water, lemon rind, and juice.

2 Bring the mixture to a boil, then reduce the heat and simmer gently for 20–25 minutes, or until the apples are reduced to a pulp and the pineapple pieces are softened.

3 Add the granulated sugar to the pan and stir well over medium heat until it is completely dissolved. Increase the heat and bring the mixture to a rapid, rolling boil.

4 Boil the fruit mixture rapidly for 20–25 minutes, stirring frequently, until the jelling point is reached (see Testing for the Jell, opposite). Skim off any froth as it rises to the surface of the jam.

THE JAM WILL start to thicken as it reaches the jelling point

5 Remove the pan from the heat and let stand for a few minutes to allow the jam to settle. Skim again if necessary.

6 Ladle the jam into hot, sterilized jars (see page 42), seal, and refrigerate; or heat process for a longer shelf life (see page 44–45).

SERVING SUGGESTION

Serve Exotic Fruit Jam with fresh scones or biscuits.

Shelf life
2 years, heat processed

MAKING FRUIT CURD

A CURD IS A CURIOUS mixture, something between a hollandaise sauce and an egg custard. It consists of fruit pulp or juice sweetened with sugar and thickened with eggs and butter. The traditional lemon curd has been made since Edwardian times, but other citrus fruit and even exotic fruits can be used. An important point to remember when making curd is that patience is needed as you wait for it to thicken, which can take anything up to 45 minutes. Heat the curd mixture over a pan of barely simmering water and stir frequently so the heat is evenly distributed. Do not try to hurry the process by increasing the heat: like custard, a fruit curd will curdle if boiled and cannot be rescued.

Pink Grapefruit Curd
(*See page 173 for recipe.*)

1 Grate the rind of one grapefruit on the fine side of a hand grater, then squeeze the juice.

2 Using a sharp knife, cut off all the peel and pith from the other grapefruit, following the curve of the fruit.

3 Carefully cut out all the segments of flesh from between the membranes and coarsely chop them.

ADD THE BUTTER in pieces so that it melts quickly

4 Put all the grapefruit juice, grated rind, and flesh in a saucepan with the lemon juice, sugar, and butter. Heat gently until the butter is melted, then transfer the mixture to a double boiler or a bowl placed over a pan of barely simmering water.

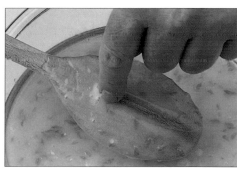

5 Strain the beaten eggs into the fruit mixture through a fine mesh sieve, stirring constantly with a wooden spoon to make sure they are evenly incorporated.

STRAIN IN THE beaten eggs to avoid lumps forming in the curd

6 Cook the mixture over very low heat, stirring frequently, for 25–40 minutes, until it is thick enough to coat the back of the spoon. Do not allow the mixture to boil or it will curdle.

―――――― TIP ――――――

• Curd does not have a long shelf life; it can be refrigerated for 3 months. To extend its shelf life to 6 months, it can be heat processed for 5 minutes (see pages 44–45).

7 Remove the pan from the heat, or take the bowl off the pan of simmering water, and stir in the orange-flower water.

8 Ladle the curd into warm, sterilized jars (see page 42) and seal immediately. Refrigerate the curd or heat process (see pages 44–45).

SERVING SUGGESTION

Use Pink Grapefruit Curd to fill cakes, tarts, and pavlovas.

Shelf life
3 months, refrigerated;
6 months, heat processed

MAKING JELLY

JELLY-MAKING IS a miraculous process – dull and cloudy fruit juice is transformed into a clear, jewel-like substance. Three elements are necessary to achieve this: pectin, which is found in varying degrees in all fruit (see Preserving Chart, page 184), acidity, and sugar. Low-pectin fruits such as cherries, peaches, and strawberries are usually supplemented with pectin-rich ones such as apples, cranberries, currants, or citrus fruit. Raspberries, used below, have a medium pectin content, so apples are included to help them jell. Recipes for jelly always used to recommend letting the pulp drip overnight, but this is usually unnecessary. Leave it until it stops dripping, which normally takes a few hours.

Raspberry Jelly

(See page 166 for recipe.)

1 Pick over the raspberries, washing them only if necessary. Remove the cores from the apples and set aside. Coarsely chop the apples.

2 Place the apples and raspberries in a food processor and process until finely chopped (you will probably need to do this in batches). Chopping the fruit in a food processor means that it requires less cooking, resulting in a jelly with a fresher, fruitier flavor.

3 Place the fruit and cores in a saucepan with water to cover. Bring to a boil, then simmer for 20–30 minutes, until the fruit is soft and pulpy.

4 Pour the fruit and liquid into a sterilized jelly bag suspended over a large bowl. Let drain for 2–3 hours, or until it stops dripping. Do not be tempted to squeeze it or the jelly will be cloudy.

5 Measure the juice and allow 2 cups (500g) sugar for every 2 cups (500ml) juice. Return the juice to the cleaned pan and add the sugar and lemon juice.

6 Heat gently, stirring from time to time with a wooden spoon, until the sugar is dissolved, then bring the liquid to a rapid boil.

ONCE THE MIXTURE has come to a rolling boil, froth will start to form on top as impurities rise to the surface

7 Skim well with a slotted spoon to remove the froth. Boil rapidly until the jelling point is reached (see page 76), starting to check after about 10 minutes.

― TIP ―

• To extract more liquid from the fruit after it has drained through the jelly bag, return the pulp to the pan and add water to cover. Simmer gently for about 30 minutes, then drain as before. Add the juice to the first batch.

8 Ladle the jelly through a jam funnel into the hot, sterilized jars. Let cool until semiset, then insert a geranium leaf into the center of each jar and seal.

SERVING SUGGESTION

Serve Raspberry Jelly on an open sandwich with sliced cold chicken breast.

 Shelf life 2 years, heat processed

MAKING FRUIT CHEESE

FRUIT CHEESES and butters are probably the earliest type of sweet preserve, dating back to pre-Roman times when fruit pulp was mixed with honey and dried in the sun. Butters are made in the same way as cheeses, but the cooking time is shorter and, sometimes, the proportion of sugar is lower, resulting in a softer, more spreadable mixture.

Jelling is achieved by boiling out the moisture, which means that any fruit can be used since pectin levels do not matter. Cheeses and butters need long, slow cooking and should be stirred frequently toward the end as they burn easily. Quinces, used below, make the best cheese as they produce a beautifully fragrant dark amber preserve.

Quince Cheese

(See page 174 for recipe.)

1 Wash the quinces well to remove any fluff, then coarsely chop them. There is no need to core them as the mixture will be strained.

2 Place the quinces in a saucepan with enough water or hard cider to cover, and add the lemon rind and juice. Bring to a boil, then reduce the heat and simmer for 30–45 minutes, until the fruit is very soft and pulpy.

3 Pass the mixture through a food mill or strainer to give a purée.

4 To calculate how much sugar to add, spoon the purée into a measuring cup. Allow 2 cups (500g) sugar for every 2 cups (500ml) purée.

5 Return the quince purée to the pan and add the sugar. Slowly bring to a boil, stirring to dissolve the sugar. Simmer for 2½–3 hours, stirring frequently. Quinces will turn a deep red color with long cooking. After a while the mixture will become very thick and will start to "plop." It is ready when a wooden spoon drawn across the bottom of the pan leaves a clear channel. Remove from the heat and let cool slightly.

WITH LONG cooking, the fruit pulp will thicken and start to "plop"

6 Brush a deep baking sheet generously with oil. Pour the cheese into the tray and smooth to an even layer, 1–1¾ in (2.5–4cm) thick. Let cool completely, then cover with a cloth and keep in a warm, dry place for 24 hours.

7 Loosen the cheese with a narrow spatula and invert onto a piece of baking parchment. Cut into squares or diamonds and dust with sugar. Arrange on baking sheets, cover, and let dry.

STORE BETWEEN layers of waxed paper in an airtight tin

SERVING SUGGESTION

Serve Quince Cheese as candy, decorated with crystallized flowers (see page 183).

Shelf life
2 years, refrigerated

PRESERVING IN ALCOHOL

PURE ALCOHOL is the ideal preservative since nothing can grow in it. It can be used on its own or mixed with a heavy syrup. The combination of fruit and alcohol is sheer indulgence: first you eat the succulent sweet fruit and then wash it down with the intoxicating perfumed liquor – a marriage made in heaven. This technique originated in the monasteries of medieval Europe. The recipe below uses peaches, but many other fruits, such as plums, apricots, cherries, and figs, can be prepared in the same way. You can use almost any kind of alcohol for preserving – rum, brandy, and eau de vie are particularly good – but make sure that it is no less than 80 proof.

Peaches in Brandy — *(See page 178 for recipe.)*

1 Blanch the peaches in boiling water for a few seconds. Refresh them in cold water for 1 minute and then peel off the skins with a small paring knife.

2 To remove the pit, run a sharp knife around the circumference of each peach. Twist the top half loose and take out the pit with a knife.

3 Put the water and 2 cups (500g) sugar in a large pan. Bring to a boil, skim any foam off the top, then reduce the heat and simmer for 5 minutes to make a syrup.

4 Gently slide the peach halves into the syrup. Return to a boil, then reduce the heat and simmer very gently for 4–5 minutes. Lift out the peaches with a slotted spoon and let cool. Meanwhile, make a spice bag (see page 47) with the vanilla pod, piece of cinnamon, cardamom pods, and cloves.

TIE THE SPICES in a piece of cheesecloth for easier removal

5 Place 2½ cups (600ml) of the syrup in a pan with the remaining sugar and spice bag. Bring to a boil, skim, then boil rapidly until the mixture reaches 219°F (104°C) on a candy thermometer. Cool slightly, remove the spice bag, then stir in the brandy.

6 Set a cherry half in the cavity of each peach, if desired, and secure with a wooden toothpick. Pack the peaches loosely into the hot, sterilized jar (see page 42).

SERVING SUGGESTION

Serve Peaches in Brandy with crystallized violets (see page 183) for a delicate dessert.

7 Pour the syrup over the peaches, shaking the jar gently to dispel any air pockets, then seal. The peaches will be ready to eat in 2 weeks, but improve the longer they are kept.

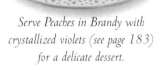

 Shelf life
2 years, refrigerated

CANDYING & CRYSTALLIZING

CANDYING CAN BE A LONG, slow process, but the end result is well worth the effort: a spectacular array of translucent, glistening, gemlike fruit. The origins of this technique are uncertain. Some maintain that it was developed in Renaissance Italy; a more likely theory is that it was invented in the royal kitchens of the Middle East during the tenth or eleventh century, and was then introduced into Europe by Arab merchants and returning Crusaders. The terms candying and crystallizing are often confused, but there is a distinction: candying refers to the process that replaces most of the fruit's moisture with a saturated sugar solution, while crystallizing (also known as glacéing) describes the sugar coating that is used as a finish for candied fruit, or the process of preserving flowers. Fruit is candied by steeping it in an increasingly concentrated syrup, a process that must be carried out slowly; otherwise, the fruit will shrink and become tough. Low-moisture fruits, such as pears, green figs, and citrus peel, are often soaked first in a strong salt or lime solution, to enable them to absorb enough sugar.

Candied Pineapple Rings (See page 182 for recipe.)

DAY ONE

1 Put the pineapple rings in a pan with enough water to cover. Bring to a boil, then reduce the heat and simmer for 15–20 minutes, until softened slightly. Drain well and place in a glass bowl.

2 Strain 4 cups (1 liter) of the cooking liquid into a pan. Add 1 cup (250g) sugar and the lemon juice. Bring to a boil, stirring until dissolved, and boil rapidly for 2–3 minutes. Skim if necessary.

3 Pour the hot sugar syrup over the pineapple rings, weight them down (see page 46) to ensure they are totally immersed, and let stand for 24 hours at room temperature.

DAY TWO

1 The next day, drain the pineapple rings well and return the sugar syrup to the saucepan.

2 Add ½ cup (100g) sugar to the syrup and bring to a boil, stirring to dissolve the sugar.

3 Boil for 1–2 minutes, then skim well and pour over the pineapple rings. Weight down and let stand 24 hours.

DAY THREE

Repeat Day Two.

DAY FOUR

Drain the pineapple rings, place the syrup in the pan, and add ⅔ cup (150g) of sugar. Bring to a boil, stirring to dissolve the sugar, and boil for 1–2 minutes, then skim and pour over the pineapple. Weight down as before and let stand 24 hours.

DAY FIVE

Repeat Day Four.

DAYS SIX & SEVEN

Drain the pineapple rings, place the syrup in the pan, and add the remaining sugar. Bring to a boil, stirring to dissolve the sugar, and boil for 1–2 minutes, then skim and pour over the pineapple. Weight down as before and let stand 48 hours.

DAY EIGHT

Place the fruit and syrup in a preserving pan and simmer for about 5 minutes. Lift out the pineapple rings with a slotted spoon. Arrange on a rack placed over a foil-lined baking sheet. Let drain and cool.

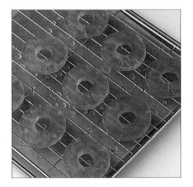

Place the rack and baking sheet in the oven preheated to 250°F (120°C), leaving the door slightly ajar. Leave for 12–24 hours, until the fruit is dry but just sticky to the touch. Let cool completely.

Dust the pineapple rings with superfine sugar to coat. Store in an airtight container, between sheets of waxed paper.

Crystallized Flowers

1 Beat an egg white with a pinch of salt and a few drops of flower water until frothy. Let stand for a few minutes. With a small, soft brush, paint the flowers evenly both inside and out with the egg white. Generously sprinkle them with sugar, being sure all surfaces are evenly coated.

2 Fill a baking sheet with a layer of superfine sugar about ½ in (1cm) deep and gently lay the sugared flowers on top. Generously sprinkle with more sugar and let dry in a warm, well-ventilated place for 1–2 days. Store the flowers in an airtight container, between layers of waxed paper.

TIPS

• Lemon juice is added to the candying syrup to prevent the sugar from recrystallizing. You could use glucose powder instead, substituting ½ cup (100g) glucose powder for the same amount of sugar in the first syrup.

• Instead of coating the flowers with egg white, you can use a cool gum arabic solution, made by dissolving 2 teaspoons gum arabic and 1 tablespoon sugar in 1 cup (250ml) water, in a bowl placed over a pan of hot water.

Shelf life
1 year for candied pineapple; 3 months for crystallized flowers

LAYER THE CANDIED FRUIT and crystallized flowers between waxed paper

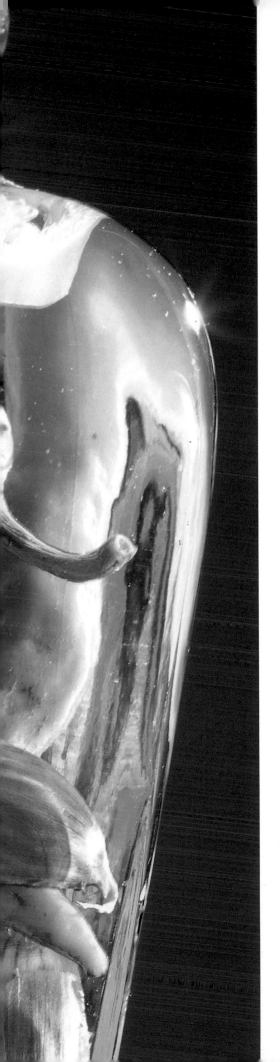

RECIPES

THIS COLLECTION of recipes contains time-honored classics, such as pickled cucumbers and tomato sauce, as well as more contemporary adaptations, like fruit piccalilli and smoky red pepper ketchup. Enticing ideas are given for both sweet and savory preserves. Learn how to make exotic, fragrant chutneys; elegant jams and jellies; aromatic spiced meat; and delicately flavored smoked fish. Serving suggestions give imaginative ways to use these delicious products.

Enjoy preserving!

PICKLES

IN THE PAST, people made the most of a seasonal glut of vegetables by preserving them in a variety of ingenious ways. This ensured a year-round supply to jazz up what might otherwise have been a monotonous diet. Today, we preserve fruit and vegetables not out of necessity, but because they taste so delicious; their pungent flavors enliven even the simplest meal. Some restaurants are in the habit of displaying jars of vividly colored pickled vegetables, Mediterranean-style, to entice passers-by. At home, too, beautiful homemade preserves tempt the appetite.

Stuffed Pickled Eggplants

Baby purple eggplants *Garlic cloves* *Celery ribs and leaves* *Carrots* *Red chilies* *Salt*

This deliciously fragrant pickle probably originated in Syria, and is still made in one form or another all over the Middle East. You will need baby eggplants — available from Indian, Oriental, and Greek greengrocers — as they are preserved whole. This recipe is my mother's; her pickled eggplants are the best I've ever tasted.

INGREDIENTS

2lb (1kg) baby purple eggplants
For the stuffing
6 garlic cloves, coarsely chopped
3–4 celery ribs and leaves, coarsely chopped
2–3 large carrots, coarsely grated
1–2 fresh red chilies, thinly sliced
1 tsp salt
For the jar
4–5 garlic cloves, peeled
2–3 fresh red or green chilies
a few grape leaves (optional)
salt
2–3 tbsp cider vinegar

1 Cut a deep slit lengthwise in each eggplant to make a pocket. Steam for 5–8 minutes, or until just softened. Remove from the heat and weight down (see page 46) to press out any moisture. Let stand overnight.

2 The next day, put all the stuffing ingredients in a bowl and mix well. Open up the pocket in each eggplant, add 1 teaspoon stuffing, and press together to hold it in place.

3 Pack the eggplants into the sterilized jar with the garlic, chilies, and grape leaves. Fill the jar with cold water, then drain it off into a measuring cup. Add 1½ teaspoons salt for every 2 cups (500ml) water, stirring until the salt is dissolved. Add the vinegar, then pour into the jar and weight down (see page 46) to keep the eggplants submerged.

4 Cover the jar with a clean cloth and let stand in a warm, well-ventilated place for 1–3 weeks, until fermentation has finished (see Brined Cucumbers, page 93), then seal the jar.

☆☆ **Degree of difficulty**
Moderate

Cooking time
5–8 minutes

Special equipment
Wide-mouth, sterilized canning jars with sealants (see pages 42–43)

Yield
About 2 pints (1kg)

Shelf life
6 months, refrigerated

TIPS

• Choose firm eggplants with a bright color and taut, shiny, unblemished skin.
• The cider vinegar and the grape leaves help speed up the fermentation process in the jar.

STUFFED PICKLED EGGPLANTS
can be served as part of a mezze, *a
wonderfully informal way of eating that
consists of a wide selection of small dishes
accompanied by copious amounts of
bread. You can also eat them as a simple
accompaniment to a plate of cold meats
and a leafy salad.*

PURPLE EGGPLANTS look
attractive, but you could
also use white or yellow
baby eggplants, or a
mixture of all three

RED CHILIES spice up the
pickle; adjust the quantity
to suit your own taste

—— VARIATION ——

◆ *Pickled Eggplants and Beets*
*Pickle the eggplants without the stuffing
and add 1 thinly sliced raw beet,
6 coarsely chopped cloves of garlic, and
2–3 chopped fresh red chilies to the jar.*

Pickled Onions

(see page 52 for technique)

It is hard to imagine some dishes being served without pickled onions. I find distilled malt vinegar a little too harsh for pickling, but it does help maintain the whiteness of the onions.

VARIATION

◆ *Pickled Beets*
Use cooked, whole baby, or cubed large beets. Omit salting, place in the jar and cover with hot vinegar.

INGREDIENTS

2½ lb (1.25kg) silverskin or small onions
salt
4 tsp mustard seed
2 bay leaves
2–4 dried red chilies (optional)
Simple Spiced Vinegar or Perfumed Vinegar, to cover (see page 129)

1 For easy peeling, blanch the onions (see page 46). Place in a glass bowl, cover with water, then drain it off into a measuring cup.

Add 1 tablespoon (75g) salt for every 4 cups (1 liter) water. Pour over the onions and weight down (see page 46). Let stand 24 hours.

2 Rinse the onions and arrange in the jars with the mustard seed, bay leaves, and chilies, if using. Pour in the vinegar to cover. Drain off and boil for 2 minutes.

3 Pour the vinegar back over the onions, making sure they are submerged, then seal. The onions will be ready in 3–4 weeks.

☆ **Degree of difficulty**
Easy

Cooking time
3–4 minutes

Special equipment
Sterilized canning jars with sealants (see pages 42–43)

Yield
About 2 pints (1kg)

Shelf life
2 years, refrigerated

Serving suggestion
Serve with cold meat, fish, and cheese

Pickled Garlic

(see page 19 for illustration)

Pickled garlic originated in Persia, where it is either served on its own or used instead of fresh garlic in cooking. Pickling mellows and changes the flavor of garlic, giving it a delicate, elusive perfume. Use fresh "green" garlic when it is in season.

INGREDIENTS

2 cups (500ml) distilled malt vinegar or white wine vinegar
2 tbsp salt
2lb (1kg) fresh garlic

1 Put the vinegar and salt in a noncorrosive saucepan. Bring to a boil and boil for 2–3 minutes, then remove the pan from the heat and let cool.

2 Separate the garlic cloves and blanch to remove the skin (see page 46). If using fresh "green" garlic, remove the outer skin and slice the bulbs crosswise in half.

3 Put the garlic in a saucepan and cover with boiling water. Blanch for 1 minute, then drain. Arrange in the sterilized jars, pour in the vinegar, then seal. The garlic will be ready to eat in 1 month.

☆ **Degree of difficulty**
Easy

Cooking time
3–4 minutes

Special equipment
Sterilized canning jars with sealants (see pages 42–43)

Yield
About 2 pints (1kg)

Shelf life
2 years, refrigerated

Pickled Green Tomatoes

(see page 15 for illustration)

An ideal way to utilize a glut of green tomatoes. This crunchy, sour pickle comes from Eastern Europe and is popular in North America, where it is an essential item in any good delicatessen.

TIP

• Try cucumbers and zucchini or fruits like gooseberries and plums. Always blanch green vegetables before pickling (see page 46).

INGREDIENTS

2lb (1kg) green tomatoes
2–3 fresh or dried red chilies
a few sprigs of dill
2–3 bay leaves
1½ tbsp mustard seed
1 tbsp black peppercorns
4–5 cloves
4 cups (1 liter) cider vinegar
½ cup (125ml) water
4 tbsp honey or sugar
1 tbsp salt

1 Lightly prick each tomato in several places with a wooden toothpick. Arrange in the hot, sterilized jars with the chilies, dill, bay leaves, and spices.

2 Put the vinegar, water, honey or sugar, and salt in a noncorrosive saucepan. Bring to a boil and boil rapidly for 5 minutes, then remove from the heat and let stand until warm.

3 Pour the warm vinegar into the jars. If there is not enough liquid to cover the tomatoes, top off with cold vinegar, then seal. The tomatoes will be ready to eat in 1 month, but improve after 2–3 months.

☆ **Degree of difficulty**
Easy

Cooking time
About 5 minutes

Special equipment
Sterilized canning jars with sealants (see pages 42–43)

Yield
About 2 pints (1kg)

Shelf life
1 year, refrigerated

Serving suggestions
Serve with meat, cheese, or with drinks

Spiced Cherry Tomatoes

(see page 15 for illustration)

A pickle with a hidden surprise — the tomato softens and bursts in the mouth when you bite down. This decorative pickle can also be made with small green or yellow tomatoes.

INGREDIENTS

2lb (1kg) firm red or yellow cherry tomatoes, preferably with stems attached

10–12 mint or basil leaves

Sugar-free Sweet Vinegar, to cover (see page 130)

1 Lightly prick each tomato in several places with a toothpick. Arrange in the sterilized jars with the mint or basil.

2 Pour the Sugar-free Sweet Vinegar into the jars, being sure that it covers the tomatoes by at least 1in (2.5cm). Poke the tomatoes with a wooden skewer to be sure there are no air pockets.

3 Weight down the tomatoes (see page 46), then seal. The tomatoes will be ready to eat in 4–6 weeks, but improve with age.

☆ **Degree of difficulty**
Easy

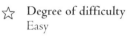 **Special equipment**
Sterilized canning jars with sealants (see pages 42–43)

Yield
About 2 pints (1kg)

Shelf life
1 year, refrigerated

Brined Cucumbers (Gherkins)

(see page 21 for illustration)

My mother, a superb pickler, maintains that the crunchiness and vivid green color of pickled cucumbers are achieved by blanching them briefly.

TIPS

• Grape leaves help the fermentation process and add their characteristic flavor to the pickle.
• The brine from this pickle and many others need not be thrown away after the gherkins have been eaten, but can be used as a base for soups, to flavor savory dishes, or to make a salad dressing.

INGREDIENTS

2lb (1kg) small, firm, pickling cucumbers

5–6 fat garlic cloves, bruised but not peeled

2–3 dill flower heads and stalks

3–4 fresh or dried red chilies

2–3 bay leaves

salt

a few grape leaves (optional)

1 Put the cucumbers in a saucepan of boiling water and blanch for 1 minute (see page 46).

2 Arrange the cucumbers, garlic, dill, chilies, and bay leaves in the sterilized jars. Fill the jars with water, then drain into a measuring cup. Add 1½ tablespoons salt for every 2 cups (500ml) water, stirring until dissolved.

3 Pour the brine into the jar, place the grape leaves on top, if using, then weight down (see page 46). Cover with a clean cloth and leave in a warm, well-ventilated place to ferment for 1–2 weeks. When fermentation starts, the brine will turn cloudy.

4 When the liquid starts to clear, indicating that fermentation is over, seal the jar tightly and store. The cucumbers are ready to eat immediately.

VARIATIONS

✦ *Fermented Tomatoes*
Use 2lb (1kg) small, firm red tomatoes and prick in several places with a toothpick. Arrange in a wide-mouth, sterilized canning jar with 3–4 fresh chilies, slit, 8 garlic cloves, 6–8 celery leaves, and 1 tablespoon black peppercorns. Cover with water and proceed as for the main recipe, adding 2 tablespoons salt for every 2 cups (500ml) water, and 2 tablespoons cider vinegar. Complete as above.

✦ *Fermented Beets*
Use 3lb (1.5kg) small, peeled beets; keep whole or cut into large chunks. Arrange in the jar and cover with the brine, as for the main recipe. Weight down, cover, and ferment. After a few days froth will start to form. Remove it every few days and wipe the top of the jar clean. The beets will be ready in about 1 month. Seal the jar. Use the liquid to make borscht. The beets can be added to borscht or eaten as a pickle.

☆ **Degree of difficulty**
Easy

Cooking time
1 minute

 Special equipment
Wide-mouth, sterilized canning jars with sealants (see pages 42–43)

Yield
About 2 pints (1kg)

Shelf life
6 months, refrigerated (3 months, refrigerated for beets)

Serving suggestions
Chop the cucumbers and add to sauces or potato salads; use to decorate canapés

Pickled Turnips or Radishes

This vividly colored pickle is popular all over the Middle East and in the southern part of Russia. In the past, pickled root vegetables were an important source of vitamins C and B during the bleak winter months. Today, they are still enjoyed for their flavor and crunchy texture.

TIP

• Any of the turnip family, such as red or white radishes or kohlrabi, can be used instead.

INGREDIENTS

1½ lb (750g) white turnips or large radishes, sliced ½ in (1cm) thick

½ lb (250g) raw beets, sliced ½ in (1cm) thick

4–5 garlic cloves, sliced

salt

3 tbsp white wine vinegar or distilled white vinegar

1 Arrange the turnips or radishes in the sterilized jars with the beets and garlic.

2 Fill the jars with enough cold water to cover the vegetables, then drain it off into a measuring cup. Add 1½ tablespoons salt for every 2 cups (500ml) water, stirring until the salt is dissolved. Add the white wine vinegar or distilled white vinegar, then pour into the jars.

3 Weight down the vegetables (see page 46), cover with a clean cloth, and leave in a warm, well-ventilated place for about 2 weeks, until fermentation is over (see Brined Cucumbers, page 93). Seal the jars. The pickle will be ready to eat in about 1 month.

☆ **Degree of difficulty**
Easy

Special equipment
Wide-mouth, sterilized canning jars with sealants (see pages 42–43)

Yield
About 2 pints (1kg)

Shelf life
3–6 months, refrigerated

Serving suggestions
Use in salads or serve as a snack with drinks

Pickled Celeriac and Carrot Salad

Earthy-looking celeriac (celery root) makes a delicious pickle. Be careful when choosing celeriac as it can become hollow and stringy when too mature. Select solid roots that are heavy for their size, and avoid any with green patches.

TIP

• I never blanch the orange rind first as I like its full, slightly bitter flavor. If you prefer, blanch the shredded rind in boiling water for 1–2 minutes, then drain and refresh in cold water before use.

INGREDIENTS

1 large celeriac, about 2lb (1kg), peeled and shredded or coarsely grated

5 large carrots, coarsely grated

2 onions, sliced into thin rings

2½ tbsp salt

2 tbsp dill seed

shredded rind and juice of 1 orange

2 cups (500ml) white wine vinegar or cider vinegar

⅔ cup (150ml) water

1 tbsp sugar (optional)

1 Mix the celeriac, carrots, and onions together in a glass bowl and sprinkle with 2 tablespoons of the salt. Mix well and let stand for about 2 hours.

2 Rinse the vegetables under cold running water, then drain well. Stir in the dill seed and orange rind, then pack loosely into the hot, sterilized jars.

3 Place the orange juice, vinegar, water, sugar, if using, and the remaining salt in a noncorrosive pan. Bring to a boil and boil for 2–3 minutes, then skim well. Pour into the jars to cover the vegetables. Poke the vegetables with a wooden skewer to be sure there are no air pockets, then seal. The pickle will be ready in 1 week.

☆ **Degree of difficulty**
Easy

Cooking time
4–5 minutes

Special equipment
Sterilized canning jars with sealants (see pages 42–43)

Yield
About 4 pints (2kg)

Shelf life
3–6 months, refrigerated

Serving suggestion
Especially good with hot or cold chicken

Chowchow

Recipes for this flavorful mustard pickle appear in many old cookbooks. This is my adaptation of a classic recipe. The pickle is traditionally made in summer when vegetables are in abundance, and any combination of fresh, colorful vegetables can be used.

INGREDIENTS

½ lb (250g) baby cucumbers

1 small cauliflower, divided into florets

½ lb (250g) green tomatoes, diced

4 medium carrots, cut into thick matchsticks

½ lb (250g) string beans, trimmed

10oz (300g) small pickling onions, peeled

4 red peppers, sliced

1 small bunch of celery, sliced

½ cup (100g) salt

For the pickling mixture

¾ cup (100g) all-purpose or whole-wheat flour

9 tbsp (75g) dry mustard powder

1½ tbsp celery seed

1½ tbsp ground turmeric

1 tbsp salt

5 cups (1.25 liters) cider vinegar or malt vinegar

1½ cups (300g) light brown or white sugar

1 If using tiny cucumbers, leave them whole; otherwise, slice into thick rings.

2 Put all the vegetables in a large glass bowl. Cover with cold water and add the salt. Mix well until the salt is dissolved, then weight down (see page 46) and let stand overnight.

3 The next day, drain the vegetables well and blanch for 2 minutes (see page 46).

4 To make the pickling mixture, combine the flour, dry mustard, celery seed, turmeric, and salt in a small bowl. Gradually add 1 cup (250ml) of the vinegar, mixing well to make a smooth, thin paste.

5 Put the remaining vinegar and the sugar in a noncorrosive saucepan and bring to a boil.

Gradually add the mustard paste, stirring all the time. Add the drained vegetables, bring back to a boil, then remove from the heat.

6 Pack the pickle into the hot, sterilized jars, then seal. It will be ready to eat in 2 weeks, but improves with age.

TIPS

• Whole-wheat flour makes a darker, more textured pickle.
• For a less crunchy pickle, simmer the vegetables in the vinegar for 5 minutes longer.

☆☆ **Degree of difficulty**
Moderate

Cooking time
About 2 minutes

Special equipment
Sterilized canning jars with sealants (see pages 42–43)

Yield
About 6 pints (3kg)

Shelf life
1 year, refrigerated

Serving suggestion
Serve as a relish with cold meats or cheese

Piccalilli

(see page 33 for illustration)

At the end of the 17th century this quintessentially British pickle was known as "pickle lila," an Indian pickle. This crunchy version is the exotic forefather of the unpleasantly harsh, bright yellow product found on supermarket shelves. For the vinegar, use any of the Spiced Vinegar recipes (see page 129).

TIPS
• Any combination of crunchy vegetables and fruits can be pickled in the same way.
• For a milder flavor, add the mustard seed to the vinegar and boil for 3–4 minutes.

INGREDIENTS
½ lb (250g) green beans, cut into bite-sized pieces

½ lb (250g) cauliflower, divided into small florets

4 medium carrots, cut into medium-thick slices

½ lb (250g) gooseberries, trimmed

½ lb (250g) honeydew melon, cut into cubes

½ lb (250g) seedless grapes

½ cup (125g) salt

13oz (400g) yellow mustard seed

4 cups (1 liter) Spiced Vinegar (see page 129)

1 tbsp ground turmeric

1 Put all the vegetables and fruit in a large glass bowl. Cover with cold water and add ⅓ cup (100g) of the salt. Mix until the salt is dissolved, then weight down (see page 46) and let stand for 24 hours.

2 The next day, coarsely grind the mustard seed in a spice mill or coffee grinder; if necessary, do this in batches.

3 Drain the vegetables and fruit, rinse under cold running water, and drain well. Taste; if too salty, cover with cold water and let soak for 10 minutes, then drain, rinse, and drain again. Add the ground mustard seed and mix well.

4 Put the Spiced Vinegar, turmeric, and remaining salt in a noncorrosive saucepan. Bring to a boil, skim well, and boil rapidly for 10 minutes.

5 Pour the boiling vinegar over the vegetables and fruit in the bowl and mix well. Pack into the hot, sterilized jars, then seal. The pickle is ready to eat immediately, but improves with age.

☆☆ **Degree of difficulty**
Moderate

Cooking time
About 12 minutes

Special equipment
Spice mill or coffee grinder; sterilized canning jars with sealants (see pages 42–43)

Yield
About 6 pints (3kg)

Shelf life
1 year, refrigerated

Serving suggestion
Delicious with cheese

Onion and Pepper Pickle

(see page 19 for illustration)

A colorful pickled salad. Use as many different colors of peppers as you can find, though green peppers lose their color very quickly. I sometimes add other vegetables such as sliced carrots or celeriac.

INGREDIENTS
2½ lb (1.25kg) onions, sliced into thin rings

2 red peppers, sliced into thin rings

2 yellow peppers, sliced into thin rings

4 tbsp salt

4 cups (1 liter) white wine vinegar or cider vinegar

½ cup (100g) sugar

2 tbsp dried mint

2 tbsp paprika

1 tbsp dill seed

2 tsp salt

1 Put the sliced onions and red and yellow peppers in a glass bowl and sprinkle with the 4 tablespoons salt. Mix well, cover with a clean cloth and let stand for 2 hours.

2 Drain off the liquid that has accumulated in the bottom of the bowl, then rinse the vegetables under cold running water and drain again.

3 Put the vinegar, sugar, mint, paprika, dill seed, and the 2 teaspoons salt in a noncorrosive saucepan. Bring to a boil, then reduce the heat and simmer for 5 minutes.

4 Pack the vegetables into the hot, sterilized jars. Pour in the boiling vinegar mixture, making sure all the vegetables are completely covered. Poke the contents of the jars with a wooden skewer to be sure there are no air pockets, then seal. The pickle will be ready to eat in about 1 week, but improves with age.

☆ **Degree of difficulty**
Easy

Cooking time
About 8 minutes

Special equipment
Sterilized canning jars with sealants (see pages 42–43)

Yield
About 4 pints (2kg)

Shelf life
6 months, refrigerated

Serving suggestion
Drain the vegetables, dress with a little oil, and serve as a refreshing salad

Bread and Butter Pickle

(see page 21 for illustration)

This delicious old-fashioned pickle was made to be spread on bread and butter, hence the name. However, some maintain that its name came about because the pickle was as common as bread and butter. This particular recipe is from New England.

INGREDIENTS

1½ lb (750g) pickling cucumbers
1¼ lb (625g) onions, sliced ¼ in (5mm) thick
¾ lb (375g) red or yellow peppers, sliced ¼ in (5mm) thick
3 tbsp salt
4 cups (1 liter) cider vinegar, white wine vinegar, or malt vinegar
2 cups (500g) light brown or white sugar
2 tsp ground turmeric
1 tbsp mustard seed
2 tsp dill seed

1 Put the cucumbers in a bowl and pour boiling water over them. Drain, refresh under cold running water, and drain again. Slice the cucumbers into ½ in (1cm) thick pieces.

2 Put the sliced cucumbers, onions, and peppers in a large glass bowl and sprinkle with the salt. Mix well, then cover the bowl with a clean cloth and let stand overnight in a cool place.

3 The next day, drain off the liquid in the bowl. Rinse the vegetables under cold running water and drain well. Taste a slice of cucumber; if it is too salty, cover the vegetables with more cold water and let stand for about 10 minutes, then drain, rinse, and drain again.

4 Put the vinegar, sugar, ground turmeric, mustard seed, and dill seed in a noncorrosive saucepan. Bring to a boil and boil rapidly for 10 minutes. Add the drained vegetables, bring back to a boil, then remove from the heat.

5 Pack the hot pickle into the sterilized jars, then seal. The pickle is ready to eat immediately.

☆ **Degree of difficulty**
Easy

Cooking time
About 15 minutes

Special equipment
Sterilized canning jars with sealants (see pages 42–43)

Yield
About 4 pints (2kg)

Shelf life
1 year, refrigerated

Serving suggestions
Serve with cold meats or spread on bread and butter with cheese

— TIP —
• The easiest way to slice the vegetables is with a mandoline.

Olive Oil Pickle

(see page 21 for illustration)

This classic pickle is easy to make and is a great standby. It is mildly sour, refreshing, and keeps extremely well. You can replace the cucumbers with thinly sliced, colorful peppers or carrots.

INGREDIENTS

1½ lb (750g) pickling cucumbers, sliced ¼ in (5mm) thick
1¼ lb (625g) onions, finely sliced
½ cup (75g) salt
2 cups (500ml) cider vinegar
⅓ cup (75ml) water
1 tbsp celery seed
1 tbsp yellow mustard seed
1 tbsp dill seed
⅓ cup (75ml) good fruity virgin olive oil

1 Put the sliced cucumbers and onions in a large glass bowl, cover with cold water, and add the salt. Mix gently until all the salt is dissolved, then weight down (see page 46). Cover the bowl with a clean cloth and let stand overnight.

2 The next day, drain and rinse the vegetables under cold running water. Drain again, squeezing out as much moisture as possible. Pack into the hot, sterilized jars.

3 Put the vinegar, water, and spices in a noncorrosive saucepan. Bring to a boil and boil for 5 minutes. Remove from the heat and allow the mixture to cool slightly, then whisk in the oil.

4 Pour the warm vinegar into the jars. Poke the vegetables with a wooden skewer to be sure there are no air pockets. Check that the oil and spices are evenly distributed, and the vegetables are covered, then seal. The pickle will be ready to eat in 2 weeks, but improves with age.

☆ **Degree of difficulty**
Easy

Cooking time
About 8 minutes

Special equipment
Sterilized canning jars with sealants (see pages 42–43)

Yield
About 3 pints (1.5kg)

Shelf life
1 year, refrigerated

Serving suggestion
Delicious with mature hard cheese such as Cheddar or Stilton

Pickled Baby Vegetables

(see page 19 for illustration)

Baby vegetables are now widely available and make a highly decorative and delicious pickle. Any mixture of vegetables can be prepared in the same way. If baby vegetables are not available, use ordinary ones, sliced into convenient-sized pieces and salted for 24 hours.

INGREDIENTS

4–5 yellow zucchini, sliced

3 baby white cabbages, quartered

3 baby cauliflowers, left whole

½ lb (250g) baby corn

½ lb (250g) shallots, peeled

½ cup (100g) salt

6 cups (1.5 liters) Spiced Vinegar of your choice, to cover (see page 129)

1 Put the zucchini, white cabbage, the cauliflowers, baby corn, and shallots in a large glass bowl and sprinkle with the salt.

2 Mix well, then cover the bowl with a clean cloth and let stand for 24–48 hours, stirring the vegetables from time to time.

3 Drain off the liquid from the bowl. Rinse the vegetables under cold running water and drain well. Cover with more cold water, let stand for 1 hour, then drain again.

4 Arrange the vegetables in decorative layers in the warm, sterilized jars, then weight down (see page 46).

5 Pour the vinegar into the jars, making sure the vegetables are covered, then seal. The pickle will be ready to eat in 4–6 weeks.

☆ **Degree of difficulty**
Easy

Special equipment
Wide-mouth, sterilized canning jars with sealants (see pages 42–43)

Yield
About 3 pints (1.5kg)

Shelf life
1 year, refrigerated

Serving suggestions
Serve as a winter salad or as the centerpiece of a cold buffet

Toby's Pickled Cucumbers

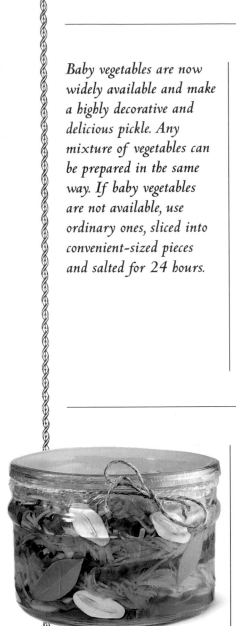

This is adapted from a recipe given to me by Toby Kay of Johannesburg, but its origins are probably Central European. It is easy to make and ready to eat in just 2 days. Drained and dressed with a little oil and chopped herbs, it makes a colorful salad.

INGREDIENTS

1 lb (500g) large cucumbers, sliced ½ in (1cm) thick

2 tbsp salt

¾ lb (375g) onions, sliced into thin rings

½ lb (275g) carrots, coarsely grated or sliced into fine julienne

4 garlic cloves, sliced

1 tsp black peppercorns

3–4 bay leaves

3 cups (750ml) water

1½ cups (350ml) white wine vinegar or distilled malt vinegar

4 tbsp sugar

1–2 dried red chilies

1 Put the sliced cucumbers in a colander and sprinkle with half the salt. Mix well and let stand for about 20 minutes. Rinse the vegetables under cold running water and drain well.

2 Mix the onion rings and carrot julienne together in a bowl, pour in boiling water to cover, then drain well.

3 Arrange a layer of sliced cucumbers in the bottom of the hot, sterilized jars. Place a few slices of garlic, a few peppercorns, and a bay leaf on top and cover with a layer of the onion and carrot mixture.

4 Repeat the layers until all the vegetables are used up. The jars should be almost full, but loosely packed.

5 Place the water, white wine vinegar, sugar, dried red chilies, and remaining salt in a noncorrosive saucepan. Bring to a boil and boil steadily for a few minutes. Skim well and remove the chilies.

6 Pour the hot vinegar mixture into the jars, filling it right to the top to make sure that the cucumbers are completely covered. Poke the vegetables with a wooden skewer to be sure there are no air pockets, then seal the jars. Keep refrigerated. The pickle will be ready to eat in 2 days.

☆ **Degree of difficulty**
Easy

Cooking time
About 5 minutes

Special equipment
Sterilized canning jars with sealants (see pages 42–43)

Yield
About 2 pints (1kg)

Shelf life
3 months, refrigerated

Serving suggestions
Serve as a salad or a snack with drinks

Pickled Okra

This pickle is based on a traditional Iranian recipe. Okra is a fascinating vegetable, with a unique flavor and texture. Do not be alarmed if the pickling liquid thickens; it is due to the glutinous quality of the okra.

INGREDIENTS

1½ lb (750g) crisp young okra
1 tbsp salt
½ lb (275g) carrots, cut into thick matchsticks
6 large garlic cloves, sliced
3–4 fresh red chilies, seeded and sliced (optional)
small bunch of mint, coarsely chopped
For the pickling mixture
4 cups (1 liter) cider vinegar
4 tbsp sugar or honey
1 tbsp salt
2 tsp ground turmeric

1 Trim any dark spots from the stem end of the okra but leave the stems attached. Prick each okra in a few places with a toothpick.

2 Lay the okra out on a large baking sheet and sprinkle with the salt. Let stand, preferably in the sun, for 1 hour.

3 Rinse the okra well under cold running water and dry on paper towels. Blanch the carrots in boiling water for 2–3 minutes (see page 46).

4 Mix together the garlic, chilies, if using, and mint. Arrange the okra and carrots in layers in the sterilized jars, evenly distributing the garlic mixture between the layers. The jars should be full, but loosely packed.

5 For the pickling mixture, put the vinegar, sugar or honey, and salt in a noncorrosive saucepan. Bring to a boil and skim well. Add the turmeric and boil for a few minutes more.

6 Pour the hot vinegar into the jars, filling them to the top to make sure the okra are completely covered. Poke the vegetables with a wooden skewer to be sure there are no air pockets, then seal. The pickle will be ready in 2 weeks.

☆ **Degree of difficulty**
Easy

Cooking time
About 6 minutes

Special equipment
Sterilized canning jars with sealants (see pages 42–43)

Yield
About 4 pints (2kg)

Shelf life
6 months, refrigerated

Serving suggestions
Serve on its own, or as a pickled salad to accompany cold meat

Hungarian Pickled Peppers ⸻ *(see page 17 for illustration)*

If you are lucky you will find "tomato" peppers — so named for their shape — in the stores in September. They are either red or pale yellow and have a dense flesh that makes them ideal for pickling. If they are unavailable, substitute small, colorful sweet peppers, but do not use green ones, which turn an unpleasant color.

INGREDIENTS

2lb (1kg) red peppers
2 small dried chilies
2 bay leaves
water
white wine vinegar
sugar
salt
For the spice bag (see page 47)
2 tsp black peppercorns
1 tsp allspice berries
2 bay leaves

1 Wash the peppers thoroughly, leaving the stems attached, then arrange them in the sterilized jars with the dried chilies and the bay leaves.

2 Fill the jars with cold water, then drain it off into a measuring cup. Drain off half the water and replace it with vinegar. For every 4 cups liquid, add 2 tablespoons each of sugar and salt.

3 Place the vinegar, water, sugar, salt, and spice bag in a noncorrosive saucepan. Bring to a boil, reduce the heat, and simmer for 10 minutes. Let cool slightly.

4 Pour the liquid into the jars, making sure the peppers are covered, then seal. After a few days check that there is enough liquid to cover the peppers — their cavities tend to absorb the vinegar. The peppers will be ready in 2 weeks.

☆ **Degree of difficulty**
Easy

Cooking time
About 12 minutes

Special equipment
Sterilized, wide-mouth canning jars with sealants (see pages 42–43)

Yield
About 2 pints (1kg)

Shelf life
1 year, refrigerated

Serving suggestion
Serve as an accompaniment to cold meats

Spiced Whole Oranges

(see page 29 for illustration)

Spiced oranges are a classic British preserve. In this elegant version, the oranges are left whole instead of being sliced. They make a welcome addition to a festive meal.

INGREDIENTS

2lb (1kg) small, thin-skinned oranges, preferably seedless

4 cups (1 liter) cider vinegar or distilled malt vinegar

3 cups (750g) sugar

juice of 1 lemon

cloves

For the spice bag (see page 47)

2 tsp cloves

2 cinnamon sticks, crushed

1 tsp cardamom pods, crushed

1 Scrub the oranges well, then remove alternate strips of rind with a vegetable peeler or paring knife and add to the spice bag.

2 Put the oranges in a noncorrosive saucepan and cover with water. Bring to a boil and simmer very gently for 20–25 minutes, or until the peel is just soft. Lift out the oranges with a slotted spoon and drain well.

3 Measure 4 cups (1 liter) of the cooking liquid and return to the pan. Add the vinegar, sugar, lemon juice, and spice bag. Bring to a boil and boil for 10 minutes. Remove from the heat and skim well. Return the oranges to the pan and let stand overnight.

4 The next day, bring the mixture back to a boil, then reduce the heat and simmer very gently for 20 minutes. Carefully remove the oranges from the liquid with a slotted spoon and let cool slightly.

5 Stud each orange with a few whole cloves and arrange in the hot, sterilized jar. Bring the syrup to a boil and boil hard until it is slightly thick. Pour the boiling syrup into the jar, making sure the oranges are completely covered, then seal. They will be ready to eat in about 1 month, but improve with age.

☆☆ **Degree of difficulty**
Moderate

Cooking time
About 1 hour

Special equipment
Wide-mouth, sterilized canning jar with sealant (see pages 42–43)

Yield
About 2lb (1kg)

Shelf life
2 years, refrigerated

Serving suggestions
Serve with cold ham (see page 134 for recipe), turkey, chicken, or other poultry

Pickled Limes

(see page 29 for illustration)

A sharp, hot pickle from the Punjab in India. This recipe can also be made with lemons or oranges.

INGREDIENTS

2lb (1kg) limes

½ cup (100g) salt

1 tsp cardamom pods

1 tsp black cumin seed (kalajeera)

1 tsp cumin seed

½ tsp cloves

2 cups (500g) light brown or white sugar

1 tbsp chili powder, or to taste

5 tbsp (75g) finely shredded fresh ginger

1 Put the limes in a bowl and cover with cold water. Let soak overnight, then drain. Cut them into slices ¼ in (5mm) thick. Place in a glass bowl and sprinkle with the salt. Mix well, cover with a clean cloth and let stand for 12 hours.

2 The next day, place the spices in the spice mill or coffee grinder and grind to a powder.

3 Drain the limes and place the liquid they have produced in a noncorrosive saucepan with the sugar and ground spices. Bring to a boil, stirring until the sugar is dissolved, and boil for 1 minute. Remove from the heat and stir in the chili powder. Let cool.

4 Add the limes and ginger to the cooled syrup and mix well. Pack into the hot, sterilized jars. Poke the limes with a wooden skewer to be sure there are no air pockets, then seal. Leave in a warm place, such as a sunny windowsill, for 4–5 days before storing. The pickle will be ready in 4–5 weeks.

☆☆ **Degree of difficulty**
Moderate

Cooking time
About 5 minutes

Special equipment
Spice mill or coffee grinder; sterilized canning jars with sealants (see pages 42–43)

Yield
About 2lb (1kg)

Shelf life
2 years, refrigerated

Serving suggestions
Serve as a relish with a selection of appetizers or spread over whole fish or fish fillets before baking

Pickled Plums

This Central European recipe makes a novel accompaniment to bread and cheese.

INGREDIENTS

2 cups (500ml) cider vinegar

⅔ cup (150ml) apple or pear concentrate

1 tbsp salt

2lb (1kg) prune plums

8 cloves

8 allspice berries

6–8 strands of finely shredded fresh ginger

2 bay leaves

1 Put the cider vinegar, fruit concentrate, and salt in a noncorrosive saucepan. Bring to a boil and boil for 1–2 minutes.

2 Prick the plums all over with a toothpick and arrange in the hot, sterilized jars with the spices and bay leaves. Pour the boiling vinegar into the jars to cover, then seal. The plums will be ready to eat in about 1 month.

☆ **Degree of difficulty**
Easy

Cooking time
3–4 minutes

Special equipment
Sterilized canning jars with sealants (see pages 42–43)

Yield
About 2lb (1kg)

Shelf life
2 years, refrigerated

Melon Pickled Like Mango

This oddity is a 17th-century British recipe. At that time mangoes were a luxury and many recipes were devised using more readily available fruits. Peppers can be prepared in the same way.

INGREDIENTS

4–5 small, underripe melons, preferably Galia or Charentais

salt

any Spiced Vinegar or Sweet Spiced Vinegar, to cover (see page 129)

For the stuffing

10oz (300g) white cabbage, finely shredded

2 medium carrots, coarsely grated

2 red peppers or a few fresh red chilies, shredded

3 celery ribs, coarsely chopped

5 tbsp (75g) finely shredded fresh ginger

2 garlic cloves, sliced

⅓ cup (100g) salt

1 tbsp mustard seed

2 tsp nigella seed (optional)

1 Prepare the melons (see step 1, below) and place in a glass bowl. Cover with cold water, then drain it off into a measuring cup. Add 4 tablespoons salt for every 4 cups (1 liter) water. Pour over the melons and let stand for 24 hours.

2 For the stuffing, place the vegetables, ginger, and garlic in a bowl. Mix well with the salt, cover, and let stand for 24 hours.

3 Drain and rinse the stuffing and melons, then rinse and drain again. Add the spices to the stuffing and fill the melons (see steps 2–3, below). Place in the jar and add vinegar to cover. Weight down (see page 46), then seal. The melons will be ready in 5–6 weeks.

☆☆☆ **Degree of difficulty**
Advanced

Special equipment
Wide-mouth, earthenware or glass sterilized canning jar with sealant (see pages 42–43)

Yield
4–5 melons

Shelf life
1 year, refrigerated

Serving suggestion
Serve as the centerpiece of a cold buffet

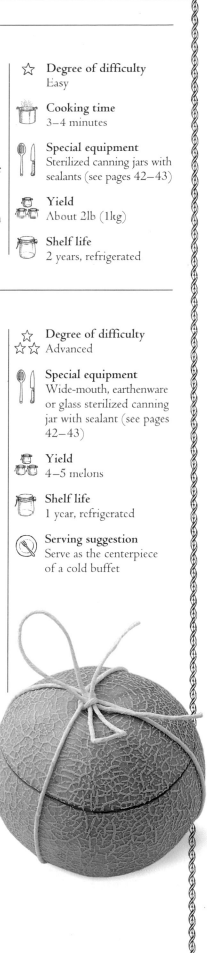

PREPARING THE MELONS

1 Cut the tops off the melons and reserve as lids. Scoop out all the seeds and fibers from the center of the fruit using a spoon.

2 Divide the drained vegetable stuffing equally between the melon halves, using a spoon to carefully pack it inside.

3 Place the lids on the stuffed melons and tie them in place with string or secure them with toothpicks.

Kiwi Fruit and Red Pepper Pickle

An exotic, colorful, and mild pickle. Be careful not to overcook the kiwi fruit as it softens very quickly. For more color, use a combination of red, yellow, and orange peppers.

INGREDIENTS

2lb (1kg) hard, unripe kiwi fruit, peeled and cut into large chunks

juice of 1 lemon

3 red peppers, cut into wide strips

1 tbsp salt

4 cups (1 liter) cider vinegar or white wine vinegar

¾ cup (200g) honey, preferably single blossom

½ cup (150g) light brown sugar or white sugar

1 tbsp black peppercorns

2 tsp juniper berries

1 tsp allspice berries

1 Put the kiwi fruit chunks in a glass bowl and sprinkle with the lemon juice. Mix gently, and let marinate for 15 minutes. Sprinkle the red peppers with the salt and leave for 15 minutes.

2 Put the vinegar, honey, sugar, and spices in a noncorrosive saucepan. Bring to a boil and boil hard for 10 minutes, until the syrup is slightly reduced.

3 Rinse the peppers under cold running water and drain well. Add to the boiling syrup. Bring back to a boil, then reduce the heat and simmer for 5 minutes. Add the kiwi fruit to the pan and simmer for 5 minutes longer.

4 Using a slotted spoon, lift the kiwi fruit and peppers out of the pan and carefully pack them into the hot, sterilized jars. Boil the syrup hard for about 10 minutes, until slightly reduced again. Pour the boiling syrup into the jars, then seal. The pickle will be ready to eat after 1 week, but improves with age.

☆☆ **Degree of difficulty**
Moderate

Cooking time
About 40 minutes

Special equipment
Sterilized canning jars with sealants (see pages 42–43)

Yield
About 3 pints (1.5kg)

Shelf life
1 year, refrigerated

Serving suggestions
Dress with olive oil and serve as a salad or use to decorate cold meat platters

Preserved Lemons

(see page 29 for illustration)

Preserved lemons are an essential ingredient in North African cooking. Salting softens the peel and gives the lemon a stronger flavor, so use with discretion.

Preserved Kaffir Limes, see tips

INGREDIENTS

2lb (1kg) small, thin-skinned lemons

salt

about 1½ cups (350ml) lemon or lime juice or acidulated water (see step 3)

1–2 tbsp olive oil

1 Wash and scrub the lemons. Slice each one lengthwise into quarters, from the pointed end, leaving the sections still attached at the stem end, so that they resemble flowers.

2 Gently open out each lemon and sprinkle with about a teaspoon of salt, then close up. Pack the lemons tightly into the sterilized jar and weight down (see page 46). Let stand in a warm place, preferably on a sunny windowsill, for 4–5 days. By then some liquid should have accumulated in the jar.

3 Pour the citrus juice or acidulated water (1½ teaspoons citric acid dissolved in 2 cups/500ml cold water) into the jar, making sure the lemons are completely covered.

4 Pour the oil into the top of the jar in a thin layer: this will prevent mold from forming. Seal the jar immediately. The brine will look cloudy at first, but should clear after 3–4 weeks, when the lemons will be ready to eat.

--- TIPS ---

• Before using the lemons, wash them well under cold running water, then slice and prepare as directed in the recipe. Some people discard the pulp and use only the peel.
• The wonderfully pungent pickling liquid can also be used to dress salads or to flavor stews.
• Limes can be preseved the same way.

☆ **Degree of difficulty**
Easy

Special equipment
Sterilized canning jar with sealant (see pages 42–43)

Yield
About 2lb (1kg)

Shelf life
2 years, refrigerated

Serving suggestions
Use to flavor tagines and couscous, or to accompany grilled fish

Pickled Watermelon Rind

Watermelon rind is very versatile — it can be preserved in syrup, candied, or fermented in brine.

INGREDIENTS

1lb (500g) watermelon rind, green skin removed, with about ¼in (5mm) of the red flesh left on

4 tbsp salt

4 cups (1kg) granulated sugar

3 cups (750ml) water

3 cups (750ml) white wine vinegar or cider vinegar

For the spice bag (see page 47)

2in (5cm) piece fresh ginger, chopped

1 cinnamon stick, broken

1 tbsp allspice berries

1 tbsp cloves

2–3 strips lemon or orange rind (optional)

1 Slice the watermelon rind into 1in (2.5cm) cubes and place in a large glass bowl with the salt. Add enough water to cover, then stir well until the salt is dissolved. Cover with a clean cloth and let stand overnight.

2 The next day, drain the watermelon rind. Place in a noncorrosive saucepan and cover with fresh water. Bring to a boil, then reduce the heat and simmer for about 15 minutes. Drain well.

3 Put the sugar, water, vinegar, and spice bag in the cleaned saucepan. Bring to a boil and cook for about 5 minutes. Skim well, add the drained watermelon rind, and return to a boil, then reduce the heat and simmer gently for 45–60 minutes, or until the rind is translucent.

4 Pack the mixture into the hot, sterilized jars, then seal. The pickle will be ready to eat in about 1 month.

☆ **Degree of difficulty**
Easy

Cooking time
1–1¼ hours

Special equipment
Sterilized canning jars with sealants (see pages 42–43)

Yield
About 3 pints (1.5kg)

Shelf life
2 years, heat processed

Serving suggestion
Delicious with poultry and cold ham

---TIP---

• Always remove all the green skin of the watermelon; it contains a laxative.

Striped Spiced Pears

This fragrant preserve is particularly attractive because of the striped appearance of the whole pears. It is especially good with game.

INGREDIENTS

juice of 1 lemon

2lb (1kg) hard pears

5 cups (1.25 liters) red wine vinegar

2 cups (500ml) red wine

2 cups (500g) sugar

¾ cup (250g) honey

For the spice bag (see page 47)

1 tbsp black peppercorns

2 tsp cloves

2 tsp allspice berries

1 tsp lavender flowers (optional)

2 bay leaves

1 large cinnamon stick

a few strips of lemon rind

1 Stir the lemon juice into a large bowl of cold water. Peel alternate strips of skin from the pears with a vegetable peeler or paring knife to give a striped effect. Put the pears in the lemon juice and water mixture.

2 Put the vinegar, wine, sugar, honey, and spice bag in a noncorrosive saucepan. Bring to a boil, skim, and boil for 5 minutes.

3 Add the pears, reduce the heat, and simmer gently for 35–40 minutes, until they have softened a little but still show some resistance when pierced with a knife. Lift the pears out of the pan with a slotted spoon and arrange them in the hot, sterilized jar.

4 Boil the syrup rapidly until it is reduced by half and slightly thickened. Remove the spice bag. Pour the hot syrup into the jar, making sure the pears are totally covered, then seal. The pears will be ready to eat in 1 month.

☆☆ **Degree of difficulty**
Moderate

Cooking time
About 50 minutes

Special equipment
Wide-mouth, sterilized canning jar with sealant (see pages 42–43)

Yield
About 2lb (1kg)

Shelf life
2 years, heat processed

Serving suggestion
Serve with game or turkey

PRESERVES IN OIL

THE PRESERVATION OF FOOD in oil is an age-old technique that is mentioned in ancient Roman writings. It is the hot country's solution to the cold country's technique of preserving food in animal fat. The oil not only acts as a sealing agent, but also imparts a delightfully mellow flavor to the preserve, so always use the best-quality oil you can afford. Cold-pressed, extra-virgin olive oil is usually too pungent for this purpose, so I usually dilute it with a mild oil, such as peanut or refined sesame oil – a good-quality, fruity, virgin olive oil could be used instead. Experiment with a mixture of oils until you find the balance of flavors that suits you best.

Mushrooms Preserved in Oil

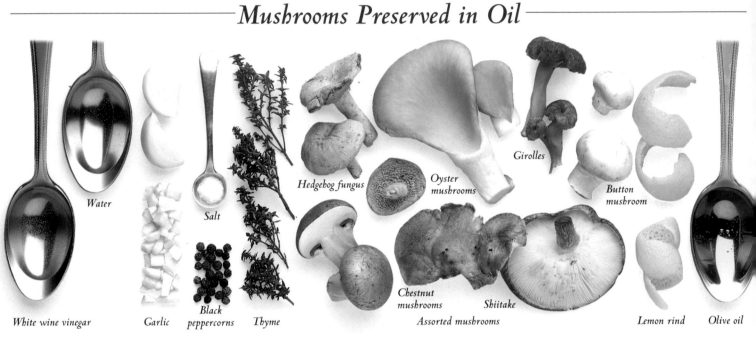

Water • Salt • Hedgehog fungus • Oyster mushrooms • Girolles • Button mushroom

White wine vinegar • Garlic • Black peppercorns • Thyme • Chestnut mushrooms • Shiitake • Assorted mushrooms • Lemon rind • Olive oil

I love mushrooms. Their flavor brings back memories of cool autumn days and the haunting scent of wood and rotting leaves. The wild mushroom season is short and one of the best ways to prolong it is to preserve a glut of mushrooms in oil.

INGREDIENTS

2 cups (500ml) white wine vinegar
1 cup (250ml) water
3–4 garlic cloves, coarsely chopped
1 tsp black peppercorns
2 tsp salt
4–6 sprigs thyme
2lb (1kg) assorted mushrooms
1–2 strips lemon rind
1 bay leaf (optional)
good-quality olive oil, to cover

1 Put the vinegar, water, garlic, peppercorns, salt, and a few sprigs of the thyme in a deep noncorrosive pan. Bring to a boil, then reduce the heat and simmer for 30 minutes.

2 Add the mushrooms to the pan and simmer for about 10 minutes, or until they are just cooked. Remove them with a slotted spoon and drain well. Remove the thyme.

3 Arrange the mushrooms, strips of lemon rind, bay leaf, if using, and remaining thyme sprigs in the hot, sterilized jar.

4 Heat the olive oil in a pan to 167°F (75°C) and pour it carefully into the jar, making sure the mushrooms are completely covered. Poke the mushrooms with a wooden skewer to be sure there are no air pockets, then seal. The mushrooms will be ready to eat in about 2 weeks.

☆ **Degree of difficulty**
Easy

Cooking time
About 45 minutes

Special equipment
Thermometer; sterilized jar with sealant
(see pages 42–43)

Yield
About 2 pints (1kg)

Shelf life
6 months, refrigerated

Serving suggestions
Serve as an hors d'oeuvre or use with a little of the oil from the jar as an instant pasta sauce

BEFORE YOU SEAL
the jar, make sure
that the mushrooms
are totally covered
with the olive oil

MUSHROOMS PRESERVED IN OIL
*make a delicious appetizer. Serve them on thick
slices of French bread that have been fried in a
little of the mushrooms' preserving oil.*

AN ASSORTMENT of
fresh wild and
cultivated mushrooms
will produce the best
flavor combination

PIECES OF LEMON rind
impart a subtle
fragrance to the
mushrooms

TIPS

• Mushrooms soak up water like a
sponge, so do not wash them unless
absolutely necessary. Just trim them,
brush off any dust and dirt, and wipe
clean with a paper towel.

• Any small edible wild mushrooms can
be used as long as they are in perfect
condition; cèpes and morels are especially
good. Small cultivated mushrooms can
be prepared in the same way.

Eggplants Preserved in Oil

An adaptation of a Lebanese recipe, this makes an unusual and very fragrant preserve. Eggplants acquire an amazingly soft, melt-in-the-mouth texture when preserved this way. The oil left in the jar is superb for dressing salads.

INGREDIENTS

2lb (1kg) baby eggplants, stems removed

salt

¼ cup (75g) pecan halves

2 lemons, finely sliced into semicircles

6 garlic cloves, cut into tiny slivers

2 cups (500ml) olive oil, to cover

1 Steam the whole eggplants for 5–7 minutes, or until just soft. Let cool.

2 Make a pocket in each eggplant by cutting a deep slit lengthwise. Sprinkle the inside of the pocket with a tiny pinch of salt and place a pecan half, a slice of lemon, and a sliver of garlic in each. Secure with a toothpick.

3 Pack the eggplants into the warm, sterilized jar. If there are any slices of lemon and garlic left over, arrange between the eggplants.

4 Heat the olive oil until it reaches 180°F (80°C). Pour it carefully into the jar, making sure the eggplants are completely covered, then seal. The eggplants will be ready to eat in 3–4 weeks.

☆☆ **Degree of difficulty**
Moderate

Cooking time
About 10 minutes

Special equipment
Steamer; wide-mouth, sterilized canning jar with sealant (see pages 42–43); thermometer

Yield
About 2 pints (1kg)

Shelf life
6 months, refrigerated

Serving suggestions
Serve as an appetizer or with drinks

Charbroiled Vegetables in Oil

Charbroiling the vegetables adds a wonderfully smoky flavor to this adaptation of a classic Sicilian recipe. Many other combinations of vegetables can be prepared in the same way.

Peppers in Oil, see variation

INGREDIENTS

1lb (500g) small eggplants, halved lengthwise, or large eggplants, sliced into thick batons

2 medium zucchini, sliced into thick batons

3 tbsp salt

4 lemons

1lb (500g) red and yellow peppers, thickly sliced

5 shallots, peeled

1 large head garlic, peeled

2½ cups (600ml) olive oil

3 tbsp capers

2–3 sprigs rosemary

2–3 sprigs thyme

1 Put the sliced eggplants and zucchini in a colander and sprinkle with 2 tablespoons of the salt. Mix well and let stand for about 1 hour. Rinse under cold running water, drain, and pat dry with paper towels.

2 Grate the rind from 1 of the lemons, then squeeze the juice from all of them. Put the rind and juice in a large glass bowl with the rest of the salt and stir until the salt is dissolved.

3 Brush the eggplants, zucchini, peppers, shallots, and garlic with 4–5 tablespoons of the oil. Cook under a hot broiler or on a barbecue for about 5 minutes on each side, or until lightly charred and blistered.

4 As soon as the vegetables are done, stir them into the lemon juice. Cover the bowl with a cloth and marinate for about 1 hour.

5 Arrange the vegetables in the hot, sterilized jar with the capers and herbs. Whisk the remaining oil with the lemon juice left over from marinating the vegetables. Place in a pan and heat until it reaches 180°F (80°C).

6 Pour the hot liquid carefully into the jar, filling it to the top and making sure all the vegetables are completely covered, then seal. The vegetables will be ready to eat in 4–6 weeks.

☆☆ **Degree of difficulty**
Moderate

Cooking time
About 12 minutes

Special equipment
Wide-mouth, sterilized canning jar with sealant (see pages 42–43); thermometer

Yield
About 4 pints (2kg)

Shelf life
1 year, refrigerated

Serving suggestion
Serve as part of an antipasto selection

VARIATION

✦ *Peppers in Oil*
Roast and skin 3lb (1.5kg) red or yellow peppers (see page 56). Marinate the warm peppers in the lemon juice with 3–4 mashed cloves of garlic. Mix well, cover, and refrigerate for 24 hours. Bring back to room temperature, drain and pack the whole peppers into a 1-quart (1-liter) sterilized jar. Finish as for main recipe.

Preserved Artichokes

Globe artichokes are popular throughout the Mediterranean, where they are eaten raw in salads, cooked in casseroles, and, of course, preserved. If you are lucky enough to find baby artichokes for this recipe, just remove any tough outer leaves and cut the artichokes in half. The tender choke can be left in.

INGREDIENTS

2 large lemons

1½ tbsp salt

1 tbsp finely chopped thyme

3lb (1.5kg) young globe artichokes

2 cups (500ml) mild olive, peanut, or refined sesame oil

1 Grate the rind from 1 of the lemons and squeeze the juice from both of them. Keep the squeezed-out lemon halves.

2 Put the lemon juice and rind, salt, and thyme in a large glass bowl and mix well until the salt is dissolved.

3 Trim the artichoke stems and peel off the leaves, trimming well to expose the heart (see steps 1–3, below). Rub the flesh with the reserved lemon halves to prevent it from discoloring. Using a grapefruit spoon, scrape out the choke (see step 4, below).

4 If the artichoke hearts are large, cut them lengthwise in half. As you finish preparing each artichoke, add it to the lemon mixture, turning to coat. Let stand for 30 minutes.

5 Pack the artichokes into the sterilized jars. Whisk the oil with the lemon juice left over from marinating the artichokes and pour into the jars, making sure the vegetables are covered, then seal. They will be ready in 6–8 weeks. Occasionally shake the jars to mix the ingredients.

 ☆☆ **Degree of difficulty**
Moderate

Special equipment
Wide-mouth, sterilized canning jars with sealants (see pages 42–43)

Yield
About 1½ pints (750g)

Shelf life
2 years, refrigerated

Serving suggestions
Serve as part of an antipasto selection or slice and serve with pasta

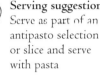

BABY ARTICHOKES are ideal for this recipe

PREPARING THE ARTICHOKES

1 Using a sharp knife, remove the tough stalk of each artichoke, cutting it off as close to the base of the head as possible.

2 Peel off the leaves, rubbing the exposed parts of the flesh with the reserved lemon half to prevent them from browning.

3 Trim the artichoke heart with a paring knife to remove any remaining tough parts. Rub the cut surfaces with the lemon again.

4 Spoon out and discard the fluffy choke from the center using a grapefruit spoon. Place the hearts in the lemon mixture.

Oven-dried Tomatoes Preserved in Oil

Dried tomatoes are the savory equivalent of raisins. They develop a strong, concentrated flavor that can be used to enhance the flavor of many dishes. In hot climates tomatoes can be dried in direct sun (see page 60). This takes about 2 days.

INGREDIENTS

2lb (1kg) beefsteak or plum tomatoes
2 tbsp salt
1 tbsp sugar
1 tbsp dried basil or mint
4 tbsp extra-virgin olive oil
1 sprig rosemary
1–2 dried chilies (optional)
1–2 garlic cloves, cut into slivers (optional)
olive oil, to cover

1 Halve the tomatoes and arrange, cut side up, on a wire rack placed over a foil-lined baking sheet. Sprinkle with the salt, sugar, and dried basil or mint and then finely drizzle the extra-virgin olive oil over the top.

2 Place the sheet in an oven set to the lowest possible temperature and leave the door slightly ajar to allow the moisture to escape. Bake for 8–12 hours, or until the tomatoes are dry but still pliable.

3 Pack the dried tomatoes into the sterilized jar along with the rosemary, dried chilies, and garlic, if using.

4 Pour olive oil into the jar, making sure the tomatoes are completely covered. Poke the contents of the jar with a wooden skewer to be sure there are no air pockets, then seal. The tomatoes will be ready to eat in 1–2 days, but improve with age.

☆ **Degree of difficulty**
Easy

Cooking time
8–12 hours

Special equipment
Sterilized canning jar with sealant (see pages 42–43)

Yield
About ¾ pint (300g)

Shelf life
2 years, refrigerated

Serving suggestions
Use to flavor salads, pasta sauces, stews, and breads; fresh from the oven, the tomatoes make a delicious first course with a yogurt dressing

Labna (Soft Cheese) (see page 54 for technique)

Labna is a refreshingly sharp yogurt cheese from the Middle East. Originally it was made with sheep's or goat's milk yogurt, but now cow's milk yogurt is more common. The cheese-making process destroys bacteria — a vital step in the days before refrigeration. Use the best virgin olive oil you can afford, as it imparts a heavenly fragrance to the cheese.

INGREDIENTS

8 cups (2 liters) plain yogurt
⅓ cup (75ml) good-quality virgin olive oil
grated rind and juice of 1 lemon
3 tbsp dried mint (optional)
1 tbsp finely chopped thyme (optional)
1 tbsp salt
olive oil, to cover

1 Place the yogurt, virgin olive oil, lemon rind and juice, dried mint, thyme, and salt in a large glass bowl. Beat with a wooden spoon until all the ingredients are thoroughly combined.

2 Line a large bowl with a double layer of sterilized cheesecloth, leaving plenty of the material overlapping the sides. Pour in the yogurt mixture.

3 Tie the ends of the cloth together and secure with string. Hang the mixture over a bowl.

4 Let the yogurt drain in a cool place, such as a cool pantry or unheated room between 42–46°F (6–8°C), for 2–3 days in winter or 2 days in summer. On hot days, you may need to keep the mixture in the bottom of the refrigerator.

5 Chill the well-drained mixture until it is firm to the touch — this makes it easier to handle. Using your fingers, shape the resulting soft cheese into 1½in (4cm) balls.

6 Chill the cheese balls again if necessary, so they keep their shape, then arrange them in the sterilized jar.

7 Pour the olive oil into the jar, making sure that the cheese balls are completely covered. Rap the jar several times on a work surface to be sure there are no air pockets, then seal. The cheese balls are ready to eat immediately.

☆☆ **Degree of difficulty**
Moderate

Special equipment
Sterilized cheesecloth; wide-mouth, sterilized canning jar with sealant (see pages 42–43)

Yield
About 2½ pints (1.25kg)

Shelf life
6 months, refrigerated

Serving suggestion
Serve the cheese balls drizzled with the oil from the jar, as part of a Middle Eastern appetizer selection

Mixed Seafood in Oil
(see page 27 for illustration)

You need as many colorful types of seafood as you can find to make this strikingly beautiful preserve. Especially suitable are small squid, octopus, clams, razor clams, mussels, and small crustaceans. If fresh seafood is not available, frozen mixed seafood can be used instead, though the flavor is not as good. There is no need to cook it; just pour the boiling stock over the defrosted seafood and marinate for 3 hours.

INGREDIENTS

1 large lemon, cut into thin wedges

1 tbsp salt

10oz (330g) small squid, cleaned and sliced into ½ in (1cm) rings

½ lb (200g) baby octopus, cleaned and left whole, or sliced large octopus

¾ lb (400g) live mussels or clams

½ lb (200g) scallops

¾ lb (400g) shrimp, heads removed, peeled if desired

2–3 dried red chilies

2–3 sprigs rosemary

1–2 bay leaves

2 cups (500ml) olive oil

For the stock

1 cup (250ml) dry white wine

1 cup (250ml) water

1 cup (250ml) white wine vinegar

1 small fennel bulb, sliced

2–3 strips lemon or orange rind

2 tsp salt

1 tsp black peppercorns

1 tsp fennel seed

1 bay leaf

1 Put the lemon wedges in a colander and sprinkle with the salt. Mix well and let stand for about 1 hour.

2 Put all the ingredients for the stock in a large, noncorrosive saucepan. Bring to a boil, then reduce the heat and simmer for 20 minutes. Add the squid rings and octopus and simmer for 15–20 minutes, or until the octopus starts to soften.

3 Add the rest of the seafood to the pan and simmer gently for about 5 minutes, or until the scallops are just done. Drain well.

4 Arrange the warm seafood in the warm, sterilized jar along with the lemon wedges, chilies, rosemary, and bay leaves. Heat the olive oil until it reaches 140°F (60°C). Pour the hot oil into the jar, filling it to the top to make sure the ingredients are completely covered, then seal. The seafood will be ready to eat in 4–6 weeks.

☆☆ **Degree of difficulty**
Moderate

Cooking time
45–55 minutes

Special equipment
Wide-mouth, sterilized canning jar with sealant (see pages 42–43); thermometer

Yield
About 2½ pints (1.25kg)

Shelf life
2–3 days, refrigerated

Serving suggestions
Serve as part of an antipasto selection or spoon over hot or cold pasta for a light main course dish

TIPS
• The mussels or clams can be removed from their shells or left on the half shell to enhance their decorative value.
• The cooking stock can be strained and used as a base for a fish soup.

Herrings in Spiced Oil
(see page 27 for illustration)

This robust, spicy preserve is my own invention and is fast becoming a favorite among chili-loving friends. Use firm-fleshed or home-salted herrings (see Salt-curing, page 74). Salted mackerel can be prepared in the same way.

INGREDIENTS

2lb (1kg) salted herrings, or about 1lb (500g) prepared herring fillets

2 cups (500ml) light olive, peanut, or refined sesame oil

2in (5cm) cinnamon stick, crushed

1 lemongrass stalk, chopped

3–4 dried red chilies, split open

4–5 cloves

4–5 cardamom pods

1 Soak the salted herrings in several changes of cold water for 24 hours, then drain well. Split in half lengthwise and remove all the bones. Rinse, dry well on paper towels, and cut into bite-sized pieces. If using prepared herring fillets, omit the soaking.

2 Put all the remaining ingredients in a saucepan and bring slowly to a boil. Keep at just below boiling point for about 20 minutes, then remove from the heat and leave until it has cooled to 120°F (50°C).

3 Arrange the herring pieces in the warm, sterilized jar. Pour the warm oil into the jar, making sure the fish are covered. Shake it gently to be sure there are no air pockets, make sure the spices are evenly distributed, then seal. The fish will be ready in 3–4 weeks.

☆ **Degree of difficulty**
Easy

Cooking time
About 25 minutes

Special equipment
Thermometer; wide-mouth, sterilized canning jar with sealant (see pages 42–43)

Yield
About 2 pints (500g)

Shelf life
2–3 days, refrigerated

Serving suggestions
Serve with chilled vodka, use to make open sandwiches, or serve as an appetizer

RELISHES, SAUCES, & SPICE MIXES

THE FOLLOWING RECIPES comprise a large and diverse family of products. Originating from various parts of the world, they are the foundation of many cuisines. Their concentrated flavor makes easy work of cooking – a dash of homemade sauce or relish will instantly lift and enhance any uninteresting dish. I always keep a selection of my own spice mixes in store as they can be used to flavor a wide variety of preserves. Make the mixes in small quantities and use as soon as possible, since once they have been ground, spices quickly lose their aroma and taste.

Tomato and Pear Relish

Beefsteak tomatoes   Pears   Shallots   Celery with leaves   Chilies   Dill seed   *Yellow mustard seed*   *Sweet paprika*   Water   Cider vinegar   Light brown sugar   Salt

While the United States is the home of the relish, this particular recipe comes from the west coast of Canada, where pears are used instead of the customary apples.

INGREDIENTS

2lb (1kg) beefsteak or plum tomatoes, peeled, seeded, and coarsely chopped
1¼ lb (625g) pears, peeled, cored, and coarsely chopped
10oz (300g) shallots or onions, finely chopped
6 celery ribs with leaves, finely chopped
2–3 fresh red chilies, seeded and finely chopped (optional)
1 tbsp yellow mustard seed
1 tbsp sweet paprika
1 tbsp dill seed
1 cup (250ml) water
4 cups (1 liter) cider vinegar or red wine vinegar
1 cup (200g) light brown or white sugar
1 tbsp salt

1 Put the tomatoes, pears, shallots or onions, celery, chilies, yellow mustard seed, paprika, dill seed, and water in a noncorrosive pan.

2 Bring to a boil and skim well. Reduce the heat and simmer, stirring frequently, for about 20 minutes, or until the pears are soft and mushy.

3 Add the vinegar, sugar, and salt. Simmer, stirring occasionally, for 1–1½ hours, or until most of the liquid evaporates and the relish is thick.

4 Remove the pan from the heat. Ladle the relish into the hot, sterilized jars, then seal. If desired, heat process, cool, and check the seals (see pages 44–45).

☆ **Degree of difficulty**
Easy

Cooking time
1½–2 hours

Special equipment
Sterilized jars with sealants (see pages 42–43)

Yield
About 3 pints (1.5kg)

Shelf life
6 months, refrigerated; 2 years, heat processed

Serving suggestions
Serve with hamburgers, in sandwiches, or with grilled fish or meat

DILL SEED and paprika give sweetness to the relish, while chilies and mustard seed add heat

TOMATO AND PEAR RELISH makes a tasty accompaniment to kebabs.

USE CANNING JARS with lids and screwbands if you wish to heat process the relish

VARIATIONS

◆ *Tomato and Quince Relish*
Replace the chopped pears with the same quantity of quince. Increase the time of cooking in step 2 to 30–35 minutes, or until the quince are soft but not mushy.

◆ *Tomato and Apple Relish*
Replace the chopped pears with the same quantity of chopped apple and flavor with crushed coriander seed instead of the dill.

Corn and Pepper Relish

(see page 17 for illustration)

Corn and Pepper Relish is a frequent offering at country fairs. It tastes clean, sweet, and sharp. If you like your relish hotter, add some sliced chilies with the vegetables.

INGREDIENTS

2 medium onions, coarsely sliced
6 celery stalks, coarsely chopped
10oz (300g) white cabbage, hard core removed, coarsely chopped
2 green peppers, coarsely chopped
2 red peppers, coarsely chopped
10 ears of corn, kernels sliced off
5 cups (1.25 liters) cider vinegar
2 cups (500g) light brown sugar
2 tbsp yellow mustard seed
1 tbsp salt

1 Finely chop the onions, celery, cabbage, and peppers in a food processor. Place all the ingredients in a noncorrosive saucepan. Bring to a boil, then simmer for 45–60 minutes, until the corn is tender and the sauce thick.

2 Pour into the hot, sterilized jars, pushing it down with a spoon so that the vegetables are covered and there are no air pockets, then seal. Heat process. The relish is ready immediately, but improves with age.

☆ **Degree of difficulty**
Easy

Cooking time
45–60 minutes

Special equipment
Food processor; sterilized canning jars with sealants (see pages 42–43)

Yield
About 6 pints (3kg)

Shelf life
1 year, heat processed; 3 months, refrigerated;

Fresh Cranberry and Orange Relish

(see page 28 for illustration)

Fresh cranberries have a refreshingly sour flavor. I use them to add color and a sharp note to many dishes, such as stuffings, salads, and fish. This recipe is the perfect accompaniment to Christmas turkey and ham.

INGREDIENTS

1lb (500g) fresh cranberries
2 oranges, coarsely chopped, seeds removed
3–4 tbsp honey
2–3 tbsp orange-flavored liqueur, such as Grand Marnier or Triple Sec
1 tsp coriander seed, freshly ground
1 tsp salt

1 Put all the ingredients in the food processor and process, using the pulse button, until the cranberries and oranges are coarsely chopped.

2 Pack into the sterilized jars, then seal and refrigerate. The relish is ready immediately. If you are using it within 2–3 days, there is no need to use sterilized jars.

☆ **Degree of difficulty**
Easy

Special equipment
Food processor; sterilized canning jars and sealants (see pages 42–43)

Yield
About 1½ pints (750g)

Shelf life
1 month, refrigerated

Tomato Sauce

(see page 15 for illustration)

Tomato sauce is one of the most popular standbys of the modern kitchen, loved by children and adults alike. Although there are plenty of ready-made sauces to choose from, none can compare with the fresh, full flavor of a homemade one. Make sure you use ripe, fleshy tomatoes, preferably vine-ripened. If you don't want to heat process the sauce, keep it refrigerated and use within 1 month.

INGREDIENTS

4 tbsp olive oil
2 medium onions, chopped
6 garlic cloves, chopped
6 celery ribs with leaves, chopped
4lb (2kg) beefsteak or plum tomatoes, skinned, seeded, and coarsely chopped
1 cup (250ml) water or dry white wine
2 tsp salt
2 tsp honey or sugar (optional)
For the herb bundle (see page 47)
3–4 sprigs thyme
4 sage leaves
2 bay leaves
2 strips orange or lemon rind (optional)

1 Heat the olive oil in a large heavy-bottomed pan, add the onions, garlic, and celery, and cook over low heat for 10 minutes, or until the onion is translucent.

2 Add the remaining ingredients to the pan. Bring to a boil, then simmer, uncovered, for 30–45 minutes, until most of the liquid evaporates.

3 Remove the herbs. Pour the sauce into the hot, sterilized bottles or jars, then seal. Heat process, cool, and check the seals (see pages 44–45). The sauce is ready to use immediately.

☆ **Degree of difficulty**
Easy

Cooking time
45–50 minutes

Special equipment
Sterilized bottles or canning jars with sealants (see pages 42–43)

Yield
About 5 cups (1.25 liters)

Shelf life
1 year, heat processed; 1 month, refrigerated

Serving suggestions
Use as a base for stews, pasta sauces, and pizzas

Red Pepper Ketchup

(see page 56 for technique)

In the past, ketchup was made from a variety of fruits and vegetables. This recipe uses red peppers to create an original sauce with an elusive smoky flavor. Yellow or orange peppers can be used instead. If you don't want to heat process the ketchup, keep it refrigerated and use within 3 months.

INGREDIENTS

4lb (2kg) red peppers
1lb (500g) shallots or onions, peeled
2 medium cooking apples, cored and coarsely chopped
2–3 fresh red chilies, seeded and coarsely chopped (optional)
6 cups (1.25 liters) water
3 cups (750ml) red wine vinegar or cider vinegar
⅔ cup (150g) white or light brown sugar
1 tbsp salt
1 tbsp arrowroot or cornstarch

For the herb bundle (see page 47)

1 sprig tarragon
2 sprigs each mint, thyme, sage, and parsley
2 strips lemon rind

For the spice bag (see page 47)

1 tbsp coriander seed
1 tbsp black peppercorns
1 tsp cloves

1 Roast and peel the peppers (see steps 1 and 2, page 56). Rinse well, then core and seed.

2 Put the peppers, shallots or onions, apples, and chilies, if using, in the food processor and process until finely chopped.

3 Transfer to a noncorrosive saucepan, add the herb bundle, spice bag, and water. Bring to a boil, then reduce the heat and simmer for 25 minutes. Remove from the heat and let cool.

4 Discard the herbs and spice bag. Pass the mixture through a sieve or food mill and place the purée in the cleaned pan. Add the vinegar, sugar, and salt. Bring to a boil, stirring to dissolve the sugar, then simmer for 1–1½ hours, until the sauce is reduced by half.

5 Mix the arrowroot or cornstarch to a thin paste with a little more vinegar. Stir into the pan and boil for 1–2 minutes. Pour into the hot, sterilized bottles, then seal. Heat process, cool, and check the seals (see pages 44–45). The ketchup is ready to use immediately.

☆☆ **Degree of difficulty**
Moderate

Cooking time
1½–2 hours

Special equipment
Food processor; sterilized canning bottles with sealants (see pages 42–43)

Yield
About 2 pints (1 liter)

Shelf life
2 years, heat processed; 3 months, refrigerated

Serving suggestions
Serve with grilled or fried fish or as a sauce for pasta

Mushroom Ketchup

This is an adaptation of an 18th-century recipe recorded in The Country Housewife and Lady's Director by Richard Bradley, who was the first professor of botany at Cambridge University. This makes a flavorful ketchup, but it is important to use only flat, fully matured mushrooms.

INGREDIENTS

4lb (2kg) large flat-cap mushrooms
1 cup (60g) dried cèpes (optional)
¾ cup (150g) salt
5 shallots, unpeeled, quartered
2in (5cm) piece dried ginger root, bruised
½ cup (125ml) port
1 tbsp cloves
2 tsp crumbled mace blades

1 Put the fresh mushrooms in the food processor and coarsely chop. Arrange in thin layers with the dried cèpes, if using, in the casserole, sprinkling each layer with some of the salt. Cover and let stand for 24 hours.

2 Bake in an oven preheated to 275°F (140°C) for 3 hours. Cool and strain through the jelly bag, squeezing to extract all the liquid. Pour into a noncorrosive saucepan with the rest of the ingredients. Bring to a boil, then simmer for 45 minutes, or until reduced by a third.

3 Strain the mixture again, return to the cleaned pan, and bring back to a boil. Pour the ketchup into the hot, sterilized bottles, then seal. Heat process, cool, and check the seals (see pages 44–45). The ketchup will be ready to use in 1 month, but improves with age.

☆☆ **Degree of difficulty**
Moderate

Cooking time
3½–4½ hours

Special equipment
Food processor; casserole; sterilized jelly bag; sterilized canning bottles with sealants (see pages 42–43)

Yield
About 1½ pints (750ml)

Shelf life
2 years, heat processed

Serving suggestions
Use in small amounts to flavor soups and stews

Mexican Chili Sauce

Chipotle chilies give this fiery sauce its characteristic smoky flavor. Chipotles are smoked jalapeño peppers and can now be bought in many shops that stock Mexican foods. If they are not available, substitute twice the quantity of charbroiled fresh chilies (see Charbroiled Vegetables in Oil, page 106).

TIPS

- When seeding or chopping chilies, wash your hands well afterward and do not touch your eyes; alternatively, wear disposable household gloves.
- For an extra-smooth sauce, pass the mixture through a fine sieve after step 3.

INGREDIENTS

2–3 chipotle chilies

2lb (1kg) plum tomatoes or other cooking tomatoes, peeled and seeded

2 medium onions, sliced

4 garlic cloves, sliced

3 cups (750ml) cider vinegar or distilled white vinegar

2 tbsp dark brown sugar

1 tbsp salt

1 tbsp ground coriander

1 tbsp arrowroot or cornstarch

large bunch of cilantro, chopped

1 Put the chilies in a bowl and pour in enough boiling water to cover them. Let stand until the water is cold. Drain, reserving the water. Slit the chilies open lengthwise, and scrape out the seeds with a knife.

2 Purée the chilies, tomatoes, onions, and garlic in the food processor. Place in a noncorrosive saucepan, adding the water from soaking the chilies. Bring to a boil, then simmer for 30 minutes, or until slightly reduced.

3 Stir in the vinegar, sugar, salt, and ground coriander. Return the mixture to a boil, then simmer for 25–30 minutes, stirring frequently, until reduced by half.

4 Mix the arrowroot to a paste with a little water and stir into the pan. Add the cilantro and cook for 1–2 minutes, stirring. Pour into the hot, sterilized bottles, then seal. Heat process, cool, and check the seals (see pages 44–45). The sauce is ready to use immediately, but improves after 3–4 weeks.

☆☆ **Degree of difficulty**
Moderate

Cooking time
About 1 hour

Special equipment
Food processor; sterilized canning bottles with sealants (see pages 42–43)

Yield
About 2 pints (1 liter)

Shelf life
1 year, heat processed

Serving suggestions
Use to add flavor to stews, soups, and dips; especially good with chicken dishes

Spicy Tomato Ketchup

This recipe produces a thick, wonderfully rich, and not-too-sweet ketchup. If you prefer a sweeter taste, increase the amount of sugar to ½ cup (100g) per 4 cups (1 liter) of pulp and omit the chilies.

INGREDIENTS

4lb (2kg) tomatoes

1lb (500g) shallots or onions, peeled

2in (5cm) piece fresh ginger, peeled

6 garlic cloves, peeled

3–4 chilies, seeded (optional)

6 celery ribs with leaves

For the spice bag (see page 47)

2 tbsp coriander seed

1 tsp cloves

1 tsp crumbled mace blades

For every 4 cups (1 liter) pulp

1 cup (250ml) cider vinegar

¼ cup (75g) brown or white sugar

2 tsp salt

1 tbsp sweet paprika

1 Process the tomatoes, shallots or onions, ginger, garlic, and chilies, if using, in the food processor until coarsely chopped.

2 Put the mixture in a large noncorrosive saucepan. Tie the celery ribs together with string and add to the pan with the spice bag. Bring to a boil, then simmer for 25 minutes, or until the shallots or onions are soft.

3 Remove the celery and spice bag. Press the mixture through a sieve or food mill, then return to the cleaned pan. Bring to a boil and cook for ¾–1 hour, or until the purée is reduced by half.

4 Measure the purée and add the appropriate quantity of vinegar, sugar, salt, and paprika. Boil for 1 hour, stirring often, until reduced and thick. Pour into the hot, sterilized bottles, then seal. Heat process, cool, and check the seals (see pages 44–45). The ketchup is ready immediately, but improves with age.

☆☆ **Degree of difficulty**
Moderate

Cooking time
2¼–2½ hours

Special equipment
Food processor; sterilized canning bottles and sealants (see pages 42–43)

Yield
About 2 pints (1 liter)

Shelf life
2 years, heat processed

Serving suggestions
Use to flavor soups, stews, and sauces or serve with pasta

VARIATION

◆ **Plum Ketchup**
Substitute 4lb (2kg) plums, pitted, for the tomatoes.

Cooked Tomato and Pepper Salsa

Salsa, *meaning sauce, is Mexican in origin. This salsa can be eaten uncooked: add the tomatoes and herbs to the chopped ingredients and marinate for 2–3 hours before using. Keep refrigerated and eat within 2 weeks.*

INGREDIENTS

1½ lb (750g) mixed sweet peppers

2–3 fresh red or green chilies, seeded

1 large red onion

2 garlic cloves, peeled

3 tbsp olive, corn, or peanut oil

3 tbsp red wine vinegar or lemon juice

2 tsp salt

1 lb (500g) firm red tomatoes, peeled, seeded, and finely chopped

3 tbsp chopped cilantro or parsley

1 Coarsely chop the vegetables, then put in the food processor with the garlic, oil, vinegar or lemon juice, and salt. Process until the vegetables are finely chopped.

2 Put in a noncorrosive saucepan with the tomatoes and herbs. Bring to a boil, then simmer for 5 minutes. Pour into the sterilized jars, then seal. Heat process, cool, and check the seals (see pages 44–45). It is ready immediately.

☆ **Degree of difficulty**
Easy

Cooking time
About 5 minutes

Special equipment
Food processor; sterilized canning jars with sealants (see pages 42–43)

Yield
About 2 pints (1kg)

Shelf life
6 months, heat processed

Chinese-style Plum Sauce

Sweet, sour, and hot, this Chinese sauce is a suitable accompaniment to roast duck as well as a flavoring for soups and stews.

INGREDIENTS

4 lb (2kg) red plums

4 cups (1 liter) red wine vinegar or rice vinegar

2 tsp salt

1 cup (250ml) dark soy sauce

1 cup (300g) honey or dark brown sugar

1 tbsp arrowroot or cornstarch

For the spice bag (see page 47)

1 tbsp star anise, lightly crushed

2 tsp Szechuan pepper, lightly crushed

1 tsp small dried red chilies, lightly crushed

1 Put the whole plums, vinegar, salt, and spice bag into a noncorrosive saucepan. Bring to a boil, then reduce the heat and simmer for about 25 minutes,

or until the plums become soft and mushy.

2 Discard the spice bag. Pass the plums through a sieve. Place the purée in the cleaned pan and stir in the soy sauce and honey or sugar. Bring to a boil, then simmer for 45 minutes, or until reduced by a quarter.

3 Mix the arrowroot or cornstarch to a paste with a little water. Stir into the sauce and simmer for 1–2 minutes, stirring. Pour into the bottles, then seal. Heat process, cool, and check the seals (see pages 44–45). The sauce is ready to use immediately, but improves with age.

☆ **Degree of difficulty**
Easy

Cooking time
About 1¼ hours

Special equipment
Sterilized canning bottles with sealants (see pages 42–43)

Yield
About 2 pints (1 liter)

Shelf life
2 years, heat processed

Serving suggestion
Use to dress salads instead of oil and vinegar

Harissa
(see page 17 for illustration)

Here is the basic recipe for this famous, fiercely hot Moroccan paste. Before using it, you can soften its flavor with a little tomato purée or puréed fresh tomatoes. Garlic, cilantro, and cumin can be added too.

INGREDIENTS

1 lb (500g) dried red chilies

⅔ cup (150ml) olive oil, plus a little more for the jars

2 tbsp salt

1 Scrape out and discard the chili seeds. Put the chilies in a bowl and add hot water to cover. Let stand for 15–20 minutes, until soft.

2 Drain the chilies and place in the food processor with ½ cup (125ml) of the soaking water. Process to a paste. Stir in the oil and salt. Pack into the sterilized jars.

3 Pour a thin layer of oil into the top of each jar, then seal and refrigerate. The harissa is ready to use immediately.

☆ **Degree of difficulty**
Easy

Special equipment
Food processor; sterilized canning jars with sealants (see pages 42–43)

Yield
About 2 pints (1kg)

Shelf life
6 months, refrigerated

Harrief

A Moroccan specialty, this is my favorite hot sauce. I make it in large quantities and use it to add instant piquancy to sauces, soups, stews, salads, and pasta, or I brush it on meat before barbecuing.

TIPS
• It is difficult to give an exact quantity for the chilies, since varieties differ greatly in heat.
• For a smoother sauce, pass the mixture through a sieve or a food mill at the end of step 2.

INGREDIENTS
4lb (2kg) sweet red peppers
½ lb (250g) fresh red chilies, seeded
½ lb (250g) garlic, peeled
⅔ cup (150ml) fruity olive oil
1 cup (250ml) cider vinegar
3 tbsp salt
1–2 tbsp chili powder (optional)
2 tbsp cumin seed, freshly ground
2 tsp arrowroot

1 Roast and peel the peppers (see steps 1 and 2, page 56). Rinse well, then core and seed. Put in the food processor with the garlic, chilies, and oil.

2 Process until the vegetables are finely chopped. Transfer to a noncorrosive saucepan and add the vinegar, salt, and spices. Bring to a boil, then reduce the heat and simmer for 1–1½ hours, until the mixture is reduced by a third.

3 Mix the arrowroot to a paste with a little vinegar and stir into the sauce. Raise the heat and boil the sauce rapidly for 1 minute, stirring constantly.

4 Pour the sauce into the hot, sterilized jars, then seal. The sauce is ready to use immediately, but improves with age.

☆☆ **Degree of difficulty**
Moderate

Cooking time
1–1½ hours

Special equipment
Food processor; sterilized canning jars with sealants (see pages 42–43)

Yield
About 2 pints (1kg)

Shelf life
1 year, refrigerated

Serving suggestion
Use as a condiment

Schug
(see page 17 for illustration)

This fiercely hot chili paste comes from Yemen, where it is used in a wide range of dishes. Extra chopped cilantro should be added just before serving. If you prefer a milder version, replace half or more of the chilies with green peppers.

INGREDIENTS
1½ lb (750g) fresh green chilies
1 large head garlic, peeled
2 bunches cilantro
1 tbsp coriander seed
2 tsp cumin seed
2 tsp black peppercorns
1 tsp cardamom pods
1 tsp cloves
1½ tbsp salt
a little olive oil, to cover

1 Put the chilies, garlic, and cilantro in the food processor and finely chop.

2 Grind all the spices to a fine powder in the spice mill or coffee grinder. Put the ground spices through a sieve into the chili and garlic mixture, then stir in the salt and mix well.

3 Pack the mixture tightly into the sterilized jars. Cover with a thin layer of oil, then seal.

☆ **Degree of difficulty**
Easy

Special equipment
Food processor; spice mill or coffee grinder; sterilized canning jars and sealants (see pages 42–43)

Yield
About 2 pints (1kg)

Shelf life
3 months, refrigerated

Serving suggestion
Use as a condiment

Date Blatjang (Date Sauce)
(see page 35 for illustration)

I came across this recipe in South Africa, where it had been introduced in the 17th century by Malay slaves. It has a hot, sharp, sweet flavor. Serve it with rice or oily fish. Other fruit, such as fresh or dried apricots, peaches, and mango, can be used instead of dates.

INGREDIENTS
5oz (150g) tamarind block
1½ cups (350ml) boiling water
1lb (500g) pitted dates, coarsely chopped
2in (5cm) piece of fresh ginger, peeled and chopped
8 garlic cloves, chopped
3–4 dried red chilies, seeded and chopped
4 cups (1 liter) red wine vinegar
2 tsp salt

1 Soak the tamarind in the boiling water for 30 minutes. Strain, then pour the liquid into a noncorrosive saucepan with the rest of the ingredients. Bring to a boil, then simmer for 10 minutes.

2 Purée in the food processor. Return to the cleaned pan and boil for 1–2 minutes. Pour into the hot, sterilized bottles, then seal. The sauce is ready immediately, but improves with age.

☆ **Degree of difficulty**
Easy

Cooking time
About 15 minutes

Special equipment
Sterilized canning bottles with sealants (see pages 42–43)

Yield
About 2 pints (1 liter)

Shelf life
2 years, heat processed

Masalas & Spice Mixes

I have borrowed the word masala *from India, but the following recipes come from all over the world. A masala is a mixture of spices, which Indian cooks use to create a rich, subtle range of flavors in their cooking. There are as many masalas as there are cooks. The whole spices are sometimes roasted, then pounded or ground to a powder and used as fresh as possible. I like making masalas in small quantities and adding them in the final stages of cooking, which helps to preserve their freshness. Use the following recipes as blueprints and create your own favorite combinations.*

TIPS
- Dried rose petals are available from some herbalists or health food stores in the form of tea. Do check that they have not been treated with chemicals. Alternatively, dry your own.
- Break nutmeg with a hammer.
- To toast whole spices, put them in a dry skillet and stir constantly over the heat until they become aromatic and start to pop.

1. CHAWAGE (YEMENITE SPICE MIX)
3 tbsp black peppercorns
3 tbsp cumin seed
2 tbsp coriander seed
1 tsp cloves
1 tsp green cardamom pods
2 tsp ground turmeric

2. GARAM MASALA
1 tbsp cumin seed, toasted
1 tbsp coriander seed, toasted
2 tsp black peppercorns
2in (5cm) cinnamon stick, crushed
1 tsp crumbled mace blades
1 tsp black cumin seed (kalajeera)
½ nutmeg, broken into pieces

3. MY FAVORITE SAVORY MASALA
2 tbsp coriander seed
2 tsp black peppercorns
2 tsp cumin seed
2 tsp caraway seed
1 tsp green cardamom pods

4. MY FAVORITE SWEET MASALA
2 tbsp coriander seed
1 tbsp allspice berries
1 tbsp cloves
1 tbsp cardamom pods
2 tsp caraway seed
1 tsp anise (optional)

5. BRITISH MIXED SPICE
2in (5cm) cinnamon stick, crushed, or 1½ tbsp ground cinnamon
1 tbsp allspice berries
2 tsp cloves
2 tsp coriander seed
1 nutmeg, broken into pieces
1–2 strips dried orange rind (optional)

6. MOROCCAN MEAT SPICING
1 tbsp black peppercorns
1 tbsp allspice berries
2 tsp crumbled mace blades
1 nutmeg, broken into pieces
1in (2.5cm) cinnamon stick, crushed
1 tbsp sweet paprika (optional)
2 tsp ground turmeric

7. RAS EL HANOUT
2 tsp black peppercorns
1 tsp coriander seed
1 tsp cumin seed
1 tsp allspice berries
2in (5cm) cinnamon stick, crushed
½ nutmeg, broken into pieces
½ tsp cloves
½ tsp cardamom pods
1 tbsp dried rose petals, crumbled (optional)
1 tsp ground ginger
½ tsp hot chili powder

1 For each masala or spice mix, place all the ingredients (except any preground spices), in the spice mill, coffee grinder, or mortar. Grind to a fine powder, then mix in any preground spices.

2 For an extra-fine powder, pass through a fine sieve, regrind the debris left in the mesh, then sieve again. Discard any bits that remain in the sieve. Transfer to a small airtight jar and seal.

 Degree of difficulty
Easy

Special equipment
Spice mill, coffee grinder, or mortar and pestle; airtight jars

Shelf life
3 months, in airtight jars

Serving suggestions
(1) goes well with meat, especially chicken; (2) may be used to flavor pickles or added to Pickled Venison (see page 132); (3) adds savor to burgers, koftas, and meatballs; use (4) or (5) to flavor mincemeat (see page 169); (6) can be added to sweet and savory dishes

CHUTNEYS

CHUTNEYS CAN BE SWEET, hot, sour, or spicy; smooth or chunky. Whatever their individual characteristics, all use sugar and vinegar as a preservative. In India, where the chutney originated, the term also includes products that are fresh marinated salads with a short shelf life, so I have included a few recipes for these too (even though they are not preserves as such). I like my chutney to have lots of texture, so I cut the ingredients into large chunks. If you prefer a smoother product, slice fruits and vegetables into smaller pieces.

Chutneys are traditionally served with meat, and their role is, perhaps, most accurately summed up by the author of the recipe below: "Chutneys are intended to act upon the taste in direct contrast to the meat with which they are eaten, and therefore spices, aromatics, and acid assume the ascendant." Use mellow vinegars for chutneys: cider, wine, or citrus vinegars are best – plain white vinegar produces too harsh a result. Keep chutneys for at least a month before using them, to allow time for their flavors to blend and mellow.

Ginger Chutney

Fresh ginger   Red peppers   Cucumber   Raisins   Onions   Lemons   *Cider vinegar*   Sugar   *Salt*

This is adapted from a recipe for Indian chutney that I found in an undated pickling book, by Marion Harris Neil, probably published about 90 years ago.

INGREDIENTS

10oz (300g) fresh ginger, shredded
2 medium red peppers, diced
1 large cucumber, quartered lengthwise and thickly sliced
1¼ cups (250g) raisins
2 large onions, coarsely chopped
4 lemons, halved lengthwise, seeds removed, thinly sliced
4 cups (1 liter) cider vinegar or white wine vinegar
2 cups (500g) granulated sugar
2 tsp salt

1 Put all the ingredients, except the sugar and salt, into a noncorrosive saucepan. Bring the mixture to a boil, then reduce the heat and simmer gently for about 30 minutes, until the fruit and vegetables are softened.

2 Add the sugar and salt to the pan, stirring until they are dissolved. Simmer gently for 30–45 minutes longer, until most of the liquid has evaporated and the chutney is thick.

3 Ladle the mixture into the hot, sterilized jars, then seal. The chutney will be ready to eat in about 1 month, but improves with age.

☆ **Degree of difficulty**
Easy

Cooking time
1–1¼ hours

Special equipment
Sterilized jars with sealants (see pages 42–43)

Yield
About 3 pints (1.5kg)

Shelf life
2 years, heat processed

Serving suggestions
Serve with game, cheese, or grilled fish

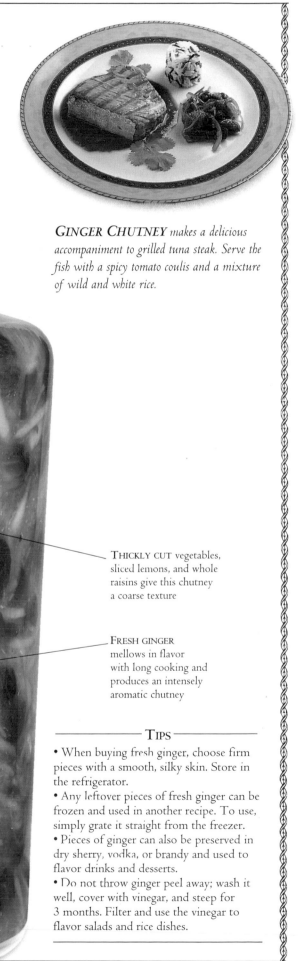

GINGER CHUTNEY *makes a delicious accompaniment to grilled tuna steak. Serve the fish with a spicy tomato coulis and a mixture of wild and white rice.*

THICKLY CUT vegetables, sliced lemons, and whole raisins give this chutney a coarse texture

FRESH GINGER mellows in flavor with long cooking and produces an intensely aromatic chutney

TIPS

• When buying fresh ginger, choose firm pieces with a smooth, silky skin. Store in the refrigerator.
• Any leftover pieces of fresh ginger can be frozen and used in another recipe. To use, simply grate it straight from the freezer.
• Pieces of ginger can also be preserved in dry sherry, vodka, or brandy and used to flavor drinks and desserts.
• Do not throw ginger peel away; wash it well, cover with vinegar, and steep for 3 months. Filter and use the vinegar to flavor salads and rice dishes.

Green Tomato Chutney
(see page 15 for illustration)

This sweet-and-sour version of a classic recipe is well worth trying. Green tomatoes are notoriously difficult to peel, so if, like me, you do not mind tomato skin in your chutney, there is no need to peel them.

INGREDIENTS
1½ lb (750g) green tomatoes
1lb (500g) cooking apples
½ lb (250g) onions, coarsely chopped
1 tbsp salt
¾ cup (125g) raisins
2 cups (500g) light brown or white sugar
1 cup (250ml) cider vinegar
grated rind and juice of 2 large lemons
2 tbsp black or yellow mustard seed
2–3 fresh red chilies, seeded and chopped (optional)

For the spice bag (see page 47)
1 tbsp coriander seed
2 tsp black peppercorns
2 tsp allspice berries
1 tsp cloves
2 cinnamon sticks, crushed

1 Blanch the tomatoes to remove the skin (see page 46), then coarsely chop. Peel, core, and chop the apples. Add the peel and cores to the spice bag.

2 Put the tomatoes, apples, onions, and salt in a noncorrosive saucepan. Bring slowly to a boil, then reduce the heat and simmer for 20 minutes.

3 Add the raisins, sugar, vinegar, lemon rind and juice, and spice bag. Return to a boil, then simmer for 30 minutes, or until thick. Add the mustard seed and chilies, if using, mix well, and remove from the heat.

4 Ladle into the hot, sterilized jars, then seal. The chutney will be ready to eat in 1 month.

☆ **Degree of difficulty** Easy

Cooking time About 1 hour

Special equipment Sterilized canning jars with sealants (see pages 42–43)

Yield About 3 pints (1.5kg)

Shelf life 1 year, heat processed

Serving suggestions Serve as an accompaniment to mature cheese or add to sandwiches

Pumpkin Chutney
(see page 58 for technique)

Pumpkin makes a superb deep golden chutney. I like it with a crunchy texture, so I cook it for less time than recommended in step 2, then leave it to mature for up to 6 weeks before eating it.

INGREDIENTS
2½ lb (1.25kg) pumpkin, peeled, seeded, and cut into 1in (2.5cm) chunks
1½ lb (750g) apples, peeled, cored, and coarsely chopped
5 tbsp (75g) finely shredded fresh ginger
3–4 fresh red chilies, seeded and sliced
2 tbsp white mustard seed
2 tbsp black mustard seed
4 cups (1 liter) cider vinegar or distilled white vinegar
1 tbsp salt
2 cups (500g) white or light brown sugar

1 Put all the ingredients, except the salt and sugar, in a noncorrosive saucepan.

2 Mix well, bring to a boil, then reduce the heat and simmer for 20–25 minutes, or until the pumpkin is just tender.

3 Add the salt and sugar and bring back to a boil, stirring until they are dissolved. Cook for 50–60 minutes, stirring frequently, until the mixture is thick and most of the liquid evaporates. Remove from the heat.

4 Ladle into the hot, sterilized jars, then seal. The chutney will be ready to eat in about 1 month, but improves with age.

VARIATION
✦ *Pineapple Chutney*
Substitute 1 medium pineapple and 1¼lb (625g) cooking apples, peeled, cored, and chopped, for the pumpkin. Cook in 1 cup (250ml) water until very soft, then add 1½ cups (350ml) vinegar, 1¼ cups (300g) sugar, and 1 tablespoon each of black and white mustard seed. Cook as in step 3, adding 6 finely sliced green chilies and 2 teaspoons caraway seed before potting.

☆ **Degree of difficulty** Easy

Cooking time 1¼–1½ hours

Special equipment Sterilized canning jars with sealants (see pages 42–43)

Yield About 4 pints (2kg)

Shelf life 2 years, heat processed

Serving suggestions Mix a few large tablespoons with plain boiled rice, or serve with cold meats and cheese

Fresh Onion Chutney

(see page 18 for illustration)

This recipe belongs to a large family of fresh, saladlike chutneys that are served to refresh the palate and revive the appetite. Grated apples, quince, carrots, and turnips can all be substituted for the onions.

INGREDIENTS

1 lb (500g) large, sweet purple or white onions, sliced into thin rings

1 tbsp salt

1–2 fresh green or red chilies, seeded and finely chopped

3 tbsp white wine vinegar or cider vinegar

2 tbsp chopped mint or cilantro

1 tsp nigella seed (optional)

1 Put the onion rings in a colander and sprinkle with the salt. Mix well and let drain for about 1 hour.

2 Squeeze the onions to extract as much moisture as possible, then mix with the rest of the ingredients. Let stand for 1 hour, to develop the flavor. The chutney is ready to eat immediately.

☆ **Degree of difficulty**
Easy

Yield
About ½ pint (250g)

Shelf life
1 week, refrigerated

Serving suggestions
Serve with curries, as an appetizer, or as a refreshing salad

Carrot and Almond Chutney

(see page 23 for illustration)

My adaptation of angel hair jam, a Middle Eastern classic made with long, thin strands of carrot. The carrot strands look translucent, which makes it particularly attractive. Full flavored, sweet and sour, this chutney goes well with mature cheese.

INGREDIENTS

2½ lb (1.25kg) carrots, grated lengthwise

¼ lb (125g) fresh ginger, shredded

1 cup (250ml) white wine vinegar

grated rind and juice of 2 large lemons

⅔ cup (150ml) water

1½ cups (400g) white or light brown sugar

4 tbsp honey

2 tbsp coriander seed, freshly ground

1 tbsp salt

3–4 dried bird's eye chilies

3 tbsp slivered almonds

1 Put the carrots in a large glass bowl with all the remaining ingredients, except the chilies and almonds. Mix well, cover, and let stand overnight.

2 The next day, put the mixture in a noncorrosive saucepan. Bring to a boil, then simmer for 20 minutes. Raise the heat and boil hard for 10–15 minutes, until most of the liquid has evaporated.

3 Grind the chilies to a powder in the spice mill or coffee grinder. Add to the pan with the almonds. Mix well. Ladle into the hot, sterilized jars, then seal. The chutney is ready in 1 month, but improves with age.

☆ **Degree of difficulty**
Easy

Cooking time
30–35 minutes

Special equipment
Spice mill or coffee grinder; sterilized canning jars with sealants (see pages 42–43)

Yield
About 3 pints (1.5kg)

Shelf life
2 years, heat processed

Serving suggestion
Serve with cold meat or just spread on bread

Squash Chutney

A simple and delicious chutney that turns the humble squash into a delicacy. If using a very large squash, remember to remove the seeds and soft center, which can turn mushy after cooking.

INGREDIENTS

2 lb (1kg) summer squash, peeled, cored, and cut into 1 in (2.5cm) cubes

2 tbsp salt

2 large onions, coarsely chopped

about 5 carrots, coarsely grated

3½ oz (100g) crystallized ginger, coarsely chopped

1–2 fresh red chilies, finely chopped

2 tbsp black mustard seed

1 tbsp ground turmeric

3 cups (750ml) cider vinegar

1 cup (250g) sugar

1 Put the squash in a colander and sprinkle with half the salt. Let stand for 1 hour. Rinse and dry. Put in a noncorrosive saucepan with all the ingredients, except the sugar and remaining salt. Bring to a boil, then reduce the heat and simmer for 25 minutes, or until the vegetables are just soft.

2 Add the sugar and salt and simmer for 1–1¼ hours, until most of the liquid evaporates and the chutney is thick. Ladle into the hot, sterilized jars, then seal. It will be ready in 1–2 months.

☆ **Degree of difficulty**
Easy

Cooking time
1½–2 hours

Special equipment
Sterilized canning jars with sealants (see pages 42–43)

Yield
About 3 pints (1.5kg)

Shelf life
2 years, heat processed

Serving suggestion
Good with cheese

Eggplant and Garlic Chutney

A soft, melt-in-the-mouth chutney that combines the mild taste of eggplant with the wonderful aroma of garlic. Use large, firm, light purple eggplants, if possible.

INGREDIENTS

2lb (1kg) eggplants, cut into 1in (2.5cm) cubes
2 tbsp salt
3 tbsp peanut, olive, or sesame oil
1 tbsp nigella seed (optional)
3 tbsp sesame seed
4 heads garlic, peeled
½ lb (250g) shallots, peeled and quartered
2–3 red or green chilies, seeded and coarsely chopped
3 cups (750ml) cider vinegar or white wine vinegar
⅔ cup (150g) light brown sugar
3 tsp sweet paprika
small bunch of mint, chopped (optional)

1 Put the eggplant cubes in a colander and sprinkle with half the salt. Mix well and let drain for 1 hour. Rinse well and pat dry on paper towels.

2 Heat the oil in a noncorrosive saucepan, add the nigella and sesame seed and cook for a minute or two, until the sesame seeds start to pop.

3 Add the eggplant, garlic, shallots, and chilies to the pan and cook, stirring frequently, for about 5 minutes.

4 Add the vinegar and bring to a boil, then reduce the heat and simmer for about 15 minutes, until the eggplant is soft. Add the sugar, paprika, and remaining salt, stirring until dissolved.

5 Increase the heat slightly and cook, stirring frequently, for 45 minutes–1 hour, until most of the liquid evaporates and the mixture is thick. Add the mint, if using, and remove from the heat.

6 Ladle the mixture into the hot, sterilized jars, then seal. The chutney is ready to eat in 1 month, but improves with keeping for 1–2 months.

☆ **Degree of difficulty**
Easy

Cooking time
1–1¼ hours

Special equipment
Sterilized canning jars with sealants (see pages 42–43)

Yield
About 3 pints (1.5kg)

Shelf life
1 year, heat processed

Serving suggestions
Especially good with chicken curry, cheese, or in sandwiches

Red Tomato Chutney

A mild and fragrant chutney. Originally jaggery (unrefined Indian sugar) was used, but since it is hard to obtain, brown sugar can be substituted.

INGREDIENTS

3 tbsp peanut or sesame oil
2 onions, coarsely chopped
1 head garlic, coarsely chopped
6 tbsp (90g) finely shredded fresh ginger
2–3 fresh red chilies, seeded and cut into thick strips (optional)
2lb (1kg) firm plum or beefsteak tomatoes, peeled, seeded, and chopped
¾ cup (125g) jaggery or light brown sugar
1 cup (250ml) red wine vinegar
6 cardamom pods
1 bunch basil or mint, chopped

1 Heat the oil in a noncorrosive saucepan and add the onions, garlic, ginger, and chilies, if using. Cook over low heat for 5 minutes, or until the onions just start to color. Add the tomatoes and cook for 15 minutes, or until soft.

2 Add the sugar and vinegar, stirring until the sugar is dissolved. Bring to a boil, then simmer for 25–30 minutes, stirring frequently, until it is thick and most of the liquid has evaporated. Remove from the heat.

3 Grind the cardamom pods in the spice mill or coffee grinder. Add to the chutney through a sieve and stir in the basil or mint.

4 Ladle into the hot, sterilized jars, then seal. The chutney will be ready to eat in about 1 month, but improves with age.

☆ **Degree of difficulty**
Easy

Cooking time
45–50 minutes

Special equipment
Spice mill or coffee grinder; sterilized canning jars with sealants (see pages 42–43)

Yield
About 2 pints (1kg)

Shelf life
1 year, heat processed

Serving suggestion
Spread a few tablespoons over the bottom of savory quiches and flan cases before adding the filling

Hot Mango Chutney

This recipe is from Bihar in India, and produces a hot, richly flavored golden preserve. Although turmeric can be used, saffron gives the chutney a unique flavor.

INGREDIENTS

4lb (2kg) unripe mangoes, peeled and cut into 1in (2.5cm) chunks (see page 175)

2 limes or lemons, sliced into semicircles

3–4 fresh red chilies, seeded and coarsely chopped

3 cups (750ml) white wine vinegar or distilled white vinegar

2 cups (500g) light brown sugar or jaggery

1 tbsp salt

1 tbsp green cardamom pods

1 tsp cumin seed

1 tsp chili powder (optional)

½ tsp saffron strands or 1 tsp ground turmeric

1 Place the mangoes, limes or lemons, chilies, and vinegar in a noncorrosive saucepan. Bring to a boil, then simmer for about 10 minutes, or until the mangoes are just tender. Add the sugar and salt. Simmer for 50–60 minutes, until the mixture is thick and most of the liquid evaporates.

2 Grind the cardamom and cumin to a powder in the spice mill or coffee grinder. Add to the chutney through a sieve, together with the chili powder and turmeric, if using. If adding saffron, soak the strands in a little hot water for a few minutes and then stir into the chutney.

3 Ladle into the hot, sterilized jars, then seal. The chutney will be ready to eat in about 1 month.

☆ **Degree of difficulty**
Easy

Cooking time
1–1¼ hours

Special equipment
Spice mill or coffee grinder; sterilized canning jars with sealants (see pages 42–43)

Yield
About 3 pints (1.5kg)

Shelf life
2 years, heat processed

Serving suggestions
Serve with pappadoms or with rice for a light supper dish

Plum Chutney

A dark red, superbly flavored chutney. The original recipe, which comes from Assam, includes 15 chilies and several spoonfuls of chili powder. I tried it and it was wonderfully hot — a real treat for chili lovers. This is a toned-down version, but you can add more chilies if you want to spice it up.

INGREDIENTS

1lb (500g) dark red plums

1lb (500g) light plums

6 large garlic cloves, coarsely chopped

6 fresh red chilies, coarsely chopped

⅓ cup (75ml) water

¼lb (125g) tamarind block or 2 tbsp tamarind paste

3 cups (750ml) malt vinegar

1½ cups (400g) light brown or white sugar

2 tsp salt

1 tsp cloves

1 tsp allspice berries

1 cinnamon stick, broken

½ tsp black cumin seed (kalajeera)

1 Cut the plums in half and remove the pits. Crack the pits with a hammer or nutcracker and tie them in a piece of cheesecloth.

2 Put the plums, cheesecloth bag, garlic, chilies, and water in a noncorrosive saucepan. Bring to a boil, then reduce the heat and simmer gently, stirring frequently, for 15–20 minutes, or until the plums are soft.

3 If using tamarind block, soak it in ½ cup (125ml) hot water for 20 minutes and then strain out and discard the large seeds.

4 Add the vinegar, sieved tamarind or tamarind paste, sugar, and salt to the pan. Bring to a boil, stirring until the sugar is dissolved. Reduce the heat and simmer for 25–30 minutes, stirring frequently, until the mixture is thick and most of the liquid evaporates. Remove from the heat and discard the pits.

5 Grind the cloves, allspice, and cinnamon to a powder in the spice mill or coffee grinder. Stir into the pan with the whole cumin. Ladle into the hot, sterilized jars, then seal. The chutney will be ready to eat in 1 month.

☆ **Degree of difficulty**
Easy

Cooking time
About 1¼ hours

Special equipment
Hammer or nutcracker; cheesecloth; spice mill or coffee grinder; sterilized canning jars with sealants (see pages 42–43)

Yield
About 2 pints (1kg)

Shelf life
2 years, heat processed

Serving suggestions
Serve with cold meat and cheese, or simply spread on bread

— TIP —
• Select firm, fleshy plums with a good color. I use a mixture of Victoria and dark red plums, but you can use just red plums if you cannot obtain Victorias.

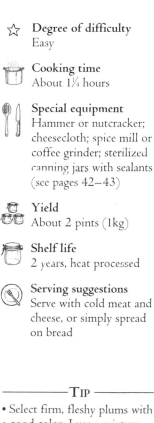

Apple Chutney

This is a classic mild, fruity chutney. You could make it with a combination of apples and pears instead of just apples. It is delicious served with cheese or can be used as an unusual sandwich filling.

INGREDIENTS

2½ lb (1.25kg) underripe cooking apples (windfalls are good), peeled, cored, and coarsely chopped

1¼ lb (625g) onions, coarsely chopped

2 lemons, finely sliced into semicircles

2 cups (300g) raisins

2 garlic cloves, finely chopped (optional)

2 cups (500ml) cider vinegar

2 cups (400g) dark brown sugar

1 tbsp salt

1 tsp ground ginger

1 tsp ground cinnamon

1 tsp ground turmeric

1 Put the apples, onions, lemons, raisins, garlic, if using, and vinegar in a noncorrosive saucepan. Bring to a boil, then simmer for 15–20 minutes, until the apples soften, but still retain some texture.

2 Add the sugar, stirring until it is dissolved. Simmer for 30–45 minutes, until the mixture is thick and most of the liquid evaporates. Remove from the heat. Add the salt and spices.

3 Ladle into the hot, sterilized jars, then seal. The chutney will be ready to eat in 1 month.

☆ **Degree of difficulty**
Easy

Cooking time
45 minutes–1 hour

Special equipment
Sterilized canning jars with sealants (see pages 42–43)

Yield
About 4 pints (2kg)

Shelf life
1 year, heat processed

Serving suggestions
Serve with cheese or spread on bread and butter

Exotic Fruit Chutney

A delightfully fresh-tasting chutney. Many other fruits can be used in this recipe, too. I tend to make it in winter and sometimes add a combination of pawpaw, kiwi fruit, and litchis to the kumquats, apples, and baby corn.

INGREDIENTS

½ lb (250g) kumquats or oranges

1 small pineapple, peeled, cored, and cut into 1in (2.5cm) chunks

1 lb (500g) cooking apples, peeled, cored, and coarsely chopped

1¼ cups (300g) dried apricots, soaked if necessary, coarsely chopped

½ lb (250g) baby corn, cut into 1in (2.5cm) lengths

4 cups (1 liter) cider vinegar or white wine vinegar

2 cups (500g) sugar

3–4 fresh red chilies, seeded and chopped

2 tbsp black mustard seed

2 tbsp salt

1 tbsp green peppercorns

1 bunch mint, coarsely chopped

1 If using kumquats, leave them whole; slice oranges in half, then cut into medium-thick slices.

2 Put all the fruit in a noncorrosive saucepan with the corn and vinegar. Bring to a boil, then simmer for 15 minutes.

3 Add the sugar, chilies, mustard seed, salt, and peppercorns. Stir until the sugar is dissolved. Simmer, stirring frequently, for 50–60 minutes, until thick and most of the liquid evaporates.

4 Remove from the heat and stir in the mint. Ladle into the hot, sterilized jars, then seal. It will be ready in 1 month, but improves with age.

☆ **Degree of difficulty**
Easy

Cooking time
1–1¼ hours

Special equipment
Sterilized canning jars with sealants (see pages 42–43)

Yield
About 6 pints (3kg)

Shelf life
1 year, heat processed

Serving suggestions
Serve with poultry or curries

Fig Chutney

I found this unusual recipe in an anonymous Victorian cookbook. It makes a dark and delicious chutney and is an ideal way to use up unripe figs.

INGREDIENTS

5 cups (1.25 liters) red wine vinegar
1 lb (500g) light brown sugar
2 tbsp salt
2 lb (1 kg) firm, slightly underripe black figs, sliced into rounds ½ in (1cm) thick
1 lb (500g) onions, sliced into thin rings
½ lb (250g) pitted dates, coarsely chopped
¼ cup (150g) finely shredded fresh ginger
2 tbsp sweet paprika
1 tbsp white mustard seed
3 tbsp chopped fresh tarragon, or 1 tbsp dried tarragon

1 Put the vinegar, sugar, and salt in a noncorrosive saucepan, stirring until the sugar is dissolved. Bring to a boil, then simmer for about 5 minutes.

2 Add the figs, onions, dates, and spices. Bring to a boil, then simmer for 1 hour, until the mixture is thick and most of the liquid evaporates.

3 Remove the pan from the heat and stir in the tarragon. Ladle into the hot, sterilized jars, then seal. The chutney will be ready to eat in 1 month.

☆ **Degree of difficulty**
Easy

Cooking time
About 1¼ hours

Special equipment
Sterilized canning jars with sealants (see pages 42–43)

Yield
About 4 pints (2kg)

Shelf life
1 year, heat processed

Serving suggestions
Use to cool down hot curries or serve with cheese and cold meats

Peach Chutney

(see page 31 for illustration)

A light, elegant, and refreshing chutney. Peaches sometimes produce a pale chutney; to correct this I add 2 tablespoons of sweet paprika, which gives it a pinkish hue, or 2 teaspoons of ground turmeric, which will add a golden yellow tint. They are added with the ground spices.

INGREDIENTS

2 lb (1 kg) peaches, peeled, pitted, and sliced 1 in (2.5cm) thick
2 medium cooking apples, peeled, cored, and chopped
½ lb (250g) seedless grapes
2 lemons, finely sliced into semicircles
½ lb (250g) shallots, coarsely chopped
3 garlic cloves, finely shredded
5 tbsp (75g) finely shredded fresh ginger
2 cups (500ml) cider vinegar or white wine vinegar
1 cup (250g) sugar
1 tsp cloves
1 tsp cardamom pods
2 in (5cm) piece of cinnamon stick
2 tsp caraway seed

1 Put all the fruit, the shallots, garlic, ginger, and vinegar in a noncorrosive saucepan. Bring to a boil, then reduce the heat and simmer for about 25 minutes, until the apples are just soft and the shallots transparent.

2 Add the sugar, stirring until it is dissolved. Simmer for 35–40 minutes, until the mixture is thick and most of the liquid evaporates. Remove the pan from the heat.

3 Grind the cloves, cardamom pods, and cinnamon stick to a powder in the spice mill or coffee grinder.

4 Add the ground spices to the chutney through a sieve (this will remove any fibers from the cardamom pods), then add the caraway seed and mix well.

5 Ladle the mixture into the hot, sterilized jars, then seal. The chutney will be ready to eat in about 1 month.

☆ **Degree of difficulty**
Easy

Cooking time
About 1¼ hours

Special equipment
Spice mill or coffee grinder; sterilized canning jars with sealants (see pages 42–43)

Yield
About 3½ pints (1.75kg)

Shelf life
6 months, heat processed

Serving suggestions
Superb with hot curries or game

TIP

• Prolonged cooking changes the character of ground spices. To maintain their freshness, add them after removing the chutney from the heat.

FLAVORED VINEGARS, OILS, & MUSTARDS

OILS AND VINEGARS readily absorb flavors: simply by adding herbs, spices, and soft fruit to oil or vinegar you can make superb condiments to dress and finish all kinds of dishes. For this purpose, do not use a strong-tasting oil, such as extra-virgin olive oil or nut oil, as they tend to mask the flavor of the steeped ingredients. I also prefer to use a clear, mild vinegar, such as cider or white wine, as its fruitiness complements the added flavorings. If you are lucky enough to have a small oak cask, you can mature vinegar in it for 2–3 years with the most wonderful results. Salad Vinegar, below, is particulary suited to this method. Mustard is one of the most ancient condiments. In the past, people would chew mustard seeds with a mouthful of meat to produce a mild, aromatic flavor. It is only when dry mustard powder is mixed with cold water that mustard produces the hot sensation we are used to today.

Salad Vinegar

White wine vinegar   Tarragon   Thyme   Chilies   Garlic   Peppercorns

As its name suggests, this mild and fragrant vinegar is perfect for making vinaigrettes and salad dressings. It improves greatly with long maturation, 2–3 years, after which it should be filtered (see page 47) and used sparingly.

INGREDIENTS

4 cups (1 liter) white wine vinegar or cider vinegar
2 sprigs tarragon
2 sprigs thyme
2 fresh or dried red chilies (optional)
2 garlic cloves, peeled and bruised
2 tsp black peppercorns

1 Put the vinegar in a non-corrosive pan. Bring to a boil and boil rapidly for 1–2 minutes. Remove from the heat and let cool to 104°F (40°C).

2 Wash the herbs only if necessary, then dry well and bruise by crushing them lightly with the flat side of a wide-bladed knife. Make a long slit in each chili, if using.

3 Divide the tarragon, thyme, chilies, garlic, and black peppercorns evenly between the sterilized bottles. Pour in the warm vinegar, then seal. Shake the bottles occasionally during storage to blend the ingredients. The vinegar will be ready to use in about 3 weeks.

☆ **Degree of difficulty**
Easy

Cooking time
3–4 minutes

Special equipment
Thermometer; sterilized bottles with sealants (see pages 42–43)

Yield
About 4 cups (1 liter)

Shelf life
2 years

SALAD VINEGAR is perfect for dressings and vinaigrettes. Its flavor complements a wide variety of fresh ingredients without overpowering them.

USE A BOTTLE with a neck wide enough for the added herbs

BRUISING THE HERBS releases extra flavor

WHOLE CHILIES add taste without imparting much heat

——— VARIATIONS ———

✦ Provençal Herb Vinegar

Use 3–4 sprigs each of rosemary, lavender, and thyme, with flowering heads if possible, and prepare following the method for the main recipe. Use this vinegar to enhance the flavor of strawberries and other fruit.

✦ Shallot Vinegar

Peel and coarsely chop 1lb (500g) of shallots and divide among the bottles. Fill with the warm vinegar, following the method for the main recipe. Use this vinegar for dressing salads or add to hollandaise sauce instead of fresh shallots.

✦ Citrus Vinegar

Peel the rind from 3–4 oranges or lemons. Remove as much white pith as possible, then secure the peel on wooden skewers and put one in each bottle. Cover with the warm vinegar and complete as for the main recipe.

Gooseberry Vinegar

This pale, yellow-green vinegar is especially delicious with fish.

INGREDIENTS

5 cups (1.25 liters) cider vinegar

2lb (1kg) tart gooseberries

4 cups (150g) sorrel or spinach leaves

a few strips of lemon rind

1 Bring the vinegar to a boil in a noncorrosive saucepan and boil rapidly for 1–2 minutes. Remove from the heat and let cool.

2 Wash the gooseberries and sorrel or spinach, then drain well. Put in the food processor and coarsely chop.

3 Transfer to a large jar and add the lemon rind. Pour in the vinegar, then cover with a clean cloth and leave in a warm place for 3–4 weeks, shaking the jar from time to time.

4 Strain through the jelly bag, then filter (see page 47). Pour into the sterilized bottles, then seal. The vinegar may be cloudy at first but the sediment should settle after a few weeks.

VARIATION

✦ *Blueberry Vinegar*
Substitute blueberries for the gooseberries, omit the sorrel or spinach and lemon rind. Increase the vinegar to 6 cups (1.5 liters). Use for salads or dilute and serve as a drink.

☆ **Degree of difficulty**
Easy

Cooking time
3–4 minutes

Special equipment
Food processor; sterilized jelly bag; sterilized canning bottles with sealants (see pages 42–43)

Yield
About 2 quarts (2 liters)

Shelf life
2 years, filtered

Serving suggestions
Add to fish dishes and sauces as a finishing touch

Strawberry Vinegar

(see page 33 for illustration)

This delightfully pink vinegar with a concentrated strawberry flavor is an ideal way to use up overripe fruit. Remember to discard any damaged berries.

TIPS

• Although the flavor of fruit vinegars improves with age, their color will eventually fade and turn brownish.
• Sometimes fruit vinegars can be cloudy. When left undisturbed in a cool, dark place, the sediment will settle to the bottom and the clear vinegar can be siphoned off. If the vinegar is still cloudy, clarify it by beating 2 egg whites with a little of the vinegar until frothy. Gradually add the mixture to the vinegar, stirring well. Bottle and let stand in a cool place for about a week. The sediment will settle at the bottom, and the clear liquid can be siphoned off.

INGREDIENTS

5 cups (1.25 liters) cider vinegar or white wine vinegar

2lb (1kg) ripe, full-flavored strawberries

a few wild or small cultivated strawberries and a few basil leaves (optional)

1 Bring the vinegar to a boil in a noncorrosive saucepan and boil rapidly for 1–2 minutes. Remove from the heat and let cool to 104°F (40°C).

2 Hull the strawberries, then finely chop in the food processor. Transfer to a large glass jar or bowl.

3 Pour the warm vinegar over the chopped berries and mix well. Cover with a clean cloth and let stand in a warm place (a sunny windowsill is ideal) for 2 weeks, stirring occasionally.

4 Strain the vinegar through the jelly bag, then filter (see page 47). Pour into the sterilized bottles, then seal.

5 To intensify the flavor of the vinegar, skewer a few wild or small cultivated strawberries and some basil leaves alternately on thin wooden skewers. Insert a skewer in each bottle and seal. The vinegar is ready to use immediately, but the flavor improves with age.

VARIATIONS

✦ *Blackberry or Black Currant Vinegar*
Substitute blackberries or black currants for the strawberries and increase the vinegar to 6 cups (1.5 liters). Omit the wild strawberries and basil. Follow the steps for the main recipe. Blackberry or Black Currant Vinegar make superb salad dressings or can be diluted and served as a refreshing drink.

☆ **Degree of difficulty**
Easy

Cooking time
3–4 minutes

Special equipment
Thermometer; food processor; sterilized jelly bag; sterilized canning bottles with sealants (see pages 42–43)

Yield
About 2 quarts (2 liters)

Shelf life
2 years, filtered

Serving suggestions
Use to dress salads, finish meat sauces, or sprinkle over fresh strawberries

Spiced Vinegars

Basic flavored vinegars like these are very easy to make and can be stored until needed. They mature and mellow with time. Any kind of vinegar can be used, but make sure it is not less than 5 percent acidity. I like cider vinegar for its fruitiness, which complements pickles. To make a sweet version, add 2–4 tablespoons of white or light brown sugar or honey to every 4 cups (1 liter) vinegar. Experiment with different combinations of spices to suit your own taste.

Perfumed Vinegar

INGREDIENTS

8 cups (2 liters) vinegar

1. SIMPLE SPICED VINEGAR

2 tbsp peppercorns

2 tbsp mustard seed

1 tbsp cloves

2 tsp crumbled mace blades

2 nutmegs, broken into pieces

2–3 dried chilies, crushed (optional)

1 cinnamon stick, crushed

2–3 bay leaves

1 tbsp salt

2. HOT AND SPICY VINEGAR

3 shallots, chopped

2½ in (6cm) piece fresh ginger, crushed

5–6 dried red chilies, crushed

1 tbsp black peppercorns

1 tbsp allspice berries

2 tsp cloves

1 cinnamon stick, crushed

2 tsp salt

3. PERFUMED VINEGAR

2in (5cm) piece of fresh ginger, sliced

2 tbsp coriander seed

1 tbsp black peppercorns

1 tbsp cardamom pods

1 tbsp allspice berries

2 cinnamon sticks, crushed

2 nutmegs, broken into pieces

1 tsp aniseed

a few strips of lemon or orange rind

1 tbsp salt

4. MILD EUROPEAN VINEGAR

1 tbsp black peppercorns

1 tbsp juniper berries

1 tbsp allspice berries

1 tbsp caraway seed

2 tsp dill or celery seed

2–3 bay leaves

2–3 garlic cloves, crushed

2–3 dried red chilies (optional)

2 tbsp salt

5. SPICY EUROPEAN VINEGAR

¼ lb (125g) shallots or onions, coarsely chopped

small bunch of fresh tarragon

4 garlic cloves, crushed

2 tsp black peppercorns

1 tsp cloves

2 tbsp salt

6. MELLOW TRADITIONAL VINEGAR

3oz (90g) fresh horseradish, peeled and sliced

1 tbsp black peppercorns

1 tbsp mustard seed

1 tbsp allspice berries

2 tsp cloves

2 pieces of dried ginger

1 cinnamon stick, crushed

2 tbsp salt

1 For each vinegar, tie all the flavorings, except the salt, in a piece of cheesecloth (see spice bags, page 47). Place in a noncorrosive saucepan with the salt and vinegar. Bring to a boil and boil for about 10 minutes.

2 Let cool, then remove the spice bag. Filter the vinegar if it is cloudy (see page 47). Pour into the sterilized bottles, then seal. The vinegar is ready immediately, but improves with age.

☆ **Degree of difficulty**
Easy

Cooking time
About 12 minutes

Special equipment
Sterilized canning bottles with sealants (see pages 42–43)

Yield
About 2 quarts (2 liters)

Shelf life
2 years, filtered

Serving suggestions
Try (2) with Pickled Onions (page 92), (3) with Pickled Garlic (page 92), (4) with Pickled Baby Vegetables (page 98), (5) with Olive Oil Pickle (page 97), or (6) with Chowchow (page 95)

Simple Spiced Vinegar

Sugar-free Sweet Vinegar

Useful for general pickling, this vinegar is sweetened with concentrated fruit juice (available from most health food stores) rather than sugar. I make large quantities of it at the beginning of winter so it will mature and be ready for use in the summer.

INGREDIENTS

4¼ quarts (4 liters) cider vinegar

1⅓ cups (300ml) concentrated apple or pear juice

2 tbsp black peppercorns

1 tbsp allspice berries

2 tsp cloves

2 tbsp coriander seed

3 cinnamon sticks

a few fresh or dried chilies (optional)

1 Put the vinegar and fruit juice in a noncorrosive saucepan. Bring to a boil and skim well. Make a spice bag with the remaining ingredients (see page 47). Add to the boiling vinegar and boil for 10 minutes.

2 Remove the spice bag, pour the vinegar into the hot, sterilized bottles, then seal. It is ready to use immediately, but improves with age.

☆ **Degree of difficulty**
Easy

Cooking time
About 12 minutes

Special equipment
Large sterilized canning bottles with sealants (see pages 42–43)

Yield
About 4½ quarts (4.3 liters)

Shelf life
Almost indefinitely, filtered

Malay Chili and Shallot Oil

In Malaysia this condiment appears on every table and has a wonderfully nutty, hot taste. Add to anything that needs extra flavor. Use in moderation to finish soups, stews, and rice dishes.

INGREDIENTS

3½ oz (100g) dried chilies, stems removed

¾ lb (350g) shallots, peeled

8–10 garlic cloves, peeled

4 cups (1 liter) peanut or refined sesame oil

1 Put the whole dried chilies, shallots, and garlic in the food processor and work until finely chopped.

2 Transfer the mixture to a saucepan and add the oil. Heat gently and cook over low heat for about 20 minutes, or until the shallots are softened and nicely browned.

3 Remove the pan from the heat and let cool. Filter the oil (see page 47), pour it into the sterilized bottles, then seal. The oil is ready to use immediately.

☆ **Degree of difficulty**
Easy

Cooking time
About 23 minutes

Special equipment
Food processor; sterilized canning bottles with sealants (see pages 42–43)

Yield
About 1 quart (1 liter)

Shelf life
6 months, filtered

Basil Oil

Herb-flavored oils are indispensable condiments in my kitchen. I use them to flavor salads or add them to soups and stews just before serving to give an extra lift. Basil oil is particularly fragrant, but many other herbs – alone or with spices and flavorings – are equally good, especially thyme with lemon and rosemary with cilantro.

INGREDIENTS

4 cups (1 liter) light olive oil

5 cups (150g) basil

1 Heat the oil gently until it reaches 104°F (40°C).

2 Lightly bruise the basil and put it in the warm, sterilized jar or bottle. Pour the warm oil into the jar, then seal. The oil will be ready to use in 3–4 weeks.

— **TIP** —

• If you plan to keep the oil for longer than a few weeks, it is best to filter it (see page 47), since the basil tends to become slimy after 3–4 months' maceration. Rebottle the oil and seal before storing.

☆ **Degree of difficulty**
Easy

Cooking time
2–3 minutes

Special equipment
Thermometer; sterilized canning jar or bottle with sealant (see pages 42–43)

Yield
About 1 quart (1 liter)

Shelf life
1 year, filtered

Serving suggestions
Use to flavor salads, sauces, and soups

Chili Oil

Red hot and wonderfully versatile, a few drops of this oil will add fire to any dish.

INGREDIENTS

3½ oz (100g) red chilies

4 cups (1 liter) peanut, sesame, or corn oil

2 tbsp sweet or hot paprika

1 Remove the stalks from the chilies. Put the chilies in the food processor and process until they are finely chopped. Transfer to a saucepan and add the oil.

2 Heat gently until the oil nearly reaches 212°F (100°C), then simmer for 15 minutes without letting the mixture get any hotter.

3 Remove the pan from the heat, cool slightly, then stir in the paprika. Let cool completely, then filter (see page 47). Pour the oil into the sterilized bottle, then seal. The chili oil is ready to use immediately.

☆ **Degree of difficulty**
Easy

Cooking time
About 18 minutes

Special equipment
Thermometer; sterilized canning bottle with sealant (see pages 42–43)

Yield
About 1 quart (1 liter)

Shelf life
1 year, filtered

Dark Spicy Mustard

Making homemade mustard is an economical way of utilizing this traditional spice. A versatile product, it can be served simply as a condiment, included in a wide variety of sauces, or used to form a tasty crust for roasted meat.

INGREDIENTS

½ cup (100g) yellow mustard seed

3 tbsp brown or black mustard seed

½ lb (250g) tamarind block, soaked in 1⅓ cups (300ml) water for 25 minutes

1 tbsp honey

1 tsp salt

1 tsp ground allspice

¼ tsp ground cinnamon

¼ tsp ground cloves

¼ tsp ground cardamom

a little brandy or whiskey

1 Grind the mustard seed in the spice mill or coffee grinder, then mix together in a bowl.

2 Strain the tamarind and add to the seeds with the honey, salt, and spices. Mix very well.

3 Pack into the sterilized jars, making sure there are no air pockets. Cover each one with a waxed paper disk that has been dipped in brandy or whiskey, then seal. The mustard will be ready to eat in a few days.

☆ **Degree of difficulty**
Easy

Special equipment
Spice mill or coffee grinder; sterilized canning jars with sealants (see pages 42–43)

Yield
About 2 pints (500g)

Shelf life
6 months

Serving suggestions
Use in dressings and sauces

Orange and Tarragon Mustard

This coarse-grained mustard is particularly good for coating meat before roasting. If you plan to use it immediately, there is no need to boil the orange juice.

INGREDIENTS

finely grated rind and juice of 2 oranges

1 cup (250g) yellow mustard seed

⅖ cup (100ml) white wine vinegar

2 tsp salt

1 tbsp chopped fresh tarragon, or 1 tsp dried tarragon

a little brandy or whiskey

1 Put the orange rind and juice in a small pan. Bring to a boil, then reduce the heat and simmer for a few seconds. (This improves the keeping qualities of the mustard.) Remove from the heat and let cool completely.

2 Coarsely grind 7oz (200g) of the mustard seed in the spice mill or coffee grinder. Place in a glass bowl with the remaining whole mustard seed, add the boiled orange juice and rind, and mix well. Let stand for about 5 minutes, then stir in the vinegar, salt, and tarragon.

3 Pack the mustard into the sterilized jars. Cover each one with a waxed paper disk that has been dipped in brandy or whiskey, then seal. The mustard will be ready to eat in a few days (this will give the whole mustard seed time to swell and soften).

☆ **Degree of difficulty**
Easy

Special equipment
Spice mill or coffee grinder; small sterilized canning jars with sealants (see pages 42–43)

Yield
About 2 pints (500g)

Shelf life
6 months

Serving suggestion
Serve with cold meat

PRESERVED MEAT

PRESERVING MEAT at home is not difficult, but it does require patience, common sense, and attention to detail. It is a rewarding skill that turns fresh meat into a superb, long-lasting delicacy. Follow each recipe closely and once a technique is mastered, you can experiment with different flavorings and ingredients – the results are worthwhile. Please read page 42 before starting.

Pickled Venison

Cardamoms

Nigella seed

| Peanut oil | Venison | Red wine vinegar | Tamarind | Salt | Jaggery | Cumin seed | Onions | Garlic | Chili | Ginger | Coriander seed |

In northern India, game, fish, and meat are preserved by being cooked in a rich mixture of spices – most of which contain natural preservatives and have antiseptic qualities. They are then kept in their cooking oil for several months – a technique akin to potting. Traditionally, mustard oil is used, but peanut or a mild olive oil can be substituted.

INGREDIENTS

1 cup (250ml) mustard or peanut oil
2lb (1kg) boneless shoulder or haunch of venison, cut into 2in (5cm) cubes
1⅓ cups (300ml) red wine vinegar
3½oz (100g) tamarind block
1 tbsp salt
1 tbsp jaggery or dark brown sugar
2 tsp green cardamom pods, lightly toasted
1 tsp nigella seed, lightly toasted
1 tsp cumin seed, lightly toasted
For the spice paste
1lb (500g) onions, coarsely chopped
5 garlic cloves, peeled
3–4 fresh chilies, seeded
2in (5cm) piece fresh ginger, coarsely chopped
2 tbsp coriander seed, freshly ground

1 Purée all the ingredients for the spice paste in the food processor. Heat the oil in a pan, add the venison, and brown on all sides. Remove from the pan.

2 Add the spice paste to the pan. Cook over high heat for a few minutes, then reduce the heat and simmer for 30 minutes, or until pale brown. Return the meat and simmer gently for 1½ hours, or until tender. If it becomes too dry, add 1–2 tablespoons water.

3 Warm the vinegar and pour it over the tamarind. Let soak for 30 minutes. Strain, then stir the salt and jaggery or sugar into the liquid. Add to the pan.

4 Bring to a boil, then simmer gently for 15 minutes, or until the oil rises to the top. Grind the cardamom pods, sieve into the pan, and add the nigella and cumin. Remove from the heat.

5 Pack into the hot, sterilized jars, then seal. The venison is ready to eat immediately, but improves after keeping for 1 week. Keep refrigerated or heat process for 35 minutes (see pages 44–45).

☆☆ **Degree of difficulty**
Moderate

Cooking time
About 2½ hours

Special equipment
Food processor; spice mill or coffee grinder; sterilized, wide-mouth jars with sealants (see pages 42–43)

Yield
About 3 pints (1.5kg)

Shelf life
5 weeks, refrigerated; 1 year, heat processed

Serving suggestion
Serve as a main course with rice

TAMARIND AND JAGGERY or dark brown sugar give the gravy an appetizing color

PICKLED VENISON *makes a delicious instant meal: simply reheat the meat and serve with warmed chapatis. Garnish with sprigs of fresh cilantro and a few sliced chilies, if desired.*

THE TOASTED SPICES complement the rich flavor of the venison

TIPS

• Lightly toasting whole spices releases their flavor. Put them in a small heated skillet, without any oil, and cook them briefly, shaking the pan frequently, until they are slightly colored and start to pop. Remove from the heat immediately and pour onto a plate. (If the seeds are left in the pan they will continue cooking in the residual heat and may burn.)

• Skim off the fat from the top of the jar before reheating the meat.

Cured Ham
(see page 64 for technique)

This recipe produces a mild-flavored ham that can be matured for a short period and then cooked, or, for a more pronounced flavor, dried more and even smoked before cooking. Instead of pork, you could use mutton or lamb. First-timers may find these meats easier, as the legs will be smaller and more manageable. Mutton is fairly hard to come by nowadays, but it has much more flavor than lamb. A good butcher will order it for you.

—— IMPORTANT NOTE ——
Before starting this recipe, please read the information on pages 42 and 64.

—————— TIP ——————
• If desired, the ham can be cold-smoked before cooking it. Smoke after step 4 or 5, below 86°F (30°C) for 18–24 hours, or longer, according to taste (see page 66).

INGREDIENTS

1 leg of pork, weighing 11–13lb (5–6kg)
2 cups (500g) salt
For the brine
3 quarts (3 liters) water, or 2 quarts (2 liters) water and 1 quart (1 liter) strong ale
3 cups (750g) salt
1½ cups (250g) dark brown sugar or light brown sugar
1 tbsp saltpeter
small bunch of thyme
3 sprigs rosemary
3 bay leaves
2 tbsp juniper berries, crushed
2 tsp cloves
For the paste
1¼ cups (150g) all-purpose flour
¼ cup (150g) salt
8–10 tsp water

1 Rub the pork all over with some of the salt, packing it firmly into the crevices. Sprinkle a layer of salt about ½in (1cm) deep in a large, noncorrosive dish. Set the meat on top and sprinkle with the rest of the salt. Cover and refrigerate for 24–48 hours.

2 Make the brine (see page 47) and cool completely. Brush the salt off the meat and place it in the crock. Strain over the brine making sure it covers the meat.

3 Weight down the meat (see page 46). Cover and refrigerate or store at or below 38°F (3°C) for 2–2½ weeks. Check the brine every day. Discard the brine if any off odors develop and cover the meat with fresh brine. (See Information Box, page 64.)

4 Remove the meat from the brine, rinse it, and then dry. Hang in a cool, dry, dark, airy place for 2–3 days (between 42–46°F/6–8°C). The ham can be cooked now, if desired (see steps below), or dried more for a stronger flavor, see step 5.

5 Mix the paste ingredients together and spread over the exposed meat, in a layer ½in (1cm) thick. Hang the meat for 2–2½ weeks, covering it with cheesecloth when the surface has dried. Cook as below.

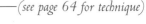

Degree of difficulty
☆ ☆ Advanced

Cooking time
25–30 minutes per 1lb (500g)

Special equipment
Large crock or noncorrosive dish; sterilized cheesecloth

Yield
8¼–9¾lb (3.75–4.5kg)

Shelf life
2 years, uncooked; 3 weeks, cooked

Serving suggestions
Serve the ham hot, with red-eye gravy or cherry sauce, or cold as the centerpiece of a buffet

✳ **Warning**
This recipe contains saltpeter, see page 42

SERVE THE HAM cold with Spiced Whole Oranges (see page 100) and Spiced Cherry Tomatoes (see page 93)

TO COOK THE HAM

SOAK THE HAM in cold water for 24 hours before cooking

1 Soak the ham for 24 hours. Place it in a pan with cold water to cover. Add an herb bundle (rosemary, thyme, bay leaves, lemon, and orange peel), some apple, onion, carrot, zucchini, peppercorns, parsley, and cloves.

2 Bring slowly to a boil, then simmer for 25–30 minutes per 1lb (500g), or a meat thermometer registers 150°F (65°C) internally.

3 If serving the ham hot, remove it from the pan. To serve cold, let cool in the water, then peel off the skin using a knife.

Smoked Chicken

(see page 24 for illustration)

Good smoked chicken is a rare delicacy — flavorful and succulent. But be sure to use only firm, fresh, free-range chicken for the best results. Many other kinds of poultry and game birds can be prepared in the same way. You need to vary the curing time according to the size of the bird.

— IMPORTANT NOTE —
Before starting this recipe, please read the information on pages 42 and 64.

INGREDIENTS

1 x 3–4lb (1.5–2kg) chicken
1 tbsp olive or peanut oil
4–5 sprigs thyme
4–5 sprigs tarragon
1 bay leaf
For the brine
2 quarts (2 liters) water
2¼ cups (600g) salt
5–6 sprigs tarragon
4–5 strips lemon rind

1 To make the brine, put all the ingredients in a noncorrosive saucepan. Bring to a boil, stirring until the salt is dissolved, then reduce the heat and simmer for about 10 minutes. Strain and let cool completely.

2 Wash and dry the chicken, then trim off any loose fat. Truss the bird as for roasting, then prick it all over with a sharp wooden skewer.

3 Put the chicken in a deep glass dish and cover with the brine. Weight down (see page 46), then refrigerate for 6–8 hours.

4 Drain the chicken well. Insert a wooden skewer through the trussed wings and tie a loop of string to it. Hang to dry in a cool, dry, dark, airy place (between 42–46°F/6–8°C) for 24 hours.

5 Brush the chicken with the oil and hang, legs down, in the smoker or place on a smoker tray. Hot-smoke for 3–3½ hours at 225–240°F (110–125°C). Halfway through smoking, add the herbs to the smoking tray.

6 To check for doneness, insert a skewer into the thickest part of the thigh — the juices should run clear without any sign of pinkness. The chicken can be served hot, but is best left until cold, then wrapped in waxed paper and refrigerated until needed.

Degree of difficulty
☆ ☆☆ Advanced

Cooking time
About 12 minutes simmering; 3–3½ hours smoking

Special equipment
Smoker

Yield
About 3lb (1.5kg)

Shelf life
1 month, refrigerated

Serving suggestions
Serve thinly sliced with a mixed green salad; or skewered with Striped Spiced Pears (see page 103) or with fresh mango as a canapé

— TIP —
• The smoked chicken can be frozen for up to 3 months.

Pastrami

New York just wouldn't be the same without pastrami on rye. This lightly smoked, deliciously piquant cured meat originated in Romania, but its roots probably lie in Turkey. Traditionally, the meat is only lightly smoked for 4 hours, but for a more intense flavor, smoke it for up to 12 hours. Fragrant fruit woods are best.

— IMPORTANT NOTE —
Before starting this recipe, please read the information on pages 42 and 64.

INGREDIENTS

6lb (3kg) lean beef brisket
1 cup (250g) salt
6 garlic cloves, crushed
4 tbsp light brown sugar
4 tbsp coarsely ground black pepper
2 tbsp coriander seed, coarsely ground
1 tbsp ground ginger
1 tsp saltpeter

1 Put the beef in a noncorrosive dish. Rub half of the salt into the meat. Cover and let stand for 2 hours, then rinse the meat and dry well.

2 Mix the remaining ingredients together, including the rest of the salt, and rub well into the meat. Return the meat to the cleaned dish. Cover and refrigerate for 1½–2 weeks, turning the meat every few days.

3 Lift the meat out and pat dry. Insert a meat hook into the beef and hang to dry in a cool, dry, dark, airy place (between 42–46°F/6–8°C) for 1 day. Cold-smoke below 100°F (50°C) for 4–6 hours (see page 66).

4 Cook the pastrami in simmering unsalted water for 2½–3 hours, or until it is tender. Remove from the cooking liquid, drain well, then serve. To serve cold, drain it well and weight down (see page 46). Let cool, then refrigerate until needed.

Degree of difficulty
☆☆ Moderate

Cooking time
4–6 hours smoking, 2½–3 hours simmering

Special equipment
Meat hook; smoker

Yield
About 4–5lb (2–2.5kg)

Shelf life
4–6 weeks, refrigerated; 6 months, frozen

Serving suggestions
Serve hot or cold, or as a sandwich filling

✳ **Warning**
This recipe contains saltpeter, see page 42

Preserved Toulouse Sausages
(see page 25 for illustration)

These simple, versatile sausages can be flavored with different herbs and spices. Traditionally, they are seasoned with just salt and pepper — white pepper rather than black, because flecks of black pepper are considered unsightly. However, I much prefer the taste of black pepper.

—IMPORTANT NOTE —

Before starting this recipe, please read the information on pages 42 and 62.

— VARIATIONS —

✦ *Herb Sausages*
Add 2 tablespoons chopped parsley or a mixture of parsley and thyme. (My favorite version also includes 1 teaspoon orange or lemon rind.)

✦ *Garlic Sausages*
Add 3 garlic cloves, crushed, and 2 tablespoons chopped herbs

✦ *Cumberland Sausages*
Add ¼ teaspoon grated nutmeg.

INGREDIENTS

4¼ lb (2.1kg) lean shoulder of pork, cubed
1¾ lb (900g) pork fatback, cubed
¼ cup (60g) salt
1 tsp freshly ground white or black pepper
½ tsp saltpeter
3¼–4¼ yards (3–4 meters) pork casing
For each jar
2 garlic cloves, blanched for 2 minutes (see page 46)
2 sprigs thyme
1 sprig rosemary
olive oil or lard to cover

1 Put the meat through the coarse disk of the meat grinder and the fat through the fine disk.

2 Put the ground meat and fat in a glass bowl with the salt, pepper, and saltpeter. Knead the mixture well with your hands to be sure the meat and fat are evenly distributed. Cover and refrigerate for at least 4 hours.

3 Prepare the casing (see steps 4 and 5, page 68). Stuff with the meat and divide into 2in (5cm) links (see step 6, page 69).

4 Fry, broil, or barbecue the sausages for 8–10 minutes per side, or until they are completely cooked through but still slightly pink and moist inside. Immediately arrange the sausages in the hot sterilized jars, along with the garlic and herbs.

5 If using olive oil to cover, heat until it reaches 194°F (90°C), pour into the jar, then seal.

6 If using lard, melt it, then let it cool. Cool the sausages, arrange in the jar, and cover with the lard. Refrigerate until the fat sets, then top off with more melted lard so that it covers the sausages by at least ½in (1cm), and seal.

7 Store in a cool, dark place (between 42–46°F/6–8°C) or the bottom of the refrigerator. The sausages will be ready to eat in 1 month. The oil or lard from the jar can be used in cooking.

☆☆ **Degree of difficulty**
Moderate

Cooking time
About 20 minutes

Special equipment
Meat grinder with sausage stuffing attachment; sterilized wide-mouth canning jars with sealants (see pages 42–43)

Yield
About 6lb (3kg)

Shelf life
1 year, refrigerated

Serving suggestions
Add to stews, bean casseroles, or cassoulet

✳ **Warning**
This recipe contains saltpeter, see page 42

—TIP —
• To eat the sausages fresh, omit the saltpeter and leave them in a coil or divide into 4in (10cm) links. Keep refrigerated and cook within 2 days (see step 4).

Dried Lamb Sausages
(see page 25 for illustration)

Different versions of this recipe are made all over the Muslim world, where pork is not eaten. The sausages may be eaten after 4 weeks when they are still very aromatic, or hung until they are hard and dry to be used for cooking.

—IMPORTANT NOTE —

Before starting this recipe, please read the information on pages 42 and 62.

INGREDIENTS

3lb (1.5kg) boned shoulder or leg of lamb, cut into large cubes
10oz (300g) lamb or beef fat, cut into large cubes
6 garlic cloves, crushed
4 tbsp olive oil
1⅓ tbsp salt
1 tbsp fennel seed
2 tbsp sweet paprika
1 tsp dried mint
1–2 tsp chili powder
½ tsp freshly ground black pepper
½ tsp saltpeter
3¼–3¾ yards (3–3.5 meters) beef casing

1 Put the lamb and fat through the coarse disk of the grinder. Add all the remaining ingredients, except the casing, and mix well. Pack into a glass bowl, making sure there are no air pockets. Cover and refrigerate for 12 hours.

2 Prepare the beef casing (see steps 4 and 5, page 68). Stuff with the meat and divide into 6in (15cm) links (see step 6, page 69). Hang in a cool, dry, dark, airy place (between 42–46°F/6–8°C) for 4–5 weeks, or until they have lost about half their original weight. Wrap in waxed paper and refrigerate.

☆☆ **Degree of difficulty**
Moderate

Special equipment
Meat grinder with sausage stuffing attachment

Yield
About 2lb (1kg)

Shelf life
6 months, refrigerated

Serving suggestions
Either barbecue the sausages or add to stews, couscous, or tagines

✳ **Warning**
This recipe contains saltpeter, see page 42

Wind-dried Duck Sausages

(see page 25 for illustration)

These curiously sweet and spicy sausages were inspired by an ancient Chinese recipe. In China, sausages like these are hung to dry in the cool, breezy mountain air, which is the ideal curing place. I hang them in my cool pantry and the results are almost as good. The same technique can be used with pure pork or a mixture of pork fat and beef or venison.

IMPORTANT NOTE

Before starting this recipe, please read the information on pages 42 and 62.

INGREDIENTS

1 x 6lb (3kg) duck, boned, skin left on
10oz (300g) veal or pork tenderloin, cubed
3 tbsp sake or fortified rice wine
3–4 fresh Thai chilies, seeded and chopped
1 tbsp salt
4–5 star anise, finely ground
1 tsp Szechuan pepper, finely ground
1 tsp fennel seed, finely ground
about 4 yards (3.8 meters) pork casing
a little peanut oil
For the cure
1 cup (250ml) soy sauce
4 tbsp honey or dark brown sugar
3 garlic cloves, crushed
2in (5cm) piece of fresh ginger, shredded
½ tsp saltpeter

1 Put all the meat in a glass bowl. Mix all the ingredients for the cure and pour over the meat, rubbing it in well. Cover with plastic wrap. Refrigerate for 24 hours, turning occasionally.

2 Put the duck breasts through the coarse disk of the grinder. Put the rest of the meat through the fine disk. Mix in the remaining ingredients, except the casing and oil. Pack into a bowl, making sure there are no air pockets. Cover and refrigerate for 12 hours.

3 Prepare the casing (see steps 4 and 5, page 68). Stuff with the meat and divide into 4in (10cm) links (see step 6, page 69).

4 Hang in a cool, dry, dark, airy place (between 42–46°F/ 6–8°C) for 4–5 weeks, or until they have lost about half their original weight. After 10 days, or when the sausages start to shrink, rub with the oil.

☆☆ **Degree of difficulty**
Moderate

Special equipment
Meat grinder with sausage stuffing attachment

Yield
About 2lb (1kg)

Shelf life
6 months, refrigerated

Serving suggestions
Serve as part of a sausage platter, or add to stir-fries and slow-cooked Chinese dishes

✳ **Warning**
This recipe contains saltpeter, see page 42

—— **TIP** ——
• To store the sausages, wrap in waxed paper and store in a cool, dry, dark place (between 42–46°F/6–8°C), refrigerate, or freeze for up to 3 months.

Landjäger

(see page 25 for illustration)

Landjäger is the German word for hunter. These flat, spicy sausages were once the favorite food to take on a hunt. Use cherry-tree chips for smoking the sausages, if possible.

IMPORTANT NOTE

Before starting this recipe, please read the information on pages 42 and 62.

INGREDIENTS

2½ lb (1.25kg) lean beef, such as chuck, shoulder, or rump, cut into large cubes
2lb (1kg) bacon
5 garlic cloves, crushed
1 tbsp salt
1 tbsp light brown sugar
½ tsp saltpeter
2 tsp coriander seed, finely ground
1 tsp freshly ground black pepper
2 tsp caraway seed
⅓ cup (75ml) kirsch
about 3¾ yards (3.5 meters) beef casing
a little peanut oil

1 Put the beef through the coarse disk of the grinder and the bacon through the fine disk.

2 Add all the remaining ingredients, except the beef casing and oil, and mix well. Pack the mixture tightly into a bowl, making sure that there are no air pockets. Cover and refrigerate for 48 hours.

3 Prepare the beef casing (see steps 4 and 5, page 68). Stuff with the meat and divide into 6in (15cm) links (see step 6, page 69). Place between two wooden boards and weight down (see page 46). Refrigerate for 48 hours.

4 Hang in a cool, dry, dark, airy place (between 42–46°F/ 6–8°C) for 24 hours, then cold-smoke for 12 hours at 86°F/30°C (see page 66).

5 Rub the sausages with a little oil. Hang to dry as before for 2–3 weeks, or until they have lost half their original weight.

☆☆ **Degree of difficulty**
Moderate

Special equipment
Meat grinder with sausage stuffing attachment; smoker

Yield
About 2½ lb (1.5kg)

Shelf life
4–5 months, refrigerated

Serving suggestion
Wonderful for picnics

✳ **Warning**
This recipe contains saltpeter, see page 42

—— **TIPS** ——
• To speed up the drying process, use an electric fan switched to the high setting.
• To store, wrap in waxed paper and keep refrigerated, or freeze for up to 3 months.

Garlic and Herb Salami

(see page 68 for technique)

Do not worry if a white deposit starts to grow on the sausages; it is a harmless mold that helps to preserve them.

IMPORTANT NOTE

Before starting this recipe, please read the information on pages 42 and 62.

INGREDIENTS

2lb (1kg) lean shoulder of pork, trimmed, all tendons removed, and cut into large cubes

1½ tbsp salt

½ tsp saltpeter

⅓ cup (75ml) vodka

¾ lb (350g) pork fatback, cut into large cubes

5 garlic cloves, finely chopped

3 tbsp finely chopped thyme

2 tsp black peppercorns

2 tsp coriander seed, coarsely ground

½ tsp freshly ground black pepper

¼ tsp allspice, freshly ground

about 2 yards (2 meters) pork casing

1 Place the pork in a glass bowl, sprinkle with the salt, saltpeter, and vodka, and mix well. Cover and refrigerate for 12 hours.

2 Put the meat through the fine disk of the grinder. Grind the fatback through the coarse disk. Mix together, adding any marinating liquid left in the bowl.

3 Add all the remaining ingredients, except the casing, and mix thoroughly but lightly. Refrigerate for at least 2 hours.

4 Prepare the casing (see steps 4 and 5, page 68). Stuff with the meat and divide into 8in (20cm) links (see step 6, page 69).

5 Hang to dry in a cool, dry, dark, airy place (between 42–46°F/6–8°C) for 5–6 weeks, or until they have lost about half their original weight. Wrap well in waxed paper and store in a cool, dry, dark place, or in the bottom of the refrigerator.

☆☆ **Degree of difficulty**
Moderate

Special equipment
Meat grinder with sausage stuffing attachment

Yield
About 1½ lb (750g)

Shelf life
4–5 months, refrigerated

Serving suggestion
Remove the skin and bake in a brioche

✳ **Warning**
This recipe contains saltpeter, see page 42

A selection of salami

Chili Salami

(see page 25 for illustration)

These spicy sausages are similar to Spanish chorizo, and can be used in cooking or eaten raw. To make milder sausages, reduce the number of chilies. For convenience, you could grind the fat on the coarse disk of a meat grinder instead of chopping it by hand, but the sausages' wonderful marbled appearance will be lost. Before serving raw, the sausages should be brought to room temperature.

IMPORTANT NOTE

Before starting this recipe, please read the information on pages 42 and 62.

INGREDIENTS

2lb (1kg) pork shoulder, cut into large cubes

1½ tbsp salt

1 tbsp light brown sugar

½ tsp saltpeter

⅓ cup (75ml) brandy

¾ lb (350g) pork fatback, cut into small, rough chunks

4–5 large, mild red chilies, very finely chopped

2 garlic cloves, crushed

2 tbsp sweet paprika

1 tsp chili powder, or to taste

1 tsp aniseed

about 2 yards (2 meters) pork casing

1 Put the pork in a large glass bowl, sprinkle with the salt, sugar, saltpeter, and brandy. Mix together with your hands. Cover and refrigerate for 12–24 hours.

2 Put the meat through the coarse disk of the grinder. Mix well with all the remaining ingredients, except the casing. Prepare the casing (see steps 4 and 5, page 68). Stuff with the meat and divide into 20in (50cm) links (see step 6, page 69).

3 Tie the ends of each sausage together to form a horseshoe. Hang in a cool, dry, dark, airy place (between 42–46°F/6–8°C) for 4–6 weeks, or until they have lost about half their original weight. Wrap in waxed paper and refrigerate until needed.

VARIATION

♦ *Smoked Chili Salami*
Dry for 1–2 days, or until the surface is just moist, then cold-smoke for 6–8 hours at 86°F/30°C (see pages 66–67). Dry as above. The smoked sausages will be ready to eat in 4–5 weeks.

☆☆ **Degree of difficulty**
Moderate

Special equipment
Meat grinder with sausage stuffing attachment

Yield
About 1½ lb (750g)

Shelf life
4–5 months, refrigerated

Serving suggestions
Slice and serve raw, or add to bean stews and casseroles

✳ **Warning**
This recipe contains saltpeter, see page 42

Jerky

Jerky conjures up images of the Wild West, yet it was eaten by Native Americans for generations before then. Pounded with fat and wild cherries, it was made into cakes called pemmican, *which were taken on long journeys to provide an instant source of energy. Unlike Biltong (see below), Jerky is not cured before drying.*

— IMPORTANT NOTE —

Before starting this recipe, please read the information on pages 42 and 62.

INGREDIENTS

2lb (1kg) bottom round or rump steak
2 tsp salt
2 tbsp coarsely ground black pepper
1 tsp chili powder

1 To slice the meat easily, put it in the freezer for 2–3 hours. Using a large, sharp chef's knife, cut the meat into ¼ in (5mm) slices along the grain, then cut into 2in (5cm) strips.

2 Mix the salt, pepper, and chili powder together, sprinkle over the meat, and rub in well.

3 Arrange the meat on a wire rack, leaving small gaps between slices. Place in the oven on the lowest possible setting, leaving the door slightly ajar.

4 After about 5 hours, turn the meat over and leave for 5–8 hours longer, or until it has lost about 75% of its original weight. The Jerky should be dry and stiff. Let cool, then store in jars or wrap in waxed paper. Keep in a cool, dry, dark place (between 42–46°F/6–8°C).

— VARIATION —

✦ *Mix together 4 tablespoons soy sauce, 4 tablespoons tomato sauce, 1 tablespoon paprika, and 1 teaspoon ground chili and rub this mixture over the meat instead of the salt, pepper, and chili. Dry as above. This is especially good made with turkey.*

☆ **Degree of difficulty**
Easy

Cooking time
10–13 hours

Yield
About 8–10oz (250–300g)

Shelf life
6 months

Serving suggestions
Serve as a snack, grate over an omelet, or rehydrate in warm water and use in stews

— TIP —

• Beef, venison, and turkey can be prepared in the same way.

Biltong

(see page 62 for technique)

Biltong is a South African specialty, made from venison, ostrich, or beef.

— IMPORTANT NOTE —

Before starting this recipe, please read the information on pages 42 and 62.

INGREDIENTS

4lb (2kg) piece of sirloin or bottom round of beef, or venison
1 cup (250g) salt
3 tbsp light brown sugar
1 tsp saltpeter
3 tbsp coriander seed, toasted and crushed
2 tbsp black peppercorns, crushed
4 tbsp malt vinegar

1 To slice the meat easily, put in the freezer for 2–3 hours. With a large, sharp chef's knife, slice the meat into long steaks 2in (5cm) thick, cutting along the grain. Cut off any sinews or loose fat.

2 Mix together all the dry ingredients. Sprinkle a layer into a large earthenware or glass dish, then add the meat. Sprinkle with the rest of the dry mix in an even layer, rubbing it in well.

3 Sprinkle the vinegar evenly over both sides of the meat and rub it in. Cover and refrigerate for 6–8 hours, turning the meat occasionally and rubbing the salt mixture into it after 2–3 hours.

4 Lift the meat out of the dish and shake off any loose salt. Hang it from meat hooks or hang it with string (see step 6, page 63). Let dry in a cool, dry, dark, airy place (between 42–46°F/6–8°C) for 1½ weeks, or until the meat is semidried and has lost nearly half its original weight. Wrap well in waxed paper and keep refrigerated.

5 Alternatively, to dry the Biltong fully, line the bottom of the oven with aluminum foil and place a shelf at the top position. Hang the meat from it and dry at the very lowest setting for 8–16 hours, or until the Biltong is fully dry, dark, and splinters when bent in two. Wrap in waxed paper and store between 42–46°F (6–8°C) or refrigerate.

☆ **Degree of difficulty**
Easy

Cooking time
8–16 hours, oven-dried

Special equipment
String and larding needle, or meat hooks

Yield
About 2lb (1kg)

Shelf life
3 weeks, semidried; 2 years, fully dried

Serving suggestion
Serve as a tasty snack

✳ **Warning**
This recipe contains saltpeter, see page 42

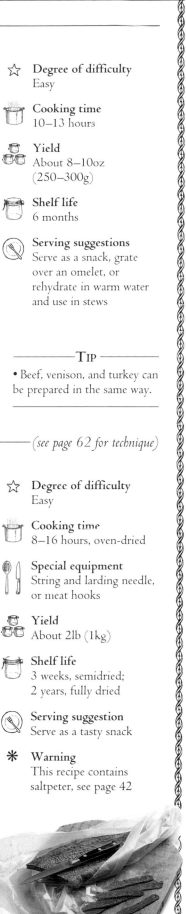

PATES & POTTED GOODS

IN THE PAST, using fat as a preservative was a convenient way to keep those cuts of meat that could not be roasted; flavored ground meats, organ meats, and other scraps were cooked and sealed in fat to last throughout the winter. Today, this technique has become a skill that gives the cook an opportunity to be creative, transforming different cuts of meat into luxurious products. Meat, when combined with herbs, spices, alcohol, and other flavorings, is ideal for making pâtés. These are delicious served simply with a relish, a glass of wine, and a chunk of bread. Always use the best raw ingredients you can afford – a cheap brandy might be less expensive, but you will need to add more of it to achieve the depth of flavor required. These products, by the nature of their ingredients, have a high fat content. After mastering this technique, you can always try reducing the fat content by replacing some of it with vegetables, such as carrots, beans, sweet potatoes, or even fruit, to retain the moisture.

Confit of Duck

Coarse salt   Saltpeter   Duck   Lard or goose or duck fat   Garlic   Cloves   Peppercorns

This specialty of south-west France is an indispensable item in the country's pantries. It is easy to make and absolutely delicious. Traditionally, goose is used, but the rich flavor of duck lends itself perfectly to this technique. Turkey, chicken, and rabbit can also be preserved in the same way.

INGREDIENTS

2 tbsp coarse salt
¼ tsp saltpeter
6 duck legs, any loose skin removed
1½ lb (750g) lard or goose or duck fat
4 garlic cloves
1 tsp black peppercorns
½ tsp cloves

1 Mix the salt and saltpeter together and rub well all over the duck. Refrigerate for 24 hours.

2 Brush the salt off the duck, then dry well, but do not wash. Gently heat the fat in a large heavy pan. Add the duck, garlic, peppercorns, and cloves. Be sure that the fat completely covers the duck. If not, melt some more fat and add to the pan to cover.

3 Cook very gently for about 2 hours, or until no liquid comes out of the meat when pierced with a skewer. Lift out and allow to cool completely.

4 Strain the fat through the cheesecloth (see page 47). Cover the bottom of the sterilized crock or jar with a little of the fat.

5 Pack the duck into the jar and cover with the remaining fat. Allow to solidify, adding more fat if necessary to cover the meat by at least ½ in (1 cm). Seal or cover with a double layer of foil. The duck is ready to eat immediately.

☆ **Degree of difficulty**
Easy

Cooking time
About 2 hours

Special equipment
Sterilized cheesecloth; sterilized earthenware crock or large jar with airtight sealant (see pages 42–43)

Yield
About 3–4lb (1.5–2kg)

Shelf life
6 months, refrigerated

Serving suggestion
Heat and serve with sautéed potatoes

✳ **Warning**
This recipe contains saltpeter, see page 42

TIP

• To serve the Confit, lift the duck out of the sealing fat and place in a dry skillet. Heat thoroughly and serve either hot or cold, accompanied by salad or mashed potatoes.

THE FAT SHOULD cover the duck in a thick layer to seal it

CONFIT OF DUCK *or goose is traditionally used in cassoulet. This delicacy of the Toulouse and Castelnaudary regions of France combines confit with beans and sausages (use Preserved Toulouse Sausages, page 136) to produce a hearty winter dish.*

COVER THE DISH with a double layer of foil or waxed paper

Rabbit Pâté

(see page 25 for illustration)

Traditional pâtés owe their moist texture to their high fat content. Some time ago, however, I was challenged to produce a low-fat pâté and devised this light, healthy version using lean meat and plenty of fresh vegetables to provide moisture. The lard used to seal the pâté is discarded before eating.

INGREDIENTS

1 large rabbit, boned, saddle fillets removed
⅔ lb (400g) lean pork, cut into large cubes
4 shallots, coarsely chopped
1 tbsp oil
3 medium carrots, finely diced
3 eggs
1 tbsp green peppercorns in brine, drained
2 tbsp salt
½ tsp freshly ground black pepper
2 tbsp finely chopped parsley
1 tbsp finely chopped thyme
1 tbsp finely chopped sage
a piece of caul fat, or ½ lb (250g) bacon slices
about 1lb (500g) lard, melted

For the marinade

⅓ cup (75ml) slivovitz, kirsch, or brandy
3–4 sprigs thyme
3–4 sage leaves
1 tsp coarsely ground black pepper
2 bay leaves, lightly toasted and crumbled (see tips, right)
1 tsp finely grated lemon rind

1 Place the rabbit fillets, the rest of the rabbit, and the pork in a bowl and mix in all the ingredients for the marinade. Cover and refrigerate for 12 hours.

2 Sweat the shallots in the oil for a few minutes until softened. Blanch the carrots in boiling water for 1 minute, then drain, refresh, and drain again (see page 46).

3 Remove the rabbit fillets from the marinade and pat dry. Put the rest of the meat and the shallots through the fine disk of the meat grinder. Strain the marinade and add to the ground meat, together with the carrots, eggs, peppercorns, salt, and pepper. Mix very well, then cover and refrigerate for 2–3 hours.

4 Mix together the chopped herbs and spread them out on a baking sheet. Roll the rabbit fillets in the herbs until they are evenly coated.

5 Line the terrine with the caul fat or bacon slices (see step 2, page 70). Spoon half the meat mixture into the terrine and smooth the surface with a narrow spatula.

6 Place the herb-coated rabbit fillets on top of the meat, in the center. Spoon in the remaining meat mixture, making sure there are no air pockets, and smooth the top. Fold over the ends of the caul fat or bacon and cover with the lid or a double layer of foil.

7 Place the terrine in a roasting pan filled with enough warm water to come about halfway up the sides of the dish. Bake in an oven preheated to 325°F/160°C for 1½–2 hours, or until the pâté has shrunk from the sides of the dish and is surrounded by liquid.

8 Remove the dish from the roasting pan. Cover the pâté with a board, then weight down (see page 46). Let cool, then refrigerate for 12 hours.

9 Remove the pâté from the terrine and wipe off the jelly or any liquid with paper towels.

10 Pour a ½ in (1cm) layer of the melted lard into the bottom of the cleaned terrine and refrigerate until set. Place the pâté on top of the set fat and pour on the remaining lard, making sure it fills the gaps down the sides and covers the pâté by about ½ in (1cm). Cover and refrigerate. The pâté will be ready to eat in 2 days.

☆ **Degree of difficulty**
☆☆ Advanced

Cooking time
1½–2 hours

Special equipment
Meat grinder; 6-cup (1.5-liter) terrine

Yield
About 3lb (1.25kg)

Shelf life
3 weeks, refrigerated

Serving suggestions
Serve with Carrot and Almond Chutney (see page 121) or Striped Spiced Pears (see page 103)

TIPS

• To toast the bay leaves, place in a heated small skillet and toast for a few minutes, until they start to color. They are then easily crumbled or pounded.
• When using fresh herbs in a marinade, bruise them first by crushing with the flat side of a large chef's knife or a cleaver.
• Check the balance of flavors when making pâté: before you put the meat mixture in the terrine, cook a spoonful in a little oil, let cool, and taste.
• To judge if the pâté is done, insert a meat thermometer in the center. It should register 167°F (75°C).
• Instead of covering the pâté with lard, you could remove it from the terrine and wrap it tightly in aluminum foil. Before serving, decorate with bay leaves, fresh sage, and thyme, if desired, then brush with melted aspic.
• Pâtés should always be brought to room temperature before serving.

Quail and Pheasant Terrine

(see page 25 for illustration)

This is just about the most complicated recipe in the whole book — a tour de force consisting of boned, stuffed quail embedded in a rich game forcemeat. A good butcher should be able to bone the birds for you, but if you prefer to do it yourself it is not complicated, requiring only patience and a sharp, flexible boning knife.

INGREDIENTS

4 quail, boned, with the skin left on
2 tbsp honey
¼ tsp salt
4 tsp brandy

For the forcemeat

1 large, pheasant, boned, all skin and tendons removed
10oz (300g) pork tenderloin or veal, cubed
½ cup (100ml) brandy
½ lb (250g) shallots, chopped
2 garlic cloves, chopped
a little oil or butter
1lb (500g) uncured slab bacon (pork belly) cut into small pieces
1 cup (250ml) dry white wine
2 eggs
1½ tsp freshly ground black pepper
1½ tsp salt
2 tbsp finely chopped thyme
15 juniper berries, coarsely ground
finely grated rind of ½ lemon

For the green forcemeat

5 cups spinach
2 tbsp finely chopped parsley

For the terrines

2 pieces of caul fat or 10oz (300g) bacon slices

1 Lay the boned quail skin side down on a board and spread evenly with the honey, salt, and brandy. Tightly roll up the birds and place in a bowl. Cover and refrigerate for 12 hours.

2 For the forcemeat, combine the pheasant and tenderloin. Add the brandy and mix well. Cover and refrigerate for 12 hours.

3 Sweat the shallots and garlic in a little oil or butter for a few minutes until soft, then allow to cool. Combine with the marinated pheasant and pork and the bacon in the food processor.

4 Process for 1–2 minutes, adding some of the wine and any leftover marinade, until it is smooth. Add the eggs, seasoning, thyme, juniper, and lemon rind. Mix in well. Measure out ½ cup (100g) of the mixture and reserve. Cover the rest and refrigerate for 2 hours.

5 For the green forcemeat, blanch the spinach in boiling water for 2 minutes (see page 46) and squeeze dry. Place in the food processor and purée. Mix with the reserved forcemeat and parsley. Refrigerate for 2 hours.

6 Unroll the quail skin side down on a board. Divide the green forcemeat between them, placing it in the center of each one. Fold over the skin flaps to encase it and reshape.

7 Line the terrines with the caul fat or bacon slices (see step 2, page 70). Spoon a quarter of the forcemeat into each terrine and smooth the surface over with a narrow spatula. Arrange the quail on top, pressing them lightly into the mixture. Spoon in the remaining forcemeat, making sure there are no air pockets, and smooth the top.

8 Fold over the ends of the caul fat or bacon and cover with the lid or a double layer of foil. Place the terrines in a roasting pan filled with enough warm water to come halfway up the sides of the dishes. Bake in an oven preheated to 325°F (160°C), for about 2 hours, or until each pâté has shrunk from the sides of its dish and is surrounded by liquid.

9 Remove the dishes from the roasting pan and let cool. Cover each pâté, then weight down (see page 46) and refrigerate overnight.

☆ **Degree of difficulty**
☆☆ Advanced

Cooking time
About 2 hours

Special equipment
Food processor; 2 x 4-cup (1-liter) terrines

Yield
About 4lb (2kg)

Shelf life
3–4 weeks, refrigerated

Serving suggestions
Serve decorated as the centerpiece of a cold buffet or with an arugula salad and Peach Chutney (see page 125) for an elegant first course

TIPS

- To serve the pâtés, decorate them with bay leaves and cranberries or brush with melted aspic or fruit jelly.
- For keeping longer than a few days, cover with melted lard or wrap tightly in foil — aspic will sour and mold.

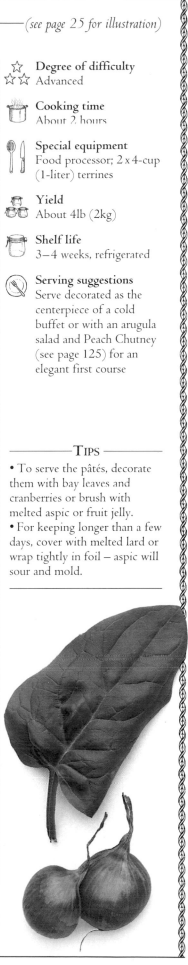

Pâté de Campagne

(see page 70 for technique)

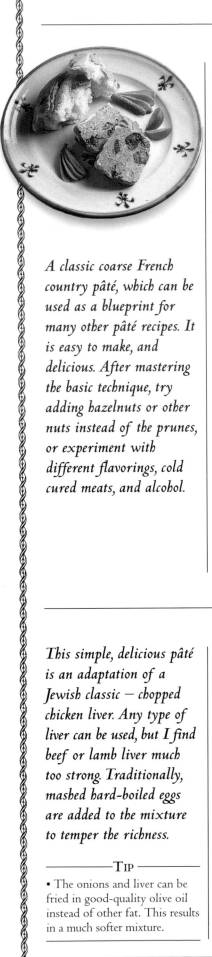

A classic coarse French country pâté, which can be used as a blueprint for many other pâté recipes. It is easy to make, and delicious. After mastering the basic technique, try adding hazelnuts or other nuts instead of the prunes, or experiment with different flavorings, cold cured meats, and alcohol.

INGREDIENTS

1 lb (500g) uncured slab bacon (pork belly) cut into large cubes
1 lb (500g) lean pork such as shoulder, tenderloin, or leg, cut into large cubes
1 lb (500g) pig's or calf's liver, sliced
¼ lb (150g) sliced bacon
1–2 garlic cloves, finely chopped
1 tsp juniper berries, crushed
½ tsp freshly ground black pepper
1 tbsp finely chopped thyme
2 tsp salt
½ cup (100g) pitted prunes, soaked in 5 tsp warm brandy for 2 hours
⅔ cup (150ml) dry white wine
2 tbsp brandy
For the terrines
2 pieces of caul fat or 10oz (300g) sliced bacon
6 thin slices of lemon or orange
4–6 bay leaves
1–1½ lb (500–750g) lard, melted
juniper berries, bay leaves, and cranberries, to garnish (optional)

1 Mix together all the meat and put through the fine disk of the grinder. Add the remaining ingredients and mix well. Cover and refrigerate for 3–4 hours.

2 Line the terrines with the caul fat or bacon slices (see step 2, page 70). Spoon half the meat into each, making sure there are no air pockets. Fold over the caul or bacon and put the citrus slices and bay leaves on top. Cover with the lids or a double layer of foil.

3 Place the terrines in a roasting pan filled with enough warm water to come halfway up the sides of the dishes. Bake in an oven preheated to 325°F (160°C) for 1½–2 hours, until each pâté has shrunk from the sides of its dish and is surrounded by liquid. Allow to cool, then weight down (see page 46) and refrigerate overnight.

4 Remove the citrus slices and bay leaves, unmold each pâté, and wipe off the jelly. Set the pâtés in the melted lard (see step 7, page 71). Garnish, if desired, then cover and refrigerate. They will be ready to eat in 2–3 days.

☆☆ **Degree of difficulty**
Moderate

Cooking time
1½–2 hours

Special equipment
Meat grinder; 2 x 4-cup (1-liter) terrines

Yield
About 4lb (2kg)

Shelf life
1 month, refrigerated

Serving suggestion
Serve with crusty bread, pickles, and a glass of wine

—— TIP ——
• The meat for this pâté is ground to give a coarse texture. If you prefer a smoother result, use a food processor.

Smooth Liver Pâté

(see page 24 for illustration)

This simple, delicious pâté is an adaptation of a Jewish classic — chopped chicken liver. Any type of liver can be used, but I find beef or lamb liver much too strong. Traditionally, mashed hard-boiled eggs are added to the mixture to temper the richness.

—— TIP ——
• The onions and liver can be fried in good-quality olive oil instead of other fat. This results in a much softer mixture.

INGREDIENTS

½ lb (250g) chicken fat, goose fat, or clarified butter (see page 73)
½ lb (250g) onions or shallots, chopped
1 lb (500g) chicken, duck, or calf's liver, trimmed and washed
1 tsp salt
½ tsp freshly ground black pepper
2 tbsp brandy (optional)
2 tbsp finely chopped parsley (optional)
½ tsp finely grated orange or lemon rind (optional)
1 garlic clove, finely mashed (optional)

1 Heat half the fat in a heavy skillet, add the onions or shallots, and cook over low heat for 15–20 minutes, or until brown. Add the liver and cook for 2 minutes on each side, or until cooked but still pink inside.

2 Cool briefly, then transfer to a food processor and process until smooth. Add the remaining ingredients and mix well.

3 Press the mixture into the dish or individual ramekins. Let cool completely, then cover and refrigerate for a few hours. Melt the remaining fat and pour over the pâté to seal. Refrigerate for at least 12 hours before serving.

☆ **Degree of difficulty**
Easy

Cooking time
About 25 minutes

Special equipment
Food processor; 2-cup (500ml) earthenware dish or 5 x ¾-cup (175ml) ramekins

Yield
About 1½ lb (750g)

Shelf life
2 weeks, refrigerated

Serving suggestions
Serve on toast or baked en croûte in puff pastry

Duck Pâté with Pistachio Nuts and Kumquats

The addition of kumquats in this classic French recipe produces a spectacular pâté. You do need to use a large, mature bird — the young, intensively reared, oven-ready ducklings commonly available nowadays just do not have the depth of flavor. Keep the duck bones to make stock and use the skin to make delicious crackling (see Tips, right).

INGREDIENTS

1 x 6lb (3kg) duck with its liver, skinned and boned
10oz (300g) pork tenderloin or lean pink veal, cut into large cubes
1lb (500g) uncured slab bacon (pork belly), cut into large cubes
2 eggs
1 cup (100g) very green pistachio nuts, skinned (see tip, right)
1 tbsp salt
1 tsp freshly ground black pepper
1 tbsp finely chopped tarragon
2 pieces of caul fat or 10oz (300g) sliced bacon
about 16 kumquats
1–1½ lb (500–750g) lard, melted
For the marinade
½ cup (100ml) brandy
2 garlic cloves, crushed
rind and juice of 1 large orange
a few sprigs of thyme, bruised

1 Put the duck meat and liver and pork tenderloin or veal in a bowl. Add all the ingredients for the marinade and mix well. Cover and refrigerate for 12 hours.

2 Remove the duck breasts and liver from the marinade and cut into ½ in (1cm) cubes. Put the remaining meat and the slab bacon through the fine disk of the meat grinder.

3 Add the cubed duck breast and liver to the ground meat, together with the marinating liquid and the eggs, nuts, salt, pepper, and tarragon. Mix well.

4 Line the terrines with the caul fat or the bacon slices (see step 2, page 70). Spoon a quarter of the meat mixture into each terrine, and smooth the surface with a narrow spatula.

5 Arrange a row of whole kumquats down the center of each pâté. Divide the remaining meat mixture between them, making sure there are no air pockets, and smooth the tops. The mixture should be about 1in (2.5cm) from the rim of each dish. Fold over the ends of the caul fat or bacon and cover each dish with its lid or a double layer of foil.

6 Place the terrines in a roasting pan filled with enough warm water to come about halfway up the sides of the dishes. Bake in an oven preheated to 325°F (160°C), for 2 hours, or until each pâté has shrunk from the sides of its dish and is surrounded by liquid.

7 Remove the dishes from the roasting pan and let cool. Cover each pâté, then weight down (see page 46) and refrigerate for 12 hours. Remove each pâté and wipe off the jelly or liquid with paper towels.

8 Set each pâté in the melted lard (see step 7, page 71), then cover and refrigerate for at least 12 hours before serving.

☆ **Degree of difficulty**
☆☆ Advanced

Cooking time
About 2 hours

Special equipment
Meat grinder; 2 x 4-cup (1-liter) terrines

Yield
About 3lb (1.45kg)

Shelf life
3 weeks, refrigerated

Serving suggestions
Serve as a first course with a salad and Shallot Confiture (see page 161) or Onion Marmalade (see page 164)

TIPS

• To skin pistachio nuts, blanch them in boiling water, then let stand until cool enough to handle and rub off the skins.
• If you prefer a smoother pâté, grind the meat twice, or process in a food processor.
• To make crackling with the duck skin, cut it into large pieces and place in a pan with 1 cup (250ml) water. Bring to a boil, then simmer very slowly until most of the water has evaporated and the fat is rendered. Increase the heat and cook until the skin is golden and crisp. Drain well, reserving the fat for future use. Serve the skin hot, sprinkled with salt and pepper. It can also be potted in its own fat and heated before serving.

Rillettes

(see page 25 for illustration)

Rillettes are the French equivalent of potted meat, except the meat is not pounded or ground but is shredded. Each region of France has its own favorite recipe, and most of them are only lightly flavored to allow the natural taste of the pork to come through. Goose, duck, and rabbit can all be prepared in the same way.

INGREDIENTS

2lb (1kg) uncured slab bacon (pork belly), cut into ½ x 2in (1 x 5cm) strips

1lb (500g) pork fatback, cut into small pieces

½ cup (125ml) water or dry white wine

2–3 sprigs thyme

2 garlic cloves, peeled

1½ tsp salt

1 tsp freshly ground black or white pepper

1 blade mace

about ½lb (250g) lard, melted, to seal

1 Place all the ingredients, except the melted lard, in a heavy pan or a deep casserole and bring slowly to a boil.

2 Cook, covered, over very low heat for about 3 hours, stirring frequently to prevent it from sticking. Uncover the pan and cook for another hour, or until the meat is very soft and falling apart.

3 Transfer the contents of the pan to a colander placed over a deep bowl. Remove the thyme, garlic, and mace and lightly squeeze the meat to extract the fat. With the aid of two forks, shred the meat until it resembles a fine, fibrous mass.

4 Place the meat in a clean saucepan and add the strained fat and cooking juices. Heat gently for about 10 minutes, mixing well to achieve a homogeneous mass.

5 Adjust the seasoning, then pack into the earthenware dish or terrine and let cool. Pour over the melted lard to seal the surface. Cover and refrigerate. The rillettes are ready to eat immediately.

☆☆ **Degree of difficulty**
Moderate

Cooking time
About 4½ hours

Special equipment
4-cup (1-liter) earthenware dish or terrine

Yield
About 2lb (1kg)

Shelf life
6 weeks, refrigerated

Serving suggestion
A wonderful picnic dish served with crusty bread

Potted Venison

(see page 72 for technique)

Venison makes the most delicious potted meat. The addition of bacon is important as it adds moisture.

INGREDIENTS

½lb (250g) sliced bacon

1½lb (750g) boned shoulder or leg of venison, trimmed well and cut into 1in (2.5cm) cubes

7 tbsp (100g) butter

2 garlic cloves, finely chopped

1 cup (250ml) port or good red wine

1 tsp juniper berries, crushed

1 tsp freshly ground black pepper

2 blades mace

½–1 cup (100–250ml) clarified butter, to seal (see page 73)

a few bay leaves and cranberries, to garnish (optional)

For the herb bundle (see page 47)

2 sprigs thyme

1 bay leaf

2–3 sage leaves

a strip of lemon rind

1 Coarsely chop the bacon and put in a deep casserole dish with all the remaining ingredients, except the clarified butter and garnish. Cover and bake in an oven preheated to 325°F (160°C) for 2½–3 hours, until the meat is very tender.

2 Remove the mace and herb bundle from the dish. Place the meat in the food processor and process until it forms a smooth paste. Pack into the dish or individual ramekins. Let cool completely. Cover and refrigerate for 2–3 hours.

3 Pour the melted clarified butter over the meat to seal (see step 5, page 73), using the larger quantity for covering the individual ramekins. Garnish with a few bay leaves and cranberries, if desired.

☆☆ **Degree of difficulty**
Moderate

Cooking time
2½–3 hours

Special equipment
Food processor; 4-cup (1-liter) dish or 6 x ¾-cup (175ml) ramekins

Yield
About 2lb (1kg)

Shelf life
1 month, refrigerated

Serving suggestion
Traditionally, potted venison is served in the dish, accompanied by toast

— **VARIATION** —

◆ Before filling the ramekins, pour 1 tablespoon melted red currant or black currant jelly over the base of each and let set.

Potted Meat

Potted meats were a great standby in Victorian times and a prudent way to extend leftovers. Cooked and raw meat were simmered with gravy and seasoning, then mixed with butter and pounded to a fine paste. This recipe is made with raw meat, but any leftover cooked beef can also be used. In this case the cooking time will be shorter.

INGREDIENTS

2lb (1kg) beef (rump or shoulder), all fat and tendons removed, cut into small pieces

1 cup (250ml) good beef stock

3–4 anchovy fillets, chopped

10 tbsp (150g) butter

2–3 sprigs of thyme

2 bay leaves

2 blades mace

1 tsp salt

½ tsp grated lemon rind

7 tbsp (100g) clarified butter (see page 73)

1 Put all the ingredients, except the lemon rind and clarified butter, in a casserole. Bring to a boil, cover tightly, then simmer over the lowest heat, or bake in an oven preheated to 325°F (160°C), for 2 hours, or until the meat is tender.

2 Remove the herbs and mace and drain the meat. Pour the cooking liquid into a pan and boil until reduced to 1 cup (250ml).

3 Process the meat and reduced liquid to a paste in the food processor. Mix in the lemon rind and season to taste. Pack into the dish or ramekins and refrigerate for 2–3 hours. Seal the top with the melted clarified butter (see step 5, page 73). Cover and refrigerate. It will be ready to eat in 2 days.

☆ **Degree of difficulty**
Easy

Cooking time
About 2 hours

Special equipment
Food processor; 6 x ¾-cup (175ml) ramekins or a 4-cup (1-liter) earthenware dish

Yield
About 1½ lb (750g)

Shelf life
5 weeks, refrigerated

Serving suggestion
Serve as a first course with watercress salad

Potted Cheese

Potting is a wonderful way to use up odd bits of good leftover cheese. Blended with butter, the cheese makes a flavorful paste that keeps for over a month. Any kind of mature hard cheese is suitable, including blue cheese.

INGREDIENTS

1lb (500g) aged Cheddar cheese, or a mixture of cheeses, finely grated

5 tbsp (75g) unsalted butter, softened

1 tbsp pale dry sherry

1 tsp English mustard

¼ tsp finely grated lemon rind

⅛ tsp freshly grated nutmeg

⅛ tsp cayenne or chili powder

¾ cup (150g) clarified butter (see page 73)

1 Put all the ingredients, except the clarified butter, in a large bowl. Beat together until smooth. Pack into the ramekins or dish, filling them to within ½ in (1cm) of the rim. Smooth the top and refrigerate for 2–3 hours.

2 Seal the top with the melted clarified butter (see step 5, page 73). Cover and refrigerate. It will be ready to eat in 2 days.

☆ **Degree of difficulty**
Easy

Special equipment
3 x ¾-cup (175ml) ramekins or a 2-cup (500ml) earthenware dish

Yield
About 1lb (500g)

Shelf life
6 weeks, refrigerated

Potted Shrimp

This classic British delicacy is tasty and easy to make. It is essential to use freshly boiled shrimp, preferably small ones, for their fresh, sweet flavor. The shells are usually removed, but I like their crunchiness and therefore only remove the heads.

INGREDIENTS

2lb (1kg) fresh raw shrimp

1¼ cups (300g) clarified butter (see page 73)

1 tsp salt

½ tsp freshly ground white or black pepper

½ tsp ground mace

⅛ tsp cayenne or chili powder

1 Cook the shrimp in boiling water for no more than 2 minutes. Drain, refresh under cold water, drain again, then peel.

2 Put the shrimp in a bowl and mix with all but 5 tablespoons of the clarified butter and all the remaining ingredients. Divide among the ramekins and bake in an oven preheated to 375°F (190°C) for 15 minutes.

3 Let cool, then refrigerate for 2–3 hours. Seal the tops with the remaining melted clarified butter (see step 5, page 73). Cover and refrigerate. The shrimp will be ready to eat in 24 hours.

☆ **Degree of difficulty**
Easy

Cooking time
About 17 minutes

Special equipment
6 x ¾-cup (175ml) ramekins

Yield
About 2lb (1kg)

Shelf life
1 month, refrigerated

PRESERVED FISH

FISH MAKE EXCELLENT preserves: they can be cured, pickled, or smoked to produce the most tasty delicacies. Do not attempt to salt-cure fish unless you have a good fishmonger who can supply you with very fresh fish; fish deteriorates quickly, especially in hot weather. Many of the following recipes use whole salted herrings, which are sometimes difficult to obtain. If you are unable to find them, use prepared salted fillets instead. These are usually sold loose, in brine or oil, in supermarkets or fish stores, or they can be bought ready-prepared in jars or cans.

Pickled Fish

Monkfish   Salt   Peanut oil   Onion rings   Red wine vinegar   Light brown sugar   Turmeric   Curry powder   Bay leaf   Dried red chilies

This delicious, piquant recipe is from the Cape of South Africa. According to the writer Laurens van der Post, it used to be made by Transvaal farmers on their summer visits to the Cape, then taken to the interior and eaten during the winter. Traditionally, Cape salmon, cod, or snoek are used, but monkfish, haddock, conger eel, and mackerel make good substitutes.

INGREDIENTS

2lb (1kg) firm, very fresh fish fillets, cut into 2in (5cm) chunks
5 tsp salt
6–7 tbsp peanut or refined sesame oil
1lb (500g) onions, sliced into thin rings
4 cups (1 liter) red or white wine vinegar
2 tbsp light brown sugar
1 tbsp mild curry powder
1 tsp ground turmeric
1in (2.5cm) piece fresh ginger, shredded
2–3 dried red chilies
1–2 bay leaves

1 Put the fish in a bowl. Sprinkle with 3 teaspoons of the salt, mixing well. Leave for 2 hours. Drain and dry on paper towels.

2 Heat 4 tablespoons of the oil in a large, heavy skillet. Add the fish, a few pieces at a time, and cook over high heat for 3 minutes on each side, or until evenly browned and just cooked through. Drain on paper towels.

3 Put the sliced onions, vinegar, sugar, curry powder, turmeric, ginger, and remaining salt in a noncorrosive pan. Bring to a boil, skim well, and boil for 5–6 minutes, until the onion is cooked but still slightly crunchy. Remove the onion with a slotted spoon and drain well.

4 Arrange the fish and onion in alternate layers in the hot, sterilized jar, adding the chilies and bay leaves, and finishing with a layer of onion. Bring the vinegar back to a boil and pour into the jar. Add the remaining oil to cover, then seal. The fish will be ready to eat in 2 days.

☆ **Degree of difficulty**
Easy

Cooking time
About 30 minutes

Special equipment
Sterilized glass or earthenware jar with sealant (see pages 42–43)

Yield
About 3lb (1.5kg)

Shelf life
3–4 months, refrigerated

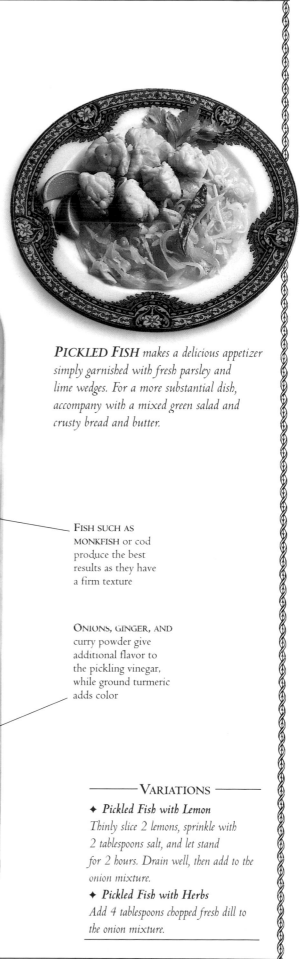

PICKLED FISH *makes a delicious appetizer simply garnished with fresh parsley and lime wedges. For a more substantial dish, accompany with a mixed green salad and crusty bread and butter.*

FISH SUCH AS
MONKFISH or cod
produce the best
results as they have
a firm texture

ONIONS, GINGER, AND
curry powder give
additional flavor to
the pickling vinegar,
while ground turmeric
adds color

VARIATIONS

✦ *Pickled Fish with Lemon*
Thinly slice 2 lemons, sprinkle with
2 tablespoons salt, and let stand
for 2 hours. Drain well, then add to the
onion mixture.

✦ *Pickled Fish with Herbs*
Add 4 tablespoons chopped fresh dill to
the onion mixture.

Pickled Salmon

(see page 27 for illustration)

In the past, when salmon was cheap and plentiful, pickled salmon was the food of the poor and was prepared in large barrels. This recipe comes from the west coast of Canada and can also be made using pike or whitefish. The bones are left in as they become soft and edible with pickling.

INGREDIENTS

4 onions, thinly sliced

2lb (1kg) salmon fillets, cut into slices 1in (2.5cm) thick

juice of 1 lemon

2½ tsp salt

¾ cup (200ml) white vinegar

2 tbsp sugar

2 bay leaves

1 tsp black peppercorns

½ tsp mustard seed

½ tsp dill seed

¼ tsp cloves

1 Place half the sliced onions in a fish kettle or large saucepan and arrange the salmon fillets on top in a single layer.

2 Add the lemon juice, 1 teaspoon of the salt, and enough cold water to cover. Bring slowly to a boil, then reduce the heat and simmer for 1 minute. Remove from the heat and let the salmon cool in the liquid.

3 Arrange alternate layers of the remaining raw onion and salmon in the hot, sterilized jar, finishing with a layer of onion.

4 Strain the cooking liquid into a noncorrosive saucepan and boil until it is reduced to about 3 cups (750ml).

5 Add the vinegar, sugar, bay leaves, black peppercorns, mustard seed, dill seed, cloves, and the remaining salt and boil for 2–3 minutes more.

6 Pour into the jar, making sure the ingredients are completely covered, then seal. The fish will be ready to eat in 3–4 days.

☆ **Degree of difficulty**
Easy

Cooking time
4–5 minutes

Special equipment
Fish kettle or large saucepan; sterilized canning jar with sealant (see pages 42–43)

Yield
About 2½lb (1.25kg)

Shelf life
3 months, refrigerated

Serving suggestion
Serve with a beet salad as a light main course

Rollmops

(see page 27 for illustration)

The best kinds of fish to use for this pickle are matjes or schmaltz herrings, although other salted herrings will do. Butterflied herrings are boned with the fillets still joined together.

TIPS

• If the whole herrings are still too salty after soaking for 12 hours, rinse them, cover with fresh water, and soak for 12 hours longer.
• Cleaning whole herrings is a messy business: wear disposable gloves or wash your hands well afterward, rubbing them with half a lemon.
• If there is not enough marinade to cover the rollmops, top off the jar with cold vinegar.

INGREDIENTS

8 whole salted herrings or 8 filleted butterflied herrings

6 tbsp strong mustard

4 large dill pickles, sliced into thick batons as long as the width of the herrings

1 large onion, thinly sliced into rings, blanched for a few seconds (see page 46)

2 tbsp capers

For the marinade

2 cups (500ml) white vinegar or cider vinegar

2 cups (500ml) water or dry white wine

2 tsp juniper berries, crushed

1 tsp allspice berries, crushed

2–3 cloves, crushed

1 To prepare the whole herrings, pour over water to cover and refrigerate for at least 12 hours, changing the water once or twice.

2 Place all the ingredients for the marinade in a non-corrosive saucepan. Bring to a boil, then simmer for 10 minutes. Let cool completely.

3 Drain and dry the herrings. Remove the heads, then fillet. Rinse and dry the prepared fillets, if using. Lay the fillets skin side down on a board and spread with the mustard. Place a piece of pickle at the wide end of each and scatter with a few onion rings and capers. Roll up like a jelly roll, securing with 2 wooden skewers.

4 Layer the fish rolls with the remaining onion in the sterilized jar, finishing with a layer of onion. Pour in the marinade, making sure the onion is totally covered, then seal and refrigerate. The fish will be ready in 1 week.

☆ **Degree of difficulty**
Easy

Cooking time
About 12 minutes

Special equipment
Sterilized wide-mouth canning jar with sealant (see pages 42–43)

Yield
About 3lb (1.5kg)

Shelf life
3 months, refrigerated

Serving suggestions
Serve as an appetizer with chilled gin or vodka, as part of a buffet; or with a warm potato salad as a light main course

Herrings in Mustard Sauce

I found this recipe on a yellowing piece of paper between the pages of an old cookbook. Although its origins are unknown, I would guess it probably came from somewhere in northern or central Europe. Select large, salted herrings, which should be soaked overnight to remove the excess salt.

TIPS

• Do not allow the egg mixture to boil or it will curdle.
• Before sealing the jar, tap it on a work surface to be sure there are no air pockets.

INGREDIENTS

6 whole, salted herrings or 12 prepared fillets

1 cup (250ml) white vinegar or distilled malt vinegar

¼ tsp cloves

2 bay leaves

1 tsp black peppercorns

3 onions, thinly sliced

4 eggs

1½ tbsp sugar

2 tbsp dry mustard

large pinch ground turmeric

1 To prepare the whole herrings, pour over water to cover and refrigerate for at least 12 hours, changing the water once or twice.

2 Place the vinegar, cloves, bay leaves, and peppercorns in a noncorrosive saucepan. Bring to a boil, reduce the heat, and simmer for a few minutes. Let cool.

3 Blanch the sliced onions for 2 minutes (see page 46). Drain and dry the herrings. Remove the heads, then fillet. Rinse and dry the prepared fillets, if using. Cut the fish into bite-sized pieces.

4 Beat the eggs with the sugar, mustard, and turmeric and add to the vinegar mixture. Transfer to the double boiler or a bowl placed over a pan of hot water. Cook gently, stirring, until the mixture is thick enough to coat the back of the spoon. Pour over the onion and let cool.

5 Add the herring and mix well. Pack into the sterilized jars, then seal and refrigerate. The fish will be ready to eat in 3 days.

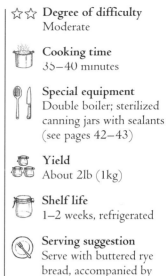

☆☆ Degree of difficulty
Moderate

Cooking time
35–40 minutes

Special equipment
Double boiler; sterilized canning jars with sealants (see pages 42–43)

Yield
About 2lb (1kg)

Shelf life
1–2 weeks, refrigerated

Serving suggestion
Serve with buttered rye bread, accompanied by chilled vodka or aquavit

Herrings in Cream Sauce

This recipe was given to me by Penny Stonfield, one of the best traditional Jewish cooks I know. She makes large quantities of this delicious salad for special occasions.

INGREDIENTS

6 whole, salted herrings or 12 prepared fillets

2 large onions, sliced into thin rings

6–8 allspice berries, crushed

2–3 dried bay leaves, crumbled

1½ cups (350ml) heavy cream

1 cup (250ml) white wine vinegar

1 tbsp sugar

1 To prepare the whole herrings, pour over water to cover and refrigerate for at least 12 hours, changing the water once or twice.

2 Drain and dry the herrings. Remove the heads, then fillet. Rinse and dry the prepared fillets, if using. Cut the fish into bite-sized pieces.

3 Blanch the sliced onions for 2 minutes (see page 46). Mix the onion with the crushed allspice berries and bay leaves. Layer with the herring in the sterilized jars, finishing with a layer of onions.

4 Stir together the cream, wine vinegar, and sugar. Pour into the jars, making sure there are no air pockets, then seal and refrigerate. The fish will be ready to eat in 2–3 days.

☆ Degree of difficulty
Easy

Special equipment
Sterilized canning jars with sealants (see pages 42–43)

Yield
About 2lb (1kg)

Shelf life
1 week, refrigerated

Serving suggestion
Serve with rye bread as a first course

TIP

• For longer shelf life, the herrings can be heat processed for 30 minutes (see pages 44–45), but this will affect their texture and might separate the cream sauce.

Smoked Salmon

(see page 66 for technique)

Freshly smoked, cured salmon is a rare delicacy. After curing, the salmon can be cold-smoked in the traditional way, or hot-smoked as it is often served in North America. The wood to use is oak, but I have used other wood like mesquite, hickory, and cherry, which also produce very good results.

VARIATION

✦ **Smoked Trout**
Do not bone the trout. Sprinkle the trout both inside and out with a thick layer of the curing mixture and refrigerate for 3–4 hours. Dry as for the salmon, then hot-smoke for 1½–2 hours. Finish as for salmon.

INGREDIENTS

1 x 4–6lb (2–3kg) fresh salmon, cleaned
1½ cups (375g) coarse salt
½ cup (125g) light brown or granulated sugar
1–2 tsps whiskey

1 Fillet the salmon and remove all the remaining bones with tweezers (see steps 1 and 2, page 66). Wash and dry the fillets.

2 Mix together the salt and sugar. Sprinkle some into a large noncorrosive dish in a layer about ¼ in (5mm) thick. Lay one fillet on top, skin side down. Sprinkle with another layer about ½ in (1cm) thick, making sure it is thinner toward the tail end.

3 Place the second fillet, skin side down, on top and sprinkle with the remaining salt mix. Cover and refrigerate for 3–3½ hours.

4 Remove the fish from the salt, wash under running water, and dry well with paper towels. Brush with the whiskey and insert a wooden skewer into the back of each fillet (see step 5, page 66).

5 Hang in a cool, dry, dark, airy place (between 42–46°F/6–8°C) for 24 hours, or until the salmon is almost dry to the touch and has a shiny salt glaze.

6 Place the fish in the smoker and hot-smoke, between 215–225°F (105–110°C) for 2–3 hours; or cold-smoke, below 86°F (30°C) for 3–4 hours. Leave until cold, then wrap in waxed paper or foil and refrigerate. It will be ready to eat in 24 hours.

☆☆ **Degree of difficulty**
Moderate

Cooking time
3–4 hours cold-smoking, or 2–3 hours hot-smoking

Special equipment
Smoker

Yield
3–4lb (1.5–2kg)

Shelf life
3 weeks, refrigerated; 3 months, frozen

Serving suggestions
Serve hot-smoked salmon thickly sliced, with a green salad and bread as a light main course; cut cold-smoked salmon into paper-thin slices and serve with cream cheese and bagels; or use to make pâté or mousse

Smoked Shrimp

Smoking gives a new dimension to shrimp, adding to their flavor and shelf life. I find oak smoke too strong for delicate shellfish and prefer to use lighter, more fragrant woods such as apple or citrus. Squid, octopus, oysters, and clams can be substituted for shrimp.

INGREDIENTS

3lb (1.5kg) large shrimp
8 cups (2 liters) water
1 tbsp salt
1 bunch of fresh dill or fennel flowers and stems, or 2 tbsp dried dill
2–3 tbsp olive or peanut oil
For the brine
6 cups (1.5 liters) water
1⅓ cups (350g) salt

1 Wash the shrimp well and let drain for 30–45 minutes.

2 For the brine, mix together the water and salt, stirring until the salt is dissolved.

3 Pour the brine over the shrimp and weight down (see page 46), making sure that they are completely submerged. Let stand for 30 minutes, then drain well. (This produces mildly salted shrimp; for a saltier flavor, let stand for up to 1 hour.)

4 Put the other measure of water and salt in a large saucepan and bring to a boil. Add the dill or fennel and simmer for 15 minutes, then add the shrimp. Simmer for 2–5 minutes, or until the shrimp are just cooked.

5 Lift out the shrimp and leave on a wire rack for 1–2 hours, or until just dry to the touch.

6 Brush the shrimp with the oil and cold-smoke below 77°F (25°C) for 2 hours (see page 66).

7 Wrap the shrimp in waxed paper and refrigerate. Alternatively, you could preserve them in oil (see Mixed Seafood in Oil, page 109).

☆☆ **Degree of difficulty**
Moderate

Cooking time
About 20 minutes simmering, 2 hours smoking

Special equipment
Smoker

Yield
About 2lb (1kg)

Shelf life
1 month, refrigerated; 3 months, frozen

Serving suggestions
Serve as a snack with drinks or as a first course; add to fish stews, risotto, and pasta dishes just before serving

Gravlax

(see page 26 for illustration)

This delicious Scandinavian recipe is the simplest and most enjoyable way to cure fish. Although salmon is almost always used, trout, mackerel, and even very fresh halibut can be prepared in the same way. Alcohol is not a traditional ingredient, but it adds flavor and helps preserve the fish.

TIP

• Brown sugar gives the fish a delightful flavor and an appetizing dark color.

INGREDIENTS

2lb (1kg) center cut of salmon, cut in half lengthwise, all bones removed
4 tbsp coarse salt
3 tbsp light brown or white sugar
1 tbsp coarsely ground black pepper
1 large bunch dill, coarsely chopped
2–3 tbsp aquavit or vodka

1 Place one half of the salmon skin side down on a large piece of aluminum foil. Mix together the salt, sugar, and pepper. Sprinkle half of the salt mixture evenly over the salmon.

2 Sprinkle with the chopped dill, the remaining salt mixture, and the aquavit or vodka. Place the other piece of salmon, skin side up, over the top. Fold the foil over and wrap well.

3 Place the foil-wrapped salmon in a shallow dish and cover with a board and a heavy weight (see page 46). Refrigerate the fish for 24–36 hours, turning it over every 12 hours.

4 Unwrap the salmon and carefully remove each fillet from the foil. Gently brush off all the salt, dill, and spices. To serve the salmon, cut into very thin slices with a long-bladed, serrated knife, angling the knife at 45 degrees.

☆ **Degree of difficulty**
Easy

Yield
About 2lb (1kg)

Shelf life
1 week, refrigerated; to keep longer, see Herrings in Spiced Oil (page 109)

Serving suggestion
Serve with a dill and mustard sauce, accompanied by a potato or beet salad

Salt-cured Sprats

(see page 74 for technique)

Salt-cured fish develop a characteristic flavor and smell and are an acquired taste. Sardines, herrings, and anchovies can be cured in the same way.

TIPS

• Choose young, fresh, even-sized fish with good, shiny, silvery skin.
• Leaving the heads on results in a stronger, more fishy taste, as they contain a lot of oil. You can remove them if you prefer.
• Other flavorings, such as juniper, allspice, and aromatic wood chips, can be added with the peppercorns and bay leaves.
• For longer shelf life, the sprats can also be kept in salt. At the end of step 6, remove from the brine and layer with coarse salt in a wooden box.
• When you want to use the sprats, remove them from the brine and soak for a few hours in water or a mixture of milk and water.

INGREDIENTS

2lb (1kg) sprats
2 cups (500g) fine salt
2–3lb (1–1.5kg) coarse salt
3–4 bay leaves
1 tbsp black peppercorns

1 Clean and gut the fish. With a small pair of scissors, snip each fish just below the gills. Make a cut down the belly, then, with your fingers, carefully pull out and discard the stomach and contents (see steps 1–3, page 74).

2 Sprinkle a little of the fine salt in the cavity of each fish and all over the outside, rubbing it in thoroughly.

3 Arrange the fish in layers in a shallow dish, adding a fine sprinkling of the sea salt to each layer. Leave in a cool place (between 42–46°F/6–8°C) or refrigerate for 4–5 hours to draw off some of the moisture. Lift out the fish and dry on paper towels.

4 Sprinkle a layer of the coarse salt over the base of a large glass or earthenware container.

5 Arrange a layer of fish on top and add a bay leaf and a few peppercorns. Cover with an even layer of coarse salt about ¼ in (5mm) thick and continue to arrange the ingredients in this way until all the sprats are used, finishing with a layer of salt.

6 Weight down (see page 46), cover, and refrigerate or leave in a cool, dark place (between 42–46°F/6–8°C). The sprats will be ready to eat in 1 week.

7 To keep the fish longer, remove the oil that has formed at the top of the container. If not enough brine has formed to cover the fish, top it off with a strong salt solution made of equal quantities of salt and water. Seal the container and refrigerate or store in a cool, dark place (between 42–46°F/6–8°C).

☆ **Degree of difficulty**
Easy

Special equipment
A sterilized earthenware or glass container with noncorrosive sealant

Yield
About 1½ lb (750kg)

Shelf life
2 years, refrigerated

Serving suggestion
Serve with a fruit vinegar and olive oil dressing, accompanied with thinly sliced raw onion and chilled vodka

VARIATIONS

✦ The filleted sprats can also be preserved in oil (see Herrings in Spiced Oil, page 109).
✦ **Anchovies in Oil**
Fillet the anchovies like the sprats, then roll each fillet around a caper and skewer onto a toothpick. Arrange in a small jar and cover with olive oil.

JAMS & OTHER SWEET PRESERVES

SUMMER IS THE TIME for making sweet preserves — long, warm days and an abundance of sweet, juicy fruit. This large family of products is divided into a number of distinct types that all use sugar as the only means of preservation. The most popular is jam, pulped fruit cooked together with sugar until it reaches a jelling point, while jelly is clear and sparkling and made from fruit juice and sugar. In the past, marmalade was made from many different kinds of fruit other than citrus fruit. I use the term for a preserve that is chunkier than jam, though not necessarily citrus based. Confiture refers to whole fruit preserved in fruit jelly. The terms preserve and conserve are interchangeable and refer to semi-candied fruit preserved in a heavy sugar syrup. Freezing destroys some of the pectin in fruit, so if you use frozen fruit to make sweet preserves, adjust the pectin content as necessary with a homemade pectin stock (see page 47) or commercial pectin; alternatively add oranges or lemons.

Grape Jam

Grapes   *Lemon*   *Sugar*   *Pecans*   *Brandy*

This is a rich confection, crunchy with nuts. Jams like this one are an essential part of the traditional Middle Eastern welcoming ceremony, when they are eaten with a spoon and accompanied by a glass of cold water.

INGREDIENTS

2lb (1kg) seedless green or red grapes
2 lemons, thinly sliced
3 cups (750g) granulated sugar
1 cup (100g) pecans, lightly toasted
⅓ cup (75ml) brandy

1 Put the grapes, lemon slices, and sugar in a noncorrosive saucepan. Mix well, cover, and let stand for a few hours, until the juices start to run.

2 Bring to a boil, then cook over moderate heat for 1–1½ hours, stirring frequently to prevent it from sticking to the bottom of the pan.

3 There is no need to test this jam for the jelling point; it is ready when it has thickened enough for a wooden spoon drawn through the center of the mixture to leave a clear channel.

4 Remove the pan from the heat and let the jam settle for a few minutes. (This keeps the fruit from sinking to the bottom of the jar.) Stir in the pecans and brandy. Ladle the jam into the hot, sterilized jars, then seal.

☆ **Degree of difficulty**
Easy

Cooking time
1¼–1¾ hours

Special equipment
Sterilized jars and sealants (see pages 42–43)

Yield
About 2½ pints (1.25kg)

Shelf life
2 years, heat processed

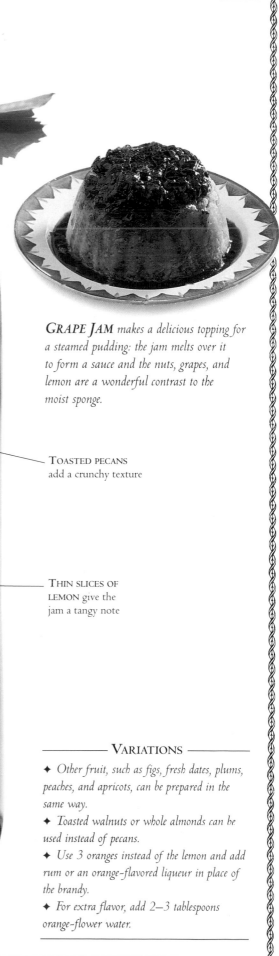

GRAPE JAM *makes a delicious topping for a steamed pudding: the jam melts over it to form a sauce and the nuts, grapes, and lemon are a wonderful contrast to the moist sponge.*

TOASTED PECANS
add a crunchy texture

THIN SLICES OF
LEMON give the
jam a tangy note

VARIATIONS

✦ *Other fruit, such as figs, fresh dates, plums, peaches, and apricots, can be prepared in the same way.*

✦ *Toasted walnuts or whole almonds can be used instead of pecans.*

✦ *Use 3 oranges instead of the lemon and add rum or an orange-flavored liqueur in place of the brandy.*

✦ *For extra flavor, add 2–3 tablespoons orange-flower water.*

Povidle (Eastern European Plum Jam)

Strictly speaking, Povidle is not a jam but a soft fruit cheese. This recipe was given to me by my mother. The amount of sugar seems small, but it results in a sharp sweet-and-sour jam.

INGREDIENTS

4lb (2kg) purple plums, preferably prune plums

4 cups (1kg) granulated sugar

1 Remove the pits from the plums, then chop the flesh coarsely. Layer the plums and sugar in a large, noncorrosive saucepan. Cover with a clean cloth and let stand for a few hours, until the juices start to run.

2 Bring the mixture to a boil, stirring until the sugar is dissolved, then reduce the heat and simmer for 1½–2 hours, stirring occasionally, until the Povidle is dark red and thick (there is no need to test for the jelling point).

3 Ladle the jam into the hot, sterilized jars, then seal. The Povidle is ready to eat immediately but improves with age.

☆ **Degree of difficulty**
Easy

Cooking time
1½–2 hours

Special equipment
Sterilized canning jars and sealants (see pages 42–43)

Yield
About 3 pints (1.5kg)

Shelf life
2 years, heat processed

Plum Jam

You can use any type of plum to make this delicious jam. Choose yellow plums for a golden jam, red ones for a crimson jam, and greengage for a greenish-yellow one.

TIP

• Red plum jam can be enlivened by the addition of 5 tbsp (75g) finely shredded fresh ginger, which should be stirred in with the sugar.

INGREDIENTS

2½ lb (1.25kg) plums, pitted and halved

1½ cups (350ml) water

4 cups (1kg) granulated sugar

1 Put the plums and water in a large, noncorrosive saucepan. Bring to a boil, then reduce the heat and simmer for 25 minutes, stirring occasionally, until the plums are soft.

2 Add the sugar, stirring until it is dissolved. Return to a boil and boil for 25–30 minutes, or until the jelling point is reached (see page 76).

3 Remove the pan from the heat and leave the jam to settle for a few minutes. Ladle the jam into the hot, sterilized jars, then seal.

VARIATIONS

✦ *Greengage Jam*
Substitute greengages for the plums. Halve and remove the pits. Place the fruit in the saucepan with the juice of 1 lemon and 1 cup (250ml) water. Complete as for the main recipe.

✦ *Damson Jam*
Substitute whole damsons for the plums. Simmer with 3 cups (750ml) water until mushy, then strain out the pits. Measure the pulp and add 2½ cups (625g) sugar for every 2 cups (500ml) pulp. Boil for 10 minutes, or until the jelling point is reached.

☆ **Degree of difficulty**
Easy

Cooking time
About 1 hour

Special equipment
Sterilized canning jars and sealants (see pages 42–43)

Yield
About 3½ pints (1.75kg)

Shelf life
2 years, heat processed

Serving suggestions
Substitute for raspberry jam in Linzer Torte or use to make a quick and easy plum crisp

Greengage Jam

Damson Jam

Plum Jam

Raspberry Jam
(see page 33 for illustration)

This is made without water to give an intensely flavored, perfumed jam.

INGREDIENTS

2 pints (1kg) raspberries

4 cups (1kg) granulated sugar

juice of 1 lemon

1 Layer the raspberries and sugar in a noncorrosive saucepan. Cover with a clean cloth and let stand overnight.

2 Add the lemon juice to the pan. Bring to a boil, stirring until the sugar is dissolved.

3 Increase the heat and boil rapidly for 20–25 minutes, or until the jelling point is reached (see page 76). Stir constantly toward the end of cooking to prevent it from sticking. If desired, pass half the jam through a sieve to reduce the seed content, then return to a boil for 5 minutes.

4 Remove the pan from the heat and let the jam settle for a few minutes. Ladle into the hot, sterilized jars, then seal.

☆ **Degree of difficulty**
Easy

Cooking time
About 45 minutes

Special equipment
Sterilized canning jars and sealants (see pages 42–43)

Yield
About 3 pints (1.5kg)

Shelf life
2 years, heat processed

Blueberry Jam
(see page 33 for illustration)

Blueberries make a soft set jam. If a more solid set is preferred, add commercial pectin or an equal quantity of apples or other high-pectin fruit. Use as a topping for cheesecakes or fold into whipped cream as a filling for sponge cakes.

INGREDIENTS

2 pints (1kg) blueberries

4 cups (1kg) granulated sugar

4 tbsp water

juice of 1 lemon

1 Place the blueberries, sugar, water, and lemon juice in a noncorrosive saucepan. Bring slowly to a boil, stirring occasionally until the sugar is dissolved. Reduce the heat and simmer for about 10 minutes.

2 Increase the heat and boil the mixture rapidly for 15–20 minutes, or until the jelling point is reached (see page 76).

3 Remove the pan from the heat and let the jam settle for a few minutes. Ladle into the hot, sterilized jars, then seal.

☆ **Degree of difficulty**
Easy

Cooking time
About 45 minutes

Special equipment
Sterilized canning jars and sealants

Yield
About 3 pints (1.5kg)

Shelf life
2 years, heat processed

Black Currant Jam

Black currants are high in pectin, which makes them ideal for jams and jellies.

INGREDIENTS

2 pints (1kg) black currants

3 cups (750ml) water

3 cups (750g) granulated sugar

a little brandy, to seal

1 Place the black currants and water in a noncorrosive saucepan. Bring slowly to a boil, then reduce the heat and simmer gently for 20–25 minutes, stirring occasionally, until the mixture is reduced by a third.

2 Add the sugar to the pan. Slowly return to a boil, stirring until the sugar is dissolved, then boil rapidly for 15–20 minutes, or until the jelling point is reached (see page 76).

3 Remove the pan from the heat and let stand until the jam is completely cold.

4 Ladle the cold jam into the sterilized jars. Cover each jar with a waxed paper disk dipped in a little brandy, then seal.

VARIATION

◆ If you prefer a smooth jam, press the pulp through a sieve at the end of step 1. Return to the cleaned pan and proceed as for the main recipe.

☆ **Degree of difficulty**
Easy

Cooking time
About 1 hour

Special equipment
Sterilized canning jars and sealants (see pages 42–43)

Yield
About 3 pints (1.5kg)

Shelf life
2 years, heat processed

Serving suggestion
Serve with thick plain yogurt as a simple dessert

Apricot Jam

Fragrant and mellow with a beautiful golden hue, apricot jam captures the essence of summer. It is a very versatile jam: use as it is to fill pastries and cakes; warmed and sieved, it makes a wonderful yellow glaze. Be sure to choose ripe but firm apricots for this recipe.

INGREDIENTS

2½ lb (1.25kg) apricots

juice of 1 lemon

4 cups (1kg) granulated sugar

1¼ cups (300ml) water

1 Halve the apricots, then remove and reserve the pits. Put the apricots in a glass bowl and sprinkle with the lemon juice. Mix well and cover until needed.

2 Crack open 10 of the apricot pits with a hammer or nutcracker and extract the kernels. Taste one – if it is very bitter use only half of them. Blanch the kernels for 1 minute in boiling water and either split into two segments or chop fine.

3 Place the sugar and water in a noncorrosive saucepan. Bring slowly to a boil, stirring until the sugar is dissolved, and boil rapidly for 3–4 minutes. Add the apricots, return to a boil, then simmer for 5 minutes.

4 Return to a boil and boil rapidly, stirring frequently, for 20–25 minutes, or until the jelling point is reached (see page 76). About 5 minutes before the jam is ready, stir in the split or chopped apricot kernels.

5 Remove the pan from the heat and let the jam settle for a few minutes. Skim well. Ladle the jam into the hot, sterilized jars, then seal.

VARIATION

✦ *To make a smooth apricot jam, follow the recipe to step 3. Let the jam cool slightly, then pass through a sieve or a food mill. Return to the cleaned pan and proceed as above. Do not add the apricot kernels if the jam is to be used as a glaze.*

☆ **Degree of difficulty**
Easy

Cooking time
45–55 minutes

Special equipment
Hammer or nutcracker; sterilized canning jars and sealants (see pages 42–43)

Yield
About 3 pints (1.5kg)

Shelf life
2 years, heat processed

Serving suggestions
Use to glaze a leg of lamb before roasting or to glaze fruit tarts

Green Tomato and Orange Jam

The earthy flavor of tomatoes and the refreshing tang of oranges combine to make a delightfully fresh breakfast jam. Sweet oranges are available all year, so this jam can be made in summer when green tomatoes are in season.

INGREDIENTS

4 large sweet oranges

2 lemons

2lb (1kg) green tomatoes

3 cups (750ml) water

4 cups (1kg) granulated sugar

1½ tbsp coriander seed, roughly crushed

1 Cut the oranges into slices and remove the seeds. Squeeze the juice from the lemons and reserve the seeds. Tie all the seeds into a piece of cheesecloth.

2 Put the tomatoes and oranges through the grinder or process them in the food processor until they are finely chopped.

3 Place the chopped tomato and orange in a noncorrosive saucepan with the water and cheesecloth bag. Bring to a boil, then reduce the heat and simmer for about 45 minutes, or until the orange peel is soft.

4 Add the sugar and the lemon juice to the pan, stirring until the sugar is dissolved.

5 Return to a boil and boil over medium heat, stirring occasionally, for 30–35 minutes, or until it is thick enough for a wooden spoon drawn through the center to leave a clear channel.

6 Remove the pan from the heat and let the jam settle for a few minutes. Skim if necessary, then remove the cheesecloth bag and stir in the crushed coriander seed. Ladle the jam into the hot, sterilized jars, then seal.

☆ **Degree of difficulty**
Easy

Cooking time
1½–1¾ hours

Special equipment
Meat grinder or food processor; sterilized canning jars and sealants (see pages 42–43)

Yield
About 4 pints (2kg)

Shelf life
1 year, heat processed

Serving suggestion
Superb on hot buttered toast

Carrot Jam

(see page 23 for illustration)

Root vegetable jams used to be made during winter, when fresh fruits were not available. Try this as a filling for jelly rolls, tarts, and sponge cakes.

TIP

• Almost any root vegetable can be used, but beets, parsnips, turnips, and kohlrabi need blanching several times first to mellow their strong flavor.

INGREDIENTS

2lb (1kg) carrots, finely grated
1½ cups (250g) golden raisins
2 cups (500ml) water
3 cups (750g) granulated sugar
rind of 2 lemons
juice of 3 lemons
2 tsp ground ginger

1 Put the carrots, golden raisins, and water in a saucepan. Bring to a boil, reduce the heat, and simmer for 10–15 minutes, or until the carrots are just soft.

2 Add the sugar and lemon rind and juice, stirring until the sugar is dissolved. Bring to a boil, reduce the heat, and cook, stirring frequently, for 1 hour, or until it is very thick (there is no need to test for the jelling point).

3 Add the ginger and remove the pan from the heat. Ladle into the sterilized jars, then seal.

☆ **Degree of difficulty**
Easy

Cooking time
About 1¼ hours

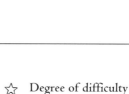

Special equipment
Sterilized canning jars and sealants

Yield
About 2 pints (1.25kg)

Shelf life
2 years, heat processed

Exotic Fruit Jam

Many types of fruit, including papaya, mango, and fragrant melon, can be used in the same way, but always add the same quantity of apple.

INGREDIENTS

1 medium pineapple, about 2½ lb (1.25kg)
2lb (1kg) cooking apples, peeled, cored, and coarsely chopped
10oz (300g) fresh litchis, peeled, pitted, and halved, or 1 x 14oz (425g) can litchis, drained and halved
1 cup (250ml) water
rind of 1 lemon
juice of 2 lemons
5 cups (1.25kg) granulated sugar

1 Peel, core, and chop the pineapple (see steps below). Process in the food processor with the apple until finely chopped.

2 Transfer to a noncorrosive saucepan and add the litchis, water, lemon rind, and juice. Bring to a boil, then reduce the heat and simmer for 20–25 minutes, or until the apples are disintegrated and the pineapple is soft.

3 Add the sugar to the pan, stirring until it is dissolved. Return to a boil and boil, stirring frequently, for 20–25 minutes, or until the jelling point is reached (see page 76).

4 Remove the pan from the heat and let the jam settle for a few minutes. Skim off any froth.

5 Ladle the mixture into the hot, sterilized jars, then seal. The jam is ready immediately but improves with age.

☆ **Degree of difficulty**
Easy

Cooking time
About 1 hour

Special equipment
Food processor; sterilized canning jars and sealants (see pages 42–43)

Yield
About 2 pints (1.5kg)

Shelf life
2 years, heat processed

Serving suggestion
Use as a filling for layer cakes

PREPARING PINEAPPLE

1 Cut the top and bottom off the pineapple with a sharp long-bladed knife.

2 To peel the pineapple, cut off the skin in sections, following the curve of the fruit.

3 To cut out the hard central core, halve the pineapple lengthwise, then cut into quarters.

4 Slice out the hard central core of the pineapple, then cut the fruit into large chunks.

Fig Konfyt (Preserved Green Figs)

This recipe comes from South Africa, where making rich preserves has been developed into a fine art. The figs should be fully mature but not ripe; otherwise, they will not withstand the cooking process.

INGREDIENTS

2lb (1kg) green, unripe figs
4 tbsp salt
1 tbsp baking soda (optional)
4 cups (1kg) granulated sugar
½ cup (125ml) water

1 Trim the stem end off each fig, then, with a small sharp knife, cut a deep cross into the top.

2 Place the figs in a large glass bowl. Cover with cold water and add the salt. Mix well until the salt is dissolved, then weight down with a plate (see page 46) and let stand overnight.

3 The next day, bring a large pan of water to a boil with the baking soda, if using (it helps preserve a good green color). Drain the figs and add to the pan.

4 Return to a boil, then reduce the heat and simmer gently for 25–30 minutes, or until the figs are just tender. Have ready a large bowl of very cold water and immediately transfer the figs to it. Let cool, then drain the figs well. Place in a large, noncorrosive saucepan.

5 Place the sugar and water in a separate pan. Bring to a boil, stirring until the sugar is dissolved, then skim well. Boil for 5 minutes, then pour over the figs. Weight down and leave overnight.

6 The next day, bring slowly to a boil, then simmer very gently for 2–2½ hours, or until the figs are translucent. Lift them out of the syrup with a slotted spoon and arrange in the hot, sterilized jars.

7 Return the syrup to a boil and boil for 10 minutes, until it has the consistency of liquid honey. Pour into the jars, then seal.

VARIATIONS

✦ Add a 2in (5cm) piece of fresh ginger, finely shredded, when you make the sugar syrup in step 5.

✦ **Melon Konfyt**
Replace the figs with 2lb (1kg) melon, peeled and cut into 1½in (4cm) chunks. Omit the baking soda. Cook for 15–20 minutes in step 4.

☆ **Degree of difficulty**
☆☆ Advanced

Cooking time
Day 2, 40–45 minutes;
Day 3, 2¼–2¾ hours

Special equipment
Sterilized canning jars and sealants (see pages 42–43)

Yield
About 2 pints (1kg)

Shelf life
2 years, heat processed

Serving suggestions
Serve as a sweet or with cream, as a dessert; use instead of glacé fruit to decorate cakes

Black Cherry Confiture

Black cherry confiture is one of the greatest European preserves — sour-sweet cherries embedded in an intensely flavored red jelly.

INGREDIENTS

2½ lb (1.25kg) black cherries, pitted
3 cups (750g) granulated sugar
1 cup (250ml) black currant or red currant juice (see Hot Crab Apple Jelly for method, page 166)
4 tbsp kirsch or cherry brandy

1 Layer the cherries and sugar in a noncorrosive saucepan. Add the black currant or red currant juice, cover, and leave for a few hours.

2 Bring the mixture slowly to a boil, occasionally shaking the pan gently. Skim well, then boil for 20–25 minutes, or until the jelling point is reached (see page 76).

3 Remove the pan from the heat and let the fruit settle for a few minutes. Stir in the kirsch or brandy. Ladle into the hot, sterilized jars, then seal.

TIPS

• The juice of 3 lemons could be used instead of the currant juice.
• Any type of sour black cherry can be used, but Morello are the best.

☆ **Degree of difficulty**
Easy

Cooking time
About 30 minutes

Special equipment
Sterilized canning jars and sealants

Yield
About 3 pints (1.5kg)

Shelf life
2 years, heat processed

Serving suggestions
Superb for breakfast or as a filling for cakes

Wild Strawberry Confiture

Wild strawberries are highly aromatic and full of flavor. Marinating, followed by careful cooking, helps maintain the texture and fragrance of this sublime confection. Use to fill tarts.

INGREDIENTS

3 cups (750g) granulated sugar

2lb (1kg) wild strawberries

1 cup (250ml) vodka (80 proof)

1 Layer the sugar and wild strawberries in a large glass bowl, starting and finishing with a layer of sugar. Pour over the vodka, cover with a clean cloth, and let stand overnight.

2 The next day, drain the liquid into a noncorrosive saucepan. Bring to a boil and boil rapidly for a few minutes, or until it reaches 240°F (116°C) on the candy thermometer.

3 Add the wild strawberries. Return to a boil and boil for 5–7 minutes, or until the jelling point is reached (see page 76). This recipe produces a soft set.

4 Remove from the heat and let the fruit settle for a few minutes. Skim well. Ladle into the hot, sterilized jars, then seal.

☆☆ **Degree of difficulty**
Moderate

Cooking time
25–30 minutes

Special equipment
Candy thermometer; sterilized canning jars and sealants (see pages 42–43)

Yield
About 2½ pints (1.25kg)

Shelf life
6 months, heat processed

Shallot Confiture
(see page 19 for illustration)

This spicy, sour-sweet confiture is my adaptation of an ancient Middle Eastern recipe. Cooked in a spiced syrup, the caramelized shallots turn a beautiful, glistening golden brown. The slow, careful cooking is important; otherwise the shallots tend to lose their shape.

INGREDIENTS

2½ lb (1.25kg) shallots

¾ cup (150g) salt

6 cups (1.5 liters) distilled white vinegar or white wine vinegar

4 cups (1kg) granulated sugar

For the spice bag (see page 47)

4 cardamom pods

2 cinnamon sticks

3 strips lemon rind

1 tbsp caraway seed

1 tbsp cloves

½ tsp bird's eye chilies

1 Peel the shallots by blanching in boiling water for a few minutes (see page 46). Make sure that the root end remains intact; otherwise the shallots will disintegrate during cooking.

2 Place the peeled shallots in a large glass bowl. Cover with cold water and add the salt. Mix well until the salt is dissolved, then weight down (see page 46) and leave for 24 hours.

3 Put the vinegar, sugar, and spice bag in a noncorrosive saucepan. Bring to a boil and boil steadily for 10 minutes, stirring occasionally. Skim well.

4 Drain the shallots, rinse well, then drain again. Carefully add them to the boiling syrup. Return to a boil, then reduce the heat to minimum and simmer very gently for 15 minutes. Remove the pan from the heat and let cool, then cover and let stand overnight.

5 The next day, bring the mixture slowly to a boil, then reduce the heat and simmer very gently for 15 minutes. Cool and let stand overnight as before.

6 The next day, bring the mixture slowly to a boil, then simmer very gently for 2–2½ hours, or until the shallots are translucent and golden brown.

7 Carefully lift the shallots out of the syrup with a slotted spoon and pack them loosely into the hot, sterilized jars. Return the syrup to a boil and boil rapidly for about 5 minutes. Pour into the jars, then seal. The shallots are ready to eat immediately, but improve with age.

☆ **Degree of difficulty**
☆☆ Advanced

Cooking time
Day 2, 30–35 minutes;
Day 3, about 20 minutes;
Day 4, 2¼–2¾ hours

Special equipment
Sterilized canning jars and sealants (see pages 42–43)

Yield
About 2½ pints (1.25kg)

Shelf life
2 years, heat processed

Serving suggestions
Especially good with venison and lamb

Eggplant Preserve

This unusual recipe comes from Morocco and makes a surprisingly fragrant sweet preserve. Traditionally, it is eaten by the spoonful and served with steaming hot tea or coffee and a glass of water.

INGREDIENTS

2lb (1kg) baby eggplants
4 tbsp salt
4 cups (1kg) granulated sugar
juice of 3 large lemons
rind of 1 lemon, cut into fine matchsticks
5 tbsp (75g) finely shredded fresh ginger
12 cloves
2 cinnamon sticks

1 Remove the green crown from around the stem of each eggplant, but leave the stem attached. Prick each eggplant in a few places with a toothpick.

2 Place the eggplants in a large glass bowl and sprinkle with the salt. Mix well, then cover and let stand for a few hours. Rinse thoroughly under cold running water.

3 Bring a large pan of water to a boil and add the rinsed eggplants. Return to a boil, then reduce the heat and simmer for 5 minutes. Lift out the eggplants and drain well.

4 Place the sugar and lemon juice in a large, noncorrosive saucepan. Bring to a boil, stirring until the sugar is dissolved, then skim well. Add the lemon rind, shredded ginger, cloves, and cinnamon sticks and boil for 5 minutes.

5 Gently slide the eggplants into the boiling syrup. Reduce the heat and simmer very gently, stirring occasionally, for 1½–2 hours, or until the eggplants have absorbed about half the syrup and look translucent.

6 Gently lift the eggplants out one at a time with a slotted spoon. Transfer to the hot, sterilized jars. Return the syrup to a boil, pour it into the jars, then seal. The preserve is ready to eat immediately, but improves with age.

☆☆ **Degree of difficulty**
Moderate

Cooking time
1¾–2¼ hours

Special equipment
Sterilized canning jars and sealants (see pages 42–43)

Yield
About 3 pints (1.5kg)

Shelf life
2 years, heat processed (the preserve may crystallize in this time but it will still be fine to eat)

Serving suggestion
Serve as a sweet, Moroccan style

TIPS

• Select very small, unblemished eggplants. Both black and light purple varieties are suitable.
• If you do not like whole spices in your preserve, tie them in a piece of cheesecloth (see spice bags, page 47), which can be lifted out at the end of cooking.

Summer Squash and Ginger Preserve

This recipe is a perfect example of the magic of preserving: it transforms humble ingredients into a delicious and versatile product.

VARIATION

◆ *Turnip Preserve*
Replace the squash with 3lb (1.5kg) peeled and cubed turnip. Cook following the main recipe.

INGREDIENTS

3lb (1.5kg) summer squash, peeled, cored, and cut into 1½ in (4cm) cubes
4 cups (1kg) granulated sugar
2 cups (500ml) water
juice of 1 lemon
2in (5cm) piece of fresh ginger, finely shredded
3–4 strips of lemon rind
1 tbsp orange-flower water (optional)

1 Put the cubed squash in a large pan and add enough cold water to cover. Bring to a boil, then reduce the heat and simmer for 10–15 minutes, or until the squash just starts to soften. Drain well.

2 Place all the remaining ingredients in a noncorrosive saucepan. Bring to a boil, stirring until the sugar is dissolved.

3 Boil for a few minutes and then add the squash. Return to a boil, then reduce the heat to minimum and simmer very gently for 2–2½ hours, or until the pieces of squash are translucent.

4 Lift the squash out of the pan with a slotted spoon. Transfer to the hot, sterilized jars. Bring the syrup to a rapid boil and boil for 5 minutes. Pour it into the jars, then seal. The preserve is ready immediately, but improves with age.

☆ **Degree of difficulty**
Easy

Cooking time
2½–2¾ hours

Special equipment
Sterilized canning jars and sealants (see pages 42–43)

Yield
About 3 pints (1.5kg)

Shelf life
2 years, heat processed

Serving suggestions
Finely chop and add to fruit cakes or serve as a topping for ice cream

Yellow Tomato Preserve

(see page 15 for illustration)

Yellow tomatoes make a wonderfully golden jam. Select sound, slightly underripe tomatoes with a good yellow color. Soft, overripe fruit will make a watery preserve.

INGREDIENTS

2lb (1kg) yellow tomatoes
2 lemons, thinly sliced into semicircles
1 lemongrass stalk, finely chopped (optional)
⅓ cup (75ml) water
3 cups (750g) granulated sugar
1 cup (250g) light brown sugar

1 Place all the ingredients in a noncorrosive saucepan (there is no need to chop the tomatoes). Bring slowly to a boil, then simmer gently for 15 minutes.

2 Return to a boil and boil steadily for 25 minutes, or until the jelling point is reached (see page 76). Stir frequently to prevent the mixture from sticking to the bottom of the pan.

3 Ladle the preserve into the hot, sterilized jars, then seal.

☆ **Degree of difficulty**
Easy

Cooking time
About 1 hour

Special equipment
Sterilized canning jars and sealants (see pages 42–43)

Yield
About 3 pints (1.5kg)

Shelf life
2 years, heat processed

Orange Marmalade with Coriander

(see page 29 for illustration)

There are literally hundreds of recipes for orange marmalade. This one is unusual since it is flavored with coriander seed and orange liqueur. Although sweet oranges can be used, for best results try to obtain bitter Seville oranges. They have a very short season and are available only in midwinter.

INGREDIENTS

2lb (1kg) Seville oranges
2 lemons
8 cups (2 liters) water
6 cups (1.5kg) granulated sugar
3 tbsp coriander seed, crushed
⅓ cup (75ml) dry orange liqueur, such as Triple Sec

1 Cut the citrus fruit in half. Remove and reserve the seeds. Slice the oranges and lemons thin (see step 1, below). Tie the seeds in cheesecloth (see step 2, below). Place the fruit and cloth bag in a bowl with the water. Cover and let stand overnight (see step 3, below).

2 The next day, transfer the oranges and water to a saucepan. Bring to a boil, then reduce the heat and simmer for 45 minutes –1 hour, or until the orange rind is just soft and the mixture is reduced by about half.

3 Add the sugar to the pan. Slowly return to a boil, stirring until the sugar is dissolved. Skim well, then stir in the crushed coriander seed.

4 Boil the mixture rapidly for 10–15 minutes, or until the jelling point is reached (see page 76). Remove the pan from the heat and let the fruit settle for a few minutes. Add the liqueur and stir in thoroughly. Ladle the marmalade into the hot, sterilized jars, then seal.

☆ **Degree of difficulty**
Easy

Cooking time
1–1½ hours

Special equipment
Sterilized canning jars and sealants (see pages 42–43)

Yield
About 4 pints (2kg)

Shelf life
2 years, heat processed

Serving suggestion
Serve on toast for breakfast

PREPARING THE FRUIT

1 Scrub the oranges and lemons well to remove any wax coating. Halve them, reserving all the seeds, then slice crosswise into thin semicircles.

2 Place all the seeds in a small square of cheesecloth. Gather up the ends of the cloth and secure with string to form a small bag.

3 Place the fruit and cold water in a noncorrosive bowl. Weight down with a plate to keep the oranges submerged.

Pumpkin Marmalade

(see page 21 for illustration)

Autumn is pumpkin time, when they appear in the market in all sizes, shapes, and colors. Pumpkin is particularly good for making jams and marmalades as it absorbs sugar beautifully.

INGREDIENTS

3lb (1.5kg) pumpkin

4 cups (1 liter) water

2 oranges, sliced into thin semicircles

3 lemons, sliced into thin semicircles

3in piece (100g) fresh ginger, finely shredded

4 cups (1kg) granulated sugar

1 Peel the pumpkin and remove all the seeds and fibers. Slice the flesh into pieces and coarsely grate so the strands are as long as possible.

2 Place the grated pumpkin in a noncorrosive saucepan with the water, oranges, lemons, and ginger. Bring to a boil, then simmer for 25–30 minutes, or until the orange peel is just soft.

3 Add the sugar, stirring until it is dissolved. Return to a boil and cook over medium heat for 25–30 minutes, or until the mixture is thick enough for a wooden spoon drawn through the center to leave a clear channel.

4 Ladle the marmalade into the hot, sterilized jars, then seal. The marmalade is ready to eat immediately, but improves with age.

☆ **Degree of difficulty**
Easy

Cooking time
About 1¼ hours

Special equipment
Sterilized canning jars and sealants (see pages 42–43)

Yield
About 3½ pints (1.75kg)

Shelf life
2 years, heat processed

Serving suggestions
Serve for breakfast or use as a tart filling

Onion Marmalade

(see page 19 for illustration)

This unusual sweet preserve is exceptionally good and, remarkably, does not taste of onions. It has a sharp, refreshing flavor and a rich color. I sometimes add dried mint. Serve with lamb or game.

INGREDIENTS

2½lb (1.25kg) onions, sliced into thin rings

3 tbsp salt

4 cups (1kg) granulated sugar

2 cups (500ml) vinegar

1½ tsp cloves tied in a piece of cheesecloth

2 tsp caraway seed

1 Sprinkle the onions with the salt. Mix well and let stand for 1 hour. Rinse and dry.

2 Place the sugar, vinegar, and spice bag in a noncorrosive saucepan. Bring to a boil, then reduce the heat and simmer for about 5 minutes. Add the onions and caraway seed. Return to a boil, skim, reduce the heat to minimum and cook for 2–2½ hours, or until the syrup is thick and the onion is translucent and golden brown.

3 Ladle the mixture into the hot, sterilized jars, then seal. The marmalade is ready to eat immediately, but improves with age.

☆ **Degree of difficulty**
Easy

Cooking time
2¼–2¾ hours

Special equipment
Sterilized canning jars and sealants (see pages 42–43)

Yield
About 3 pints (1.5kg)

Shelf life
2 years, heat processed

Red Tomato Marmalade

(see page 15 for illustration)

Tomatoes make an extraordinarily tasty marmalade, with an elusive flavor that will intrigue and surprise you.

INGREDIENTS

2 lemons

2lb (1kg) firm, ripe tomatoes, peeled, seeded, and coarsely chopped

4 cups (1kg) granulated sugar

1½ tbsp coriander seed, coarsely crushed (optional)

1 Thinly peel the lemons and slice the rind into fine julienne strips. Squeeze out the juice.

2 Place the tomatoes in a noncorrosive saucepan with the sugar and lemon rind and juice. Bring slowly to a boil, then simmer for 5 minutes. Skim and add the coriander seed, if using.

3 Return the mixture to a boil and boil, stirring frequently, for 30 minutes, until the jelling point is reached (see page 76). Ladle into the jars, then seal.

☆ **Degree of difficulty**
Easy

Cooking time
About 50 minutes

Special equipment
Sterilized canning jars and sealants (see pages 42–43)

Yield
About 3 pints (1.5kg)

Shelf life
2 years, heat processed

Vanilla-flavored Peach Marmalade

Although this fragrant conserve is rather fussy to make, the results justify all the work. Select firm, unblemished, almost ripe peaches and handle them gently — they bruise easily.

INGREDIENTS

2½lb (1.25kg) firm, just ripe, white or yellow peaches

4 cups (1kg) granulated sugar

juice of 2 lemons

4 tbsp good-quality cognac

1–2 vanilla pods, cut into 3in (7cm) lengths

1 Peel the peaches by blanching in boiling water (see page 46). Halve them, remove the pits, and cut the flesh into thick slices.

2 Put the peach slices in a noncorrosive saucepan with the sugar and lemon juice. Cover the pan and let stand for 2–3 hours.

3 Bring the mixture to a boil, then reduce the heat and simmer gently for 20 minutes, or until the peaches are just soft.

4 Return to a boil and boil rapidly, stirring frequently, for 20–25 minutes, or until the jelling point is reached (see page 76). The peaches produce a soft-set marmalade.

5 Remove the pan from the heat, skim well, and let cool for about 10 minutes. Stir in the cognac.

6 Ladle the preserve into the hot, sterilized jars, inserting a piece of vanilla pod into each, then seal. The marmalade will be ready to eat in about 1 month, but improves with age.

— **TIP** —

• Skim the marmalade very well at all stages of cooking as peaches tend to produce a large amount of froth.

☆ **Degree of difficulty**
Easy

Cooking time
50 55 minutes

Special equipment
Sterilized canning jars and sealants (see pages 42–43)

Yield
About 2 pints (1kg)

Shelf life
1 year, heat processed

Serving suggestion
Heavenly with croissants for breakfast

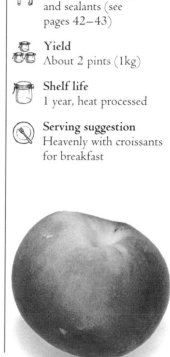

Old-fashioned Black Currant Jelly

Although it is fairly lengthy, this method produces an intensely flavored and very colorful jelly.

INGREDIENTS

2lb (1kg) black currants

granulated sugar

1 Place the black currants in the stone jar or casserole. Cover and bake in the oven at 275°F (140°C) for 1 hour, or until they are mushy and juicy. Alternatively, place the container in a pan of simmering water and simmer for 1 hour.

2 Pour the fruit and liquid into the sterilized jelly bag (see page 80). Leave to drain until it stops dripping.

3 Transfer the pulp from the jelly bag to a noncorrosive saucepan and add enough cold water to just cover it. Bring to a boil, then reduce the heat and simmer for 20 minutes. Drain through the jelly bag as before.

4 Combine the two batches of juice and measure it. Allow 2 cups (500g) sugar for every 2 cups (500ml) juice.

5 Return the fruit juice with the sugar to the cleaned saucepan. Heat slowly, stirring until the sugar is dissolved, then increase the heat and bring to a boil.

6 Skim well and boil rapidly for 10 minutes, or until the jelling point is reached (see page 76). Pour the liquid into the hot, sterilized jars, then seal.

☆☆ **Degree of difficulty**
Moderate

Cooking time
About 1¼ hours

Special equipment
Stone jar or casserole; sterilized jelly bag; sterilized canning jars and sealants (see pages 42–43)

Yield
About 3 pints (1.5kg)

Shelf life
2 years, heat processed

Serving suggestions
Fold into whipped cream to make a simple dessert, or use to glaze a leg of lamb before roasting

Raspberry Jelly

(see page 80 for technique)

This clear, red jelly has a geranium leaf in the center of each jar. The jelly is left to cool in the jar until semi-set, then a leaf is gently inserted into it. Be careful not to create any air bubbles.

INGREDIENTS

1lb (500g) cooking apples
2 pints (1kg) raspberries
2 cups (500ml) water
granulated sugar
juice of 1 lemon
scented geranium leaves (optional)
a little brandy, to seal

1 Remove the cores from the apples and set aside. Coarsely chop the apples, then place in the food processor with the raspberries and process until finely chopped.

2 Place the chopped fruit in a noncorrosive saucepan with the apple cores and water. Bring to a boil, then reduce the heat and simmer for 20–30 minutes, or until the fruit is soft and pulpy.

3 Pour the fruit and liquid into the sterilized jelly bag (see page 80). Leave to drain until it stops dripping. Measure the juice and allow 2 cups (500g) sugar for every 2 cups (500ml) juice.

4 Place the fruit juice, sugar, and lemon juice in the cleaned pan. Heat gently, stirring until the sugar is dissolved. Bring to a boil, then reduce the heat and skim well. Return to a rapid boil for 10 minutes, or until the jelling point is reached (see page 76).

5 Pour the liquid jelly into the hot, sterilized jars, then seal if not adding the geranium leaves.

6 To add the geranium leaves, allow the jelly to cool in the jars until semi-set. Gently insert a leaf into the center of each jar. Pierce any air pockets that form by prodding with a long, thin wooden skewer. Cover each jar with a waxed paper disk dipped in a little brandy, then seal.

☆☆ **Degree of difficulty**
Moderate

Cooking time
45–55 minutes

Special equipment
Food processor; sterilized jelly bag; sterilized canning jars and sealants (see pages 42–43)

Yield
About 4 pints (2kg)

Shelf life
2 years, heat processed

Serving suggestions
Good with cold lamb and chicken

VARIATION

◆ **Red Currant Jelly**
Replace the raspberries with red currants and omit the apples. Cook with 2½ cups (600ml) water, crushing the fruit against the pan. Complete following the main recipe. Omit the geranium leaves.

Hot Crab Apple Jelly

Crab apples make a firm jelly that can be flavored in many ways. Here, red chilies are used to give a piquant, sweet-hot jelly.

INGREDIENTS

2lb (1kg) crab apples, cut in half
4–5 fresh or dried red chilies, coarsely chopped, plus 1 fresh chili for each jar
granulated sugar
a little brandy, to seal

1 Place the crab apples and the chopped chilies in a noncorrosive saucepan and add cold water to cover. Bring to a boil, then simmer for 25 minutes, or until the fruit is pulpy.

2 Pour the fruit and liquid into the sterilized jelly bag (see page 80). Let drain for 2–3 hours, or until it stops dripping.

3 Measure the juice and allow 2 cups (500g) sugar for every 2 cups (500ml) juice. Place the juice and sugar in the cleaned pan. Bring slowly to a boil, stirring until the sugar is dissolved. Skim well, then boil for 15 minutes, or until the jelling point is reached (see page 76).

4 Remove the pan from the heat and let settle for a few minutes. Skim well. Pour the liquid jelly into the hot, sterilized jars.

5 Slit the chilies lengthwise and trim off the stems. When the jelly is semi-set, carefully insert a chili into each jar. Pierce any air pockets that form by prodding with a long, thin wooden skewer. Cover each jar with a waxed paper disk dipped in a little brandy, then seal.

☆☆ **Degree of difficulty**
Moderate

Cooking time
50–55 minutes

Special equipment
Sterilized jelly bag; sterilized canning jars and sealants (see pages 42–43)

Yield
About 2½ pints (1.25kg)

Shelf life
2 years, heat processed

Serving suggestions
Serve with meat, add to sandwiches, or stir a tablespoonful into game casseroles just before serving

Minted Apple Jelly

Apples are nature's gift to jelly-making, since they contain just the right balance of acidity and pectin for a good set. Pure apple jelly is rather insipid, so enliven the flavor with other ingredients such as fragrant tea leaves or herbs. Some of my favorites are mint, thyme, tarragon, and lavender flowers.

INGREDIENTS

small bunch of mint
a few strips of lemon rind
2lb (1kg) apples, coarsely chopped
7 cups (1.75 liters) water or hard cider
granulated sugar
juice of 1 lemon
3–4 tbsp finely chopped mint
a little brandy, to seal

1 Tie the mint and lemon rind together with string. Place in a noncorrosive saucepan with the apples and 5 cups (1.25 liters) of the water or cider.

2 Bring to a boil, then simmer, stirring occasionally, for about 25 minutes, or until the apples are very soft and pulpy. Pour into the sterilized jelly bag. Leave for 2–3 hours, until it stops dripping.

3 Remove the pulp from the jelly bag and return it to the cleaned pan. Add the remaining water or cider. Bring to a boil, then simmer for 20 minutes. Drain through the jelly bag as before.

4 Combine the two batches of juice and measure it. Allow 2 cups (500g) sugar for every 2 cups (500ml) juice. Pour the juice into the cleaned pan and add the lemon juice.

5 Bring to a boil and boil for 10 minutes. Add the sugar, stirring until it is dissolved, and boil rapidly for 8–10 minutes, or until the jelling point is reached (see page 76).

6 Remove the pan from the heat and allow to cool for about 10 minutes. Stir in the chopped mint, then pour into the hot, sterilized jars and let cool completely. Cover each jar with a waxed paper disk dipped in a little brandy, then seal.

☆ **Degree of difficulty**
Easy

Cooking time
About 1¼ hours

Special equipment
Sterilized jelly bag; sterilized canning jars and sealants (see pages 42–43)

Yield
About 2½ pints (1.25kg)

Shelf life
2 years, heat processed

Serving suggestion
Wonderful with lamb

TIP
• There is no need to core the apples if you chop them by hand; if you are using a food processor, remove the cores first as broken seeds can impart a bitter flavor to the jelly. Remember to put the cores in the pan with the apples, as they contain a large amount of pectin.

Red Plum Jelly

This jelly has an interesting hint of bitter almonds. Use a dark red variety of plums.

INGREDIENTS

2lb (1kg) red plums
15 bitter almonds, coarsely pounded, or 1 tsp bitter almond extract
granulated sugar
4 tbsp slivovitz (or other plum brandy)
a few blanched bitter almonds for each jar (optional)

1 Place the whole plums in a noncorrosive saucepan with the bitter almonds or almond extract and add enough cold water to just cover. Bring to a boil, then reduce the heat and simmer for 20–25 minutes, or until pulpy.

2 Pour the fruit and liquid into the sterilized jelly bag. Leave for 2–3 hours, until it stops dripping. Measure the juice and allow 2 cups (500g) sugar for every 2 cups (500ml) juice.

3 Place the juice and sugar in the cleaned pan. Bring to a boil, stirring until the sugar is dissolved. Boil for a few minutes, then reduce the heat and skim well. Boil rapidly for 10 minutes, or until the jelling point is reached (see page 76). Let cool for 5 minutes.

4 Skim well and stir in the slivovitz. Pour into the hot, sterilized jars, then seal if not adding the almonds.

5 If adding almonds, allow the jelly to semi-set, then place a few in each jar. Cover each jar with a waxed paper disk dipped in a little slivovitz, then seal.

☆ **Degree of difficulty**
Easy

Cooking time
40–50 minutes

Special equipment
Sterilized jelly bag; sterilized canning jars and sealants (see pages 42–43)

Yield
About 2½ pints (1.25kg)

Shelf life
2 years, heat processed

Serving suggestions
Serve with roast lamb, venison, or cold chicken

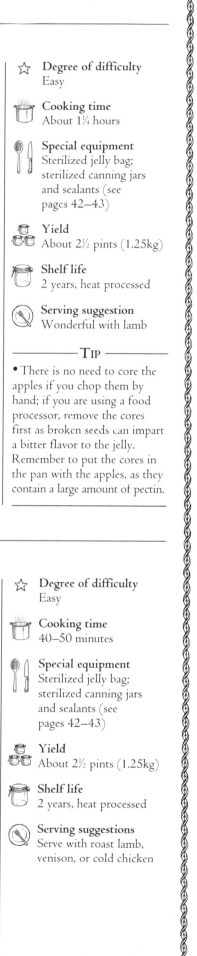

Pineapple and Orange Jelly

A clear, bright-yellow jelly with a hint of orange and a concentrated pineapple flavor. There is no need to peel and core the fruit for this recipe. If desired, you can add 1½ tablespoons of coriander seed to the jelly in step 1.

INGREDIENTS

1 small pineapple, about 1lb (500g), sliced
1lb (500g) apples, sliced
2 oranges, sliced
6 cups (1.5 liters) water
granulated sugar

1 Place all the ingredients, except the sugar, in a non-corrosive saucepan. Bring slowly to a boil, then reduce the heat and simmer for 30 minutes, or until the fruit is soft and pulpy.

2 Pour the fruit and liquid into the sterilized jelly bag (see page 80). Let drain for 2–3 hours, or until it stops dripping.

3 Remove the fruit pulp from the jelly bag, return it to the pan, and add enough cold water to cover. Bring to a boil, then simmer for 30 minutes.

4 Drain through the jelly bag as before. Combine the two batches of juice and measure it. Allow 2 cups (500g) sugar for every 2 cups (500ml) juice.

5 Place the juice and sugar in the cleaned pan. Bring slowly to a boil, stirring until the sugar is dissolved. Boil for a few minutes, then reduce the heat and skim well. Return to a boil, and boil rapidly for 10–12 minutes, or until the jelling point is reached (see page 76).

6 Remove the pan from the heat and let the jelly settle for a few minutes. Skim very well. Pour the liquid jelly into the hot, sterilized jars, then seal.

—— VARIATION ——

✦ *Quince Jelly*
Put 2lb (1kg) quinces and 5 cups (1.25 liters) water in a noncorrosive saucepan. Bring to a boil, then simmer gently for 1–1½ hours. Top off with boiling water if necessary to keep the fruit covered. Strain through the jelly bag and return the pulp to the pan as for the main recipe. In step 5 add the juice of 2 lemons to the quince juice and sugar. Boil rapidly for 1–2 minutes, skim well, then boil rapidly for 10–15 minutes, or until the jelling point is reached. Serve with game and other dark meat.

☆☆ **Degree of difficulty**
Moderate

Cooking time
About 1½ hours

Special equipment
Sterilized jelly bag; sterilized canning jars and sealants (see pages 42–43)

Yield
About 2½ pints (1.25kg)

Shelf life
2 years, heat processed

Serving suggestions
Use as a yellow glaze for cooked hams or fresh fruit tarts

Guava Jelly

Guavas are a subtropical fruit with a haunting, exotic perfume. They are delicious eaten raw and also make a very elegant rust-red jelly. Do not use white guavas as the color is too insipid.

—— TIP ——
• Do not worry if the jelly seems to be too soft. It will be firmer in a day or two.

INGREDIENTS

2lb (1kg) firm guavas, coarsely chopped
1 lime, coarsely chopped
granulated sugar

1 Place the chopped guavas and lime in a noncorrosive saucepan, and add enough cold water to cover. Bring slowly to a boil, then reduce the heat and simmer for about 30 minutes, or until the fruit is soft and pulpy.

2 Pour the fruit and liquid into the sterilized jelly bag (see page 80). Let drain until it stops

dripping. Measure the juice and allow 1½ cups (325g) sugar for every 2 cups (500ml) juice.

3 Place the fruit juice and sugar in the cleaned pan. Bring slowly to a boil, stirring until the sugar is dissolved, then reduce the heat and skim well.

4 Return to a boil and boil rapidly for 10–12 minutes, or until the jelling point is reached (see page 76).

5 Pour the liquid jelly into the hot, sterilized jars, then seal.

☆ **Degree of difficulty**
Easy

Cooking time
45–55 minutes

Special equipment
Sterilized jelly bag; sterilized canning jars and sealants (see pages 42–43)

Yield
About 2 pints (1kg)

Shelf life
2 years, heat processed

Serving suggestions
Spread on bread or serve with cold meat and cheese

Spicy Prickly Pear Jelly
(see page 35 for illustration)

The recipe for this soft-set jelly was given to me by Ya'akove Lishansky, who lives in Haifa, Israel. Now over 80 years old, he produces some of the most delicious preserves I have ever tasted. Prickly pears are available throughout the summer from many ethnic food shops and some large supermarkets. Purple ones are especially good in this recipe.

INGREDIENTS

2lb (1kg) purple, red, or orange prickly pears

2 medium cooking apples, chopped

3 cups (750ml) water

2 cups (500ml) cider vinegar or white wine vinegar

½ cup (125ml) lemon juice

granulated sugar

1 tbsp arrack, ouzo, or Pernod

For the spice bag (see page 47)

1 tsp allspice berries, lightly crushed

4–6 dried bird's eye chilies, including the seeds, crushed

3 dried bay leaves, crumbled

1 Using gloved hands, trim the prickly pears top and bottom with a sharp knife. Run the knife the length of the fruit, cutting through the thick skin, then remove it. Wash the fruit and place in a bowl. Crush to a pulp with a potato masher.

2 Place in a noncorrosive saucepan with the apples and water. Bring slowly to a boil, then simmer for 25 minutes, or until the fruit is soft and pulpy.

3 Pour the fruit and liquid into the sterilized jelly bag (see page 80). Let drain until it stops dripping. Add the vinegar and lemon juice to the prickly pear juice and measure the liquid. Allow 2 cups (500g) sugar for every 2 cups (500ml) liquid.

4 Place the liquid, sugar, and spice bag in the cleaned pan. Bring slowly to a boil, stirring until the sugar is dissolved. Boil for 25 minutes, or until the jelling point is reached (see page 76).

5 Remove the pan from the heat and discard the spice bag. Stir in the arrack, ouzo, or Pernod. Pour the liquid jelly into the hot, sterilized jars, then seal.

☆☆ **Degree of difficulty**
Moderate

Cooking time
About 1 hour

Special equipment
Sterilized jelly bag; sterilized canning jars with sealants (see pages 42–43)

Yield
About 3 pints (1.5kg)

Shelf life
2 years, heat processed

Serving suggestions
Delicious with cold meats or stirred into steamed vegetables

Rich Mincemeat

Mincemeat is one of the most glorious inventions of the British medieval kitchen. In the past, it contained fatty mutton, and suet is still considered indispensable for providing moisture and texture. I make my mincemeat once every two years and add grated chilled butter — about ¼ lb (125g) per 2lb (1kg) — just before use.

INGREDIENTS

2 medium cooking apples, coarsely grated

½ lb (200g) carrots, finely grated

¾ cup (125g) dried apricots, coarsely chopped

¾ cup (125g) prunes, coarsely chopped

¾ cup (125g) glacé cherries, coarsely chopped

¾ cup (125g) fresh ginger, finely grated

1½ cups (8oz) dark raisins

1½ cups (8oz) golden raisins

1½ cups (8oz) currants

1¼ cups (175g) mixed peel

grated rind and juice of 2 lemons

grated rind and juice of 2 oranges

½ cup (125g) honey or dark brown sugar

2–3 tbsp Sweet Masala (see page 117) or your favorite sweet spice mix

1 cup (250ml) brandy, plus extra for the jars

1 Place all the ingredients in a large bowl and mix very well. Cover with a clean cloth and let stand in a warm kitchen for 2–3 days.

2 Pack the mincemeat tightly into the hot, sterilized jars and cover with waxed paper disks. Pour 1–2 tablespoons of brandy into each jar, then seal and refrigerate.

3 Every 6 months or so, open the jars, pour a little brandy over the top, and reseal.

TIP
• If possible, use whole candied citrus peel rather than prechopped peel, and cut it yourself. Of course, you could always make your own candied peel (see page 181).

☆ **Degree of difficulty**
Easy

Special equipment
Sterilized canning jars and sealants (see pages 42–43)

Yield
About 5 pints (2.5kg)

Shelf life
2 years, heat processed

Serving suggestions
Use to make mince pies or tarts, or to fill baked apples; for sheer indulgence, serve topped with whipped cream

VARIATION
✦ *For a milder mincemeat, add a quarter of its weight of grated apples or quince, ground almonds, or a mixture of these before use.*

FRUIT BUTTERS, CURDS, & CHEESES

THESE ARE CLOSELY related to jams and jellies, where a fruit pulp is cooked, together with sugar, to a thick consistency. Cheeses are more solid and are usually molded and served in chunks. With butters, the concentration of sugar is lower, they are cooked for less time, and consequently are softer and have a shorter shelf life. Curds are softer still, and are made from fruit juice thickened with eggs and butter. Traditionally, fruit cheeses and butters were served as sweet spreads as well as an accompaniment to roasts and cold meats. All these products are essential for the pantry. They are delicious spread thickly on bread and butter, make instant fillings for cakes and tarts, or can be mixed with cream cheese, farmer cheese, or sour cream for quick and simple dessert toppings.

Orchard Fruit Butter

Apple

Pear

Peach

Hard cider

Light brown sugar

Allspice berries

Cloves

Cinnamon

This is a convenient way to preserve a glut of orchard fruit. You can try using different combinations, but it is important to remember that at least half the quantity of fruit should be apples. Any type will do, from sweet apples to windfalls. Orchard Fruit Butter is shown layered with Kiwi Fruit Butter and Mango Butter in the jar, opposite.

INGREDIENTS

2½ lb (1.25 kg) apples, chopped (no need to peel and core)
1¼ lb (625 g) pears, chopped (no need to peel and core)
1¼ lb (625 g) peaches, halved and pitted
4 cups (1 liter) hard cider or water
2 lb (1 kg) light brown or white sugar
1 tsp allspice berries
½ tsp cloves
2 tsp ground cinnamon

1 Put the chopped apples, pears, and peaches in a noncorrosive saucepan with the cider or water. Bring to a boil, then skim well, reduce the heat, and simmer for 1 hour, or until all the fruit is very soft and mushy.

2 Either press the fruit through a strainer or pass it through a food mill. Return the purée to the cleaned pan. Add the sugar, stirring until it is dissolved. Bring to a boil, then simmer, stirring frequently, for 1½–2 hours, or until the mixture is reduced and becomes very thick.

3 Grind the allspice and cloves in the spice mill or coffee grinder. Add to the pan with the cinnamon and continue to cook for a minute or two. Pour into the sterilized jars, then seal.

☆ **Degree of difficulty**
Easy

Cooking time
2¾–3¼ hours

Special equipment
Spice mill or coffee grinder; sterilized canning jars and sealants (see pages 42–43)

Yield
About 3 pints (1.5 kg)

Shelf life
2 years, heat processed

Serving suggestions
Use as a filling for cakes or tarts; serve with cold meats

MANGO BUTTER can be flavored with orange, vanilla, or cinnamon

ORCHARD FRUIT BUTTER is lightly spiced with a warming hint of allspice, cloves, and cinnamon

TIP

• To make this attractive layered preserve, place 1¼ cups (300g) Kiwi Fruit Butter (see page 172) in a small pan and heat gently until it comes to a boil. To prevent it from burning, add 1–2 tablespoons water. Pour into a warm, sterilized jar and let cool. Repeat with the Orchard Fruit Butter and the Mango Butter (see page 172 for recipe). Cover the surface with a waxed paper disk dipped in a little brandy, then seal and refrigerate or heat process.

ORCHARD FRUIT BUTTER makes an unusual filling for a jelly roll.

KIWI FRUIT BUTTER has a slightly sharp flavor

Mango Butter
(see page 34 for illustration)

Wonderfully golden and fragrant, this simple butter is an ideal way to use up very ripe mangoes. Try adding different flavorings, such as grated orange rind, vanilla, or cinnamon.

INGREDIENTS

4lb (2kg) ripe mangoes

1⅓ cups (300ml) hard cider or water

4½ cups (1kg) granulated sugar

grated rind and juice of 2 lemons

1 Prepare the mango flesh (see page 175).

2 Place the mango and cider or water in a noncorrosive saucepan. Bring to a boil, then simmer for 15–20 minutes, until the fruit is soft and pulpy. Either press the mixture through a sieve or pass through a food mill. Return the purée to the cleaned pan.

3 Add the sugar and lemon rind and juice, stirring until the sugar has dissolved. Bring to a boil, then simmer, stirring frequently, for 35–40 minutes, or until it is reduced and thickened. Pour into the warm, sterilized jars, then seal.

☆ **Degree of difficulty**
Easy

Cooking time
About 1 hour

Special equipment
Sterilized canning jars and sealants (see pages 42–43)

Yield
About 3 pints (1.5kg)

Shelf life
2 years, heat processed

Melon Butter
(see page 21 for illustration)

Melon makes a very pleasant butter with a subtle, fruity scent. Use fragrant varieties such as Ananas or Galia, or ripe cantaloupe for a beautiful deep-orange color.

INGREDIENTS

4lb (2kg) ripe melons, peeled, seeded, and chopped

2 cups (500ml) hard cider or water

4½ cups (1kg) granulated sugar

juice of 2 lemons

2 lemongrass stalks, finely chopped (optional)

1 tbsp orange-flower water

1 Put the melon in a noncorrosive saucepan with the cider or water. Bring to a boil, skim, then simmer for 40 minutes, until soft.

2 Either press the mixture through a sieve or pass it through a food mill. Return the purée to the cleaned pan.

3 Add the sugar, lemon juice, and lemongrass, if using. Bring to a boil, then simmer, stirring frequently, for 1 hour, or until reduced and thick.

4 Remove the pan from the heat and stir in the flower water. Pour into the warm, sterilized jars, then seal.

☆ **Degree of difficulty**
Easy

Cooking time
About 1¾ hours

Special equipment
Sterilized canning jars and sealants (see pages 42–43)

Yield
About 2 pints (1kg)

Shelf life
2 years, heat processed

Serving suggestion
Use as a filling for cakes

Kiwi Fruit Butter
(see page 34 for illustration)

Don't worry if this delightful butter doesn't thicken much in the pan; it will thicken considerably once it has cooled.

INGREDIENTS

2lb (1kg) ripe kiwi fruit, chopped (no need to peel)

3 cups (750ml) hard cider or water

juice and grated rind of 1 lemon

5 tbsp (75g) finely shredded fresh ginger

granulated sugar

1 tsp freshly ground black pepper (optional)

1 Place the kiwi fruit, cider or water, and lemon juice in a noncorrosive saucepan. Bring to a boil, reduce the heat and simmer for 15–20 minutes, until the fruit is soft and mushy.

2 Either press the mixture through a sieve or pass it through a food mill. Measure the purée and allow 1½ cups (400g) sugar for every 2 cups (500ml) purée. Return the purée to the cleaned pan.

3 Add the lemon rind, ginger, sugar, and pepper, if using, stirring until the sugar is dissolved. Bring to a boil, reduce the heat and simmer, stirring frequently, for 30–35 minutes, or until the mixture is the consistency of a soft-set jam. Pour into the warm, sterilized jars, then seal.

☆ **Degree of difficulty**
Easy

Cooking time
About 1 hour

Special equipment
Sterilized canning jars and sealants (see pages 42–43)

Yield
About 2 pints (1kg)

Shelf life
2 years, heat processed

Serving suggestions
Use as a filling for tarts or spread on bread

Passion Fruit Curd

The passion fruit seeds add a surprisingly crunchy texture to this curd, which for me is part of its attraction. However, if you prefer a smooth curd, use 2lb (1kg) of fruit and strain it before adding the eggs.

———— TIP ————
• Choose wrinkled passion fruit; they are riper and contain more juice.

INGREDIENTS
1½ lb (750g) passion fruit

juice of 1 lemon

1¼ cups (325g) granulated sugar

¾ cup (150g) butter, softened

4 eggs, beaten

1 Slice the passion fruit in half and scoop out the seeds and pulp; there should be about 2 cups (500ml).

2 Place in a small pan, add the lemon juice and sugar, and heat gently, stirring until the sugar is dissolved. Add the softened butter and stir until melted.

3 Transfer the mixture to the double boiler or a bowl placed over a pan of simmering water. Strain in the eggs and cook over barely simmering water, stirring frequently, for 25–40 minutes, until it is thick enough to coat the back of a spoon. Do not let the mixture boil or it will curdle.

4 Pour the curd into the warm, sterilized jars, then seal.

☆☆ **Degree of difficulty**
Moderate

Cooking time
30–45 minutes

Special equipment
Double boiler; sterilized canning jars and sealants (see pages 42–43)

Yield
About 2 pints (1kg)

Shelf life
3 months, refrigerated

Serving suggestion
Use to fill tarts

Lemon Curd
(see page 29 for illustration)

Lemon curd can be used to create a wide range of sweet delicacies, such as meringue pies, pavlovas, and trifles. This recipe uses less sugar than usual; if you prefer a sweeter curd, increase the quantity by up to a third.

INGREDIENTS
grated rind and juice of 6 lemons

1½ cups (375g) granulated sugar

¾ cup (150g) butter, softened

5 eggs, beaten

1 Place the lemon rind and juice in a small pan with the sugar. Heat gently, stirring until the sugar is dissolved. Add the butter and stir until melted.

2 Transfer the mixture to the double boiler or a bowl placed over a pan of simmering water. Strain in the eggs and cook over barely simmering water, stirring often, for 25–40 minutes, until it is thick enough to coat the back of a spoon. Do not let the mixture boil or it will curdle.

3 Pour the curd into the warm, sterilized jars, then seal.

☆☆ **Degree of difficulty**
Moderate

Cooking time
30–45 minutes

Special equipment
Double boiler; sterilized canning jars and sealants

Yield
About 1½ pints (750g)

Shelf life
3 months, refrigerated

Pink Grapefruit Curd
(see page 78 for technique)

A delicious, delightfully pink curd with an interesting texture. Try to find ruby red grapefruits, which have an intense color; the ordinary pink grapefruits make an anemically pale product. This curd takes time to thicken, so be patient — the results are well worth it.

INGREDIENTS
grated rind and juice of 1 ruby red or pink grapefruit

segmented flesh of 1 ruby red or pink grapefruit (see steps 2 and 3, page 78)

juice of 2 lemons

1½ cups (375g) granulated sugar

7 tbsp (100g) butter, softened

4 eggs and 2 egg yolks, beaten

3 tbsp orange-flower water

1 Place the grapefruit rind, juice, and flesh, the lemon juice, and sugar in a small pan. Heat gently, stirring until the sugar is dissolved. Add the softened butter and stir until melted.

2 Transfer the mixture to the double boiler or a bowl placed over a pan of simmering water. Strain in the eggs and cook over barely simmering water, stirring often, for 25–40 minutes, until the mixture coats the back of a spoon. Do not let it boil or it will curdle.

3 Remove from the heat and stir in the orange-flower water. Pour the curd into the warm, sterilized jars and seal.

☆☆ **Degree of difficulty**
Moderate

Cooking time
30–45 minutes

Special equipment
Double boiler; sterilized canning jars and sealants (see pages 42–43)

Yield
About 2 pints (1kg)

Shelf life
3 months, refrigerated

Serving suggestion
Use to fill pavlovas

Quince Cheese

(see page 82 for technique)

Quinces make the best cheese — translucent, dark amber, and beautifully fragrant. A Spanish specialty, Quince Cheese is traditionally eaten as a sweet snack.

INGREDIENTS

3lb (1.5kg) ripe quinces
about 8 cups (2 liters) water or hard cider
2–3 strips of lemon rind
juice of ½ lemon
granulated sugar
mild oil, such as almond or peanut, for brushing
superfine sugar for dusting

1 Wash the quinces well to remove any fluff, then chop coarsely. Place in a noncorrosive saucepan with enough water or cider to cover and add the lemon rind and juice. Bring to a boil, then simmer for 30–45 minutes, until the fruit is very soft.

2 Press the mixture through a sieve or pass it through a food mill. Measure the purée and allow 1½ cups (375g) sugar for every 2 cups (500ml) purée.

3 Return the purée to the cleaned pan and add the sugar.

Bring slowly to a boil, stirring until the sugar is dissolved. Reduce the heat and simmer, stirring frequently, for 2½–3 hours, until the mixture "plops" and is very thick. Remove from the heat and let cool slightly.

4 Brush a baking sheet or roasting pan with plenty of oil. Pour the cooled cheese onto the sheet and smooth to an even layer 1–1½ in (2.5–4cm) thick. Let cool completely, then cover loosely with a clean cloth and leave in a warm, dry place for 24 hours.

5 Loosen the cheese with a narrow spatula, then turn out onto waxed paper. Cut into squares or diamonds and dust with superfine sugar. Arrange on baking sheets and let dry, loosely covered with baking parchment.

6 To store, arrange the cheese in layers between sheets of waxed paper in an airtight container.

☆☆ **Degree of difficulty**
Moderate

Cooking time
3–3¾ hours

Special equipment
Airtight container

Yield
About 4½ lb (2.25kg)

Shelf life
2 years, refrigerated

Serving suggestion
Serve as a sweetmeat

Pear and Tomato Cheese

A curious combination of sweet and savory, this cheese is traditionally made for the Christmas table. Instead of pears, either apples or quinces can be used.

INGREDIENTS

2lb (1kg) plum tomatoes, coarsely chopped
1½lb (750g) ripe pears, cored and coarsely chopped
½lb (250g) apples, cored and coarsely chopped
1 lemon, coarsely chopped
2 cups (500ml) water
granulated sugar
1 tsp freshly ground black pepper
1 tsp ground coriander
½ tsp ground cinnamon
¼ tsp ground cloves

1 Place the tomatoes, pears, apples, lemon, and water in a noncorrosive saucepan. Bring to a boil, then reduce the heat and

simmer for about 30 minutes, until the fruit is soft and mushy.

2 Press the mixture through a sieve or pass it through a food mill. Measure the resulting purée and allow 1½ cups (400g) sugar for every 2 cups (500ml) purée.

3 Return the purée to the cleaned pan and add the sugar and spices. Bring to a boil, then simmer, stirring frequently, for 1–1½ hours, until it is reduced and becomes very thick.

4 Ladle into the sterilized jars, then seal, or pack into the oiled molds, let cool, then cover with plastic wrap.

☆ **Degree of difficulty**
Easy

Cooking time
2–2½ hours

Special equipment
Sterilized canning jars and sealants (see pages 42–43) or individual gelatin molds, oiled

Yield
About 2½ lb (1.25kg)

Shelf life
2 years, refrigerated in sealed jars

Serving suggestions
Good with cold roast meats, especially turkey, or spread on bread

Fruit Leathers

Sun-dried pulped fruit (leather) was probably the predecessor to jam-making. This convenient and delicious source of energy can be made from almost any ripe fruit: apricots, litchis, and peaches are very good, as are tomatoes.

TIP
• If the leather is too brittle, add more sugar the next time you make it.

INGREDIENTS
2lb (1kg) fully ripe fruit, e.g., mangoes, peeled, cored, and coarsely chopped

1 tbsp lemon juice

2–3 tbsp sugar, or more to taste

1 Purée the prepared fruit (see steps 1 and 2, below) in the food processor or food mill. Add the lemon juice and sugar, stirring until the sugar is dissolved.

2 Line a large, dampened baking sheet with plastic wrap or foil, allowing about 1in (2.5cm) to overhang the edge. Pour onto the sheet.

3 Spread the purée out (see step 3, below). Place in an oven preheated to 225°F (110°C) for 12–14 hours, leaving the oven door slightly ajar, or until it is dry but pliable (see step 4, below).

4 Let the leather cool, peel off the plastic wrap, then roll up in waxed paper. Store in an airtight container.

5 Alternatively, dry the fruit in the sun for 1–2 days, until it is dry to the touch and pulls easily away from the baking sheet. Invert the leather directly onto the sheet and dry for one more day.

☆ **Degree of difficulty**
Easy

Cooking time
12–14 hours in an oven; 2–3 days outdoors

Special equipment
Food processor

Yield
About 5oz (150g)

Shelf life
2 years, in an airtight container

Serving suggestion
Spread with cream cheese, roll up, and cut into slices

MANGO LEATHER

SPREAD THE PURÉE in an even layer about ¼in (5mm) thick by tilting the sheet. The purée should reach almost to the edge.

1 Cut the mango flesh from both sides of the large central pit and score into squares.

2 Turn the mango halves inside out and cut off the cubes of flesh. Purée the flesh.

3 Pour the purée into the center of the lined baking sheet. Tilt to spread it out in an even layer.

4 Dry the purée as directed. It should be dry yet pliable. Peel off the plastic wrap when cool.

FORM THE FRUIT LEATHER into a horn of plenty and fill with dried and candied fruit as a centerpiece for the dessert table.

PRESERVED FRUIT & FRUIT SYRUPS

STEEPING IN ALCOHOL is probably the easiest way to preserve different types of ripe fruit. The result is an appetizing concoction that yields the most delicious combination of intoxicating flavors. Candied and crystallized fruit add color, texture, and flavor to fruit cakes and make succulent treats, especially for Christmas. Fruit syrups can be diluted with water to make refreshing, thirst-quenching drinks or used "neat" to add sweetness to a wide variety of desserts.

Clementines in Brandy

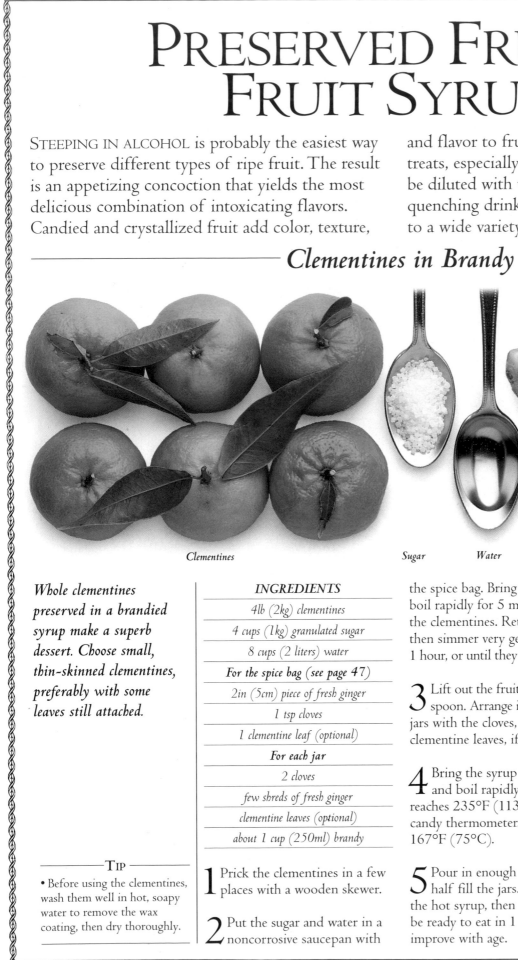

Clementines   Sugar   Water   Fresh ginger   Cloves   Brandy

Whole clementines preserved in a brandied syrup make a superb dessert. Choose small, thin-skinned clementines, preferably with some leaves still attached.

TIP
• Before using the clementines, wash them well in hot, soapy water to remove the wax coating, then dry thoroughly.

INGREDIENTS

4lb (2kg) clementines
4 cups (1kg) granulated sugar
8 cups (2 liters) water
For the spice bag (see page 47)
2in (5cm) piece of fresh ginger
1 tsp cloves
1 clementine leaf (optional)
For each jar
2 cloves
few shreds of fresh ginger
clementine leaves (optional)
about 1 cup (250ml) brandy

the spice bag. Bring to a boil and boil rapidly for 5 minutes. Add the clementines. Return to a boil, then simmer very gently for about 1 hour, or until they are soft.

3 Lift out the fruit with a slotted spoon. Arrange in the sterilized jars with the cloves, ginger, and clementine leaves, if using.

4 Bring the syrup to a boil and boil rapidly until it reaches 235°F (113°C) on the candy thermometer. Let cool to 167°F (75°C).

5 Pour in enough brandy to half fill the jars. Top off with the hot syrup, then seal. They will be ready to eat in 1 month, but improve with age.

1 Prick the clementines in a few places with a wooden skewer.

2 Put the sugar and water in a noncorrosive saucepan with

☆ **Degree of difficulty**
Easy

Cooking time
About 1¼ hours

Special equipment
Candy thermometer; Sterilized canning jars with sealants (see pages 42–43)

Yield
About 4lb (2kg)

Shelf life
2 years, refrigerated

Serving suggestion
Serve in the syrup with thick cream

VARIATIONS

✦ **Kumquats in Brandy**
*Use the same quantity of washed and pricked
kumquats and cook for about 25 minutes, or until
the fruit is just soft. Continue as for the main recipe.*
✦ *Other alcohol, such as vodka, rum, or eau de vie,
can be used instead of brandy.*

CLEMENTINES IN BRANDY
*make a delicious dessert, served in their
own syrup, for special and festive occasions.
Accompany with whipped cream for an
indulgent treat.*

A FEW FRESH
clementine leaves and
spices add decoration
as well as flavor

THE FRUIT
may have a
wrinkled appearance
once it has matured

Peaches in Brandy

(see page 84 for technique)

A perfect match of alcohol and fruit — sweet, succulent peaches with fragrant brandy. Although cheap cooking brandy will suffice, the better the brandy, the tastier the end product. Many other fruits, such as pitted apricots, whole plums, peeled and pitted nectarines, and peeled and cored pears, can be used.

INGREDIENTS

3lb (1.5kg) firm peaches
4 cups (1 liter) water
3lb (1.5kg) granulated sugar
1⅓ cups (300ml) good-quality brandy
½ cup (100g) glacé cherries, halved (optional)

For the spice bag (see page 47)

1 vanilla pod
small piece of cinnamon stick
3–4 cardamom pods
4 cloves

1 Blanch the peaches (see page 46), then cut them in half and remove the pits.

2 Put the water and 1lb (500g) of the sugar in a large pan. Bring to a boil, skim off any froth, then reduce the heat and simmer for 5 minutes to make a syrup.

3 Gently slide the peach halves into the syrup. Return to a boil, then simmer very gently for 4–5 minutes. Remove the peaches with a slotted spoon and let cool.

4 Place 2½ cups (600ml) of the syrup in a small pan with the remaining sugar and the spice bag. Bring to a boil, stirring until the sugar is dissolved. Skim, then boil rapidly until it reaches 219°F (104°C) on the candy thermometer. Cool slightly, then add the brandy.

5 Place a cherry half in the cavity of each peach, if desired, and secure with a toothpick. Pack the peaches loosely into the hot, sterilized jars.

6 Remove the spice bag from the pan and pour the syrup into the jars, making sure the peaches are completely covered. Shake the jars gently to be sure there are no air pockets, then seal. The peaches will be ready to eat in 2 weeks, but improve with age.

☆☆ Degree of difficulty
Moderate

Cooking time
About 15 minutes

Special equipment
Candy thermometer; sterilized, wide-mouth canning jars and sealants (see pages 42–43)

Yield
About 2lb (1kg)

Shelf life
2 years, refrigerated

Serving suggestions
Use to make a superb open tart, serve with cream or ice cream with plenty of the brandied juice

Rumtopf

This ingenious Christmas dish is made by layering fresh fruit with alcohol and sugar in an earthenware pot, topping it off with more fruit as different varieties come into season. In Germany, where this dish originated, special Rumtopf pots are available, but you could use a large earthenware casserole or a glass jar.

INGREDIENTS

selection of fresh ripe fruit (see tip, below)

For every 2lb (1kg) prepared fruit

1 cup (250g) granulated sugar
about 4 cups (1 liter) light rum

1 To prepare the fruit, remove any stems and bruised parts. Quarter large fruit, such as pears. Peaches should be blanched and peeled (see page 46).

2 Mix the prepared fruit with the sugar in a large bowl. Cover and let stand for about 30 minutes.

3 Spoon into the Rumtopf pot and pour over the rum. Cover with plastic wrap and the lid.

4 Every week or so, mix the contents by shaking the pot.

5 As more fruits come into season, prepare as above and add to the pot, together with the appropriate amount of sugar and rum. When the last fruit is added, it will be ready to eat in 3 months.

TIPS

• Any ripe, perfect juicy fruit can be used, such as strawberries and other berries, black, red, and white currants, peaches, pears, plums, and cherries.
• The amount of sugar called for makes a slightly tart rumtopf; for a sweeter version use up to 1½ cups (400g) sugar for every 2lb (1kg) fruit.
• If using a pot or jar, keep the Rumtopf in a dark place as light affects the color of the fruit.

☆ Degree of difficulty
Easy

Special equipment
Rumtopf pot or large jar or casserole with lid

Yield
As the size of pot or jar

Shelf life
2 years or longer, refrigerated

Serving suggestions
Serve as a topping on ice cream and other desserts, or eat the fruit with a spoon, washing it down with the liquor

Pears in Eau de Vie

(see page 31 for illustration)

In France pear buds are inserted into slim-necked bottles and allowed to grow in their individual greenhouse. The bottles are then filled with alcohol and left to mature. The result is a heady, flavored liqueur and a fragrant, alcoholic pear. This is my homage to that tradition.

INGREDIENTS

3–4 ripe pears

1¼–1½ cups (325–375g) granulated sugar

1 vanilla pod

about 4 cups (1 liter) eau de vie

1 Wash the pears, dry, and prick in a few places with a needle or a sharp wooden skewer.

2 Arrange the pears in the sterilized jars. Add the sugar and vanilla pod and pour in enough eau de vie to fill the jars.

3 Cover the jars tightly and leave in a cool, dark place for 3–4 months, gently shaking the jars from time to time to help dissolve the sugar.

TIPS

• Pear brandy or vodka can be substituted for eau de vie.

• For sweeter results, up to 2 cups (500g) sugar can be added.

☆ **Degree of difficulty**
Easy

Special equipment
Sterilized, wide-mouth canning jars and sealants (see pages 42–43)

Yield
About 2lb (1kg)

Shelf life
2 years, refrigerated

Serving suggestion
Serve as a dessert to cheer up a cold winter night

Pineapple in Kirsch

(see page 35 for illustration)

When this luscious fruit is stored in alcohol, its delicate fragrance is preserved — and so too is the enzyme it contains that aids digestion. Vodka, eau de vie, and white rum are also suitable. Serve with cream as the ultimate dessert.

INGREDIENTS

4–5 small pineapples, peeled, cored, and cut into rings ½ in (1cm) thick

3–4 cinnamon sticks

3–4 strips of orange peel

1¼–2 cups (325–500g) granulated sugar

5–6 bitter almonds, blanched (optional)

about 4 cups (1 liter) kirsch

1 Arrange the pineapple with the cinnamon and orange peel in the sterilized jars. Add the sugar and almonds, if using. I find that 1¼ cups (300g) sugar is sufficient, but if you prefer the pineapple to be sweeter, add the larger amount.

2 Pour enough kirsch into the jars to cover the pineapple, then seal. It will be ready to eat in 2–3 months. For the first few weeks, shake the jars every few days to help dissolve the sugar.

☆ **Degree of difficulty**
Easy

Special equipment
Sterilized, wide-mouth canning jars with sealants (see pages 42–43)

Yield
About 2lb (1kg)

Shelf life
2 years, refrigerated

Cassis

This traditional French black currant liqueur is extremely delicious and very easy to make.

TIPS

• Make sure the fruit is ripe and pick it over well, discarding any damaged or moldy berries.

• Do not throw away the pulp left in the jelly bag after straining the fruit. If you cook it with an equal quantity of sugar and a little water it makes a delightfully boozy jam.

• Other berries, such as strawberries, red currants, blueberries, and raspberries, can be treated in the same way.

INGREDIENTS

2lb (1kg) black currants, washed

2 cups (500ml) brandy

1½–2 cups (350–500g) granulated sugar

1 Place the black currants in the sterilized jar and crush them well with a potato masher.

2 Pour over the brandy, then cover the jar tightly. Leave in a cool, dark place for about 2 months, shaking the jar from time to time.

3 Pour the fruit and liquid into the sterilized jelly bag. Leave for a few hours, until it stops dripping. Squeeze the bag to extract as much liquid as possible. Filter the juice through a double layer of cheesecloth (see page 47), then return it to the jar.

4 Add the sugar to taste (I prefer the smaller amount), then seal. Leave in a cool, dark place for about 2 weeks, shaking the jar every few days until all the sugar is dissolved and the liquid is clear.

5 Filter the liquid again if necessary. Pour into sterilized bottles, then seal. The liqueur can be used immediately, but improves with age.

☆ **Degree of difficulty**
Easy

Special equipment
Sterilized, wide-mouth canning jar, jelly bag, bottles, and sealants (see pages 42–43)

Yield
About 4 cups (1 liter)

Shelf life
Keeps indefinitely; once opened, consume within 3 months

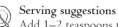 **Serving suggestions**
Add 1–2 teaspoons to a glass of dry white wine or Champagne to make Kir or Kir Royale; or pour over ice cream

Raspberry Syrup

Making syrup is a good way to use up soft fruits that are too ripe for jams or jellies. The hot method used here is easier than the cold method (*see Black Currant Syrup, opposite*), but does not produce the same intensity of flavor. Any ripe, juicy berries can be prepared in the same way, but discard any that are bruised or moldy.

INGREDIENTS

2 pints (1kg) raspberries
⅓ cup (75ml) water
granulated sugar

1 Put the raspberries and water in a bowl and mash well. Set over a pan of simmering water for 1 hour, mashing occasionally.

2 Pour into the jelly bag (see page 80). Leave for a few hours, until it stops dripping. Squeeze the bag to extract as much liquid as possible. Filter the juice through a double layer of cheesecloth (see page 47).

3 Measure the juice and allow 1½ cups (375g) sugar for every 2 cups (500ml) juice.

4 Place in a saucepan and bring slowly to a boil, stirring until the sugar is dissolved. Skim off all the froth and boil for 4–5 minutes. Do not overcook or it will start to jell. Pour into the bottles, then seal.

☆ **Degree of difficulty**
Easy

Cooking time
About 1¼ hours

Special equipment
Sterilized jelly bag and cheesecloth; sterilized bottles (see pages 42–43)

Yield
About 3 cups (750ml)

Shelf life
2 years, heat processed

Cassis

Black Currant Syrup

Pomegranate Syrup

Raspberry Syrup

Serving suggestions
Dilute with water to make a drink; pour over desserts and ice cream. The syrup makes a pleasant treat when frozen

Pomegranate Syrup

(see page 35 for illustration)

A wonderful ruby-red syrup. Sour pomegranates are preferable (available from Indian or Middle Eastern grocers), but if sweet ones are all you can find, add the juice of 3 lemons or 1 teaspoon of citric acid.

INGREDIENTS

4lb (2kg) very red pomegranates

1½ cups (375g) granulated sugar

1 tsp orange-flower water (optional)

1 Cut the pomegranates in half and use a lemon squeezer to extract all the juice; you should end up with about 2 cups (500ml) juice.

2 Filter the juice through a double layer of cheesecloth (see page 47) into a pan. Add the sugar and bring slowly to a boil, stirring until the sugar is dissolved.

3 Boil for 10 minutes, then skim and stir in the orange-flower water, if using. Pour into the hot, sterilized bottles, filling them to 2in (5cm) from the top, then seal.

☆ **Degree of difficulty**
Easy

Cooking time
About 15 minutes

Special equipment
Sterilized bottles and sealants (see pages 42–43)

Yield
About 2 cups (500ml)

Shelf life
2 years, heat processed

Black Currant Syrup

Black currants make the best syrup — perfumed and refreshing. This recipe extracts the juice when cold, which produces a very fresh flavor. The slight fermentation period before draining the fruit is necessary to destroy as much of the pectin as possible; otherwise, the syrup will start to set.

INGREDIENTS

2lb (1kg) ripe black currants

granulated sugar

1 Put the black currants in the food processor and blend to a purée. Transfer to a bowl, cover with a clean cloth, and let stand for 24 hours.

2 Pour the fruit purée into the sterilized jelly bag (see page 80), let stand for a few hours, or until it stops dripping. Squeeze

the bag to extract as much liquid as possible. Filter the juice through a double layer of sterilized cheesecloth (see page 47).

3 Measure the juice and add 1½ cups (400g) sugar for every 2 cups (500ml) juice. Stir well until the sugar is dissolved.

4 Pour the syrup into the sterilized bottles, filling them to within 2in (5cm) of the top. Heat-process, let cool, and check the seals (see pages 44–45).

☆ **Degree of difficulty**
Easy

Cooking time
About 20 minutes

Special equipment
Food processor; sterilized jelly bag and cheesecloth; sterilized bottles and sealants (see pages 42–43)

Yield
About 3 cups (750ml)

Shelf life
2 years, heat processed

Candied Citrus Peel

This recipe is a wonderful way to use citrus peel. Traditionally, some of the outer skin was removed to make the peel less bitter, but I find it unnecessary. Any thick-skinned citrus fruit can be used, such as orange, grapefruit, citron, and pomelo. The last two are especially good.

INGREDIENTS

2lb (1kg) citrus peel, cut into 2in (5cm) strips

4 cups (1kg) granulated sugar

1½ cups (350ml) water

1 Put the peel in a noncorrosive saucepan with enough water to cover. Bring to a boil, then simmer for 10 minutes. Drain, discard the cooking liquid, and cover with fresh water. Bring back to a boil, then simmer for 20 minutes and drain again.

2 Place the cooked peel in a large bowl, cover with cold water, and let stand for 24 hours.

3 Drain well. Place the sugar and water in a pan. Bring to a boil, stirring until the sugar is dissolved. Add the peel, reduce the heat, and simmer over very low heat for 2–3 hours, or until the peel is translucent and most of the syrup absorbed. Stir frequently to prevent sticking.

4 To preserve the peel in syrup, spoon the mixture into the jars, then seal. Alternatively, lift the peel out of the syrup, arrange on wire racks and dry in the oven (see Candied Pineapple, page 182). Dust with superfine sugar and store in an airtight container, between layers of waxed paper.

☆ **Degree of difficulty**
Easy

Cooking time
2¾–3¾ hours

Special equipment
Sterilized jars or airtight container (see pages 42–43)

Yield
About 3lb (1.5kg)

Shelf life
2 years in syrup; 1 year with a crystallized finish

Serving suggestions
Cover with chocolate, use for decoration or add to fruit cakes

Candied Pineapple Rings

(see page 86 for technique)

Technically, candying is an easy process, but it takes a long time to complete. The results, however, are really worth the trouble – sweet fruits that last for a long time. Select slightly under-ripe, unblemished fruits that will withstand the long preparation. Apricots, figs, cherries, kiwi fruit, plums, peaches, kumquats, clementines, pears, and angelica also candy well.

INGREDIENTS

1 large pineapple, peeled, cut into slices ⅝ in (1.5cm) thick, and cored

4 cups (1kg) granulated sugar

juice of 1 lemon

superfine sugar for dusting

1 Place the pineapple in a pan with enough water to cover. Bring to a boil, reduce the heat, and simmer for 15–20 minutes, or until the pineapple is starting to soften. Lift the rings out, drain well, and place in a glass bowl.

2 Measure 4 cups (1 liter) of the cooking liquid. Strain it through a cheesecloth-lined sieve into a noncorrosive saucepan. Add 1 cup (250g) of the sugar and the lemon juice. Bring to a boil, stirring until the sugar is dissolved. Skim and boil rapidly for 2–3 minutes.

3 Pour the sugar syrup over the pineapple and weight down with a plate (see page 46). Leave for 24 hours at room temperature.

4 Drain the pineapple rings. Return the syrup to the pan and add ½ cup (100g) of the sugar. Bring to a boil, stirring until the sugar is dissolved, and boil for 1–2 minutes. Skim well and pour back over the pineapple. Weight down and let stand for 24 hours.

5 Repeat step 4.

6 Drain the rings. Return the syrup to the pan and add ½ cup (150g) of the sugar. Bring to a boil, stirring until the sugar has dissolved. Boil for 1–2 minutes, skim well, and pour back over the pineapple. Weight down and let stand for 24 hours.

7 Repeat step 6.

8 Drain the pineapple. Return the syrup to the pan and add the remaining sugar. Bring to a boil, stirring until the sugar is dissolved. Boil for 1–2 minutes, skim well, and pour over the rings. Weight down and let stand for 48 hours.

9 Place the fruit and syrup in the noncorrosive saucepan. Simmer for about 5 minutes, then remove from the heat. Lift out the pineapple rings with a slotted spoon and arrange on a wire rack placed over a foil-lined baking sheet. Let drain and cool.

10 Place the rack and sheet in an oven preheated to 250°F (120°C), leaving the door slightly ajar. Dry for 12–24 hours, or until the pineapple rings are dry but just sticky to the touch.

11 Remove the pineapple rings from the oven and let cool completely. Dust with superfine sugar. Store between sheets of waxed paper in an airtight container. Instead of dusting the pineapple rings with the sugar, you could preserve them in their syrup (see Candied Apricots, step 8, opposite).

☆ **Degree of difficulty**
☆☆ Advanced

Cooking time
Day 1, about 30 minutes; Days 2–6, 5 minutes each day; Day 8, 5 minutes plus 12–24 hours drying

Yield
About 2lb (1kg)

Shelf life
3 months with crystallized finish; 2 years in syrup

Serving suggestions
Dice and fold into cakes and ice cream; coat in chocolate and serve as candy

Candied Apricots

This a simplified method for candying. The fruit does not keep so well, lasting for only a few months. To prevent deterioration, keep it in the heavy syrup or crystallize just before use. The fruit should be slightly underripe with a good color. Keep soft fruits, such as apricots, whole, to maintain their shape. Firmer fruits, like pears or peaches, can be halved and pitted.

TIP

• To hasten the sugar absorption process, first steep the pricked fruit in a strong salt solution (¼ cup/75g salt per 2 cups/ 500ml water) for 24–48 hours.

INGREDIENTS

2lb (1kg) apricots
6 cups (1.5kg) granulated sugar
1 cup (250ml) water
juice of 1 lemon or 1 tsp citric acid

1 Prick each apricot a few times with a toothpick.

2 Place 4 cups (1kg) of the sugar in a noncorrosive saucepan with the water and lemon juice or citric acid. Bring to a boil, stirring until the sugar has dissolved, then skim well and boil until it reaches 230°F (110°C) on the candy thermometer.

3 Slide the apricots into the pan and simmer for 3 minutes. Remove with a slotted spoon and place in a large glass bowl. Return the syrup to a boil and boil for 5 minutes. Pour over the apricots, weight down with a plate (see page 46) and leave for 24 hours.

4 Drain the apricots. Return the syrup to the pan, adding 1 cup (250g) of the sugar. Bring slowly to a boil, stirring until the sugar has dissolved. Skim well and boil for about 5 minutes.

5 Add the apricots to the pan. Return to a boil, then reduce the heat and simmer over very low heat for about 5 minutes. Remove the apricots with a slotted spoon and place in the bowl. Return the syrup to a boil and boil for 5 minutes. Pour over the apricots, weight down, and let stand for 24 hours.

6 Drain the apricots. Return the syrup to the pan and add the rest of the sugar. Bring to a boil, stirring until it has dissolved. Skim, then boil for 2–3 minutes.

7 Add the apricots to the pan. Return to a boil, then reduce the heat to minimum and simmer very gently (the syrup should only bubble occasionally) for 3–4 hours, or until the fruit looks clear and candied.

8 Arrange the fruit in the hot sterilized jars, top off with the hot syrup, then seal. Alternatively, lift the fruit out of the syrup onto wire racks. Leave for 24 hours, or until dry to the touch. Sprinkle with superfine sugar, then dry in the oven for 12–24 hours (see Candied Pineapple, opposite).

☆ **Degree of difficulty**
☆☆ Advanced

Cooking time
Day 1, about 10 minutes;
Day 2, about 5 minutes;
Day 3, about 15 minutes;
Day 4, 3¼–4¼ hours

Special equipment
Candy thermometer;
sterilized, wide-mouth canning jars and sealants or airtight container

Yield
About 3lb (1.5kg)

Shelf life
2 years in syrup;
3–4 months with a crystallized finish

Serving suggestions
Use to decorate cakes, cookies, and desserts; or serve as a candy

Crystallized Flowers

(see page 87 for technique)

The most suitable flowers for crystallizing are strongly perfumed roses, violets, pansies, orange blossom, and the blossom orchard fruits such as apples and pears. Edible leaves can also be crystallized in the same way. Vary the quantities of egg white and sugar to match the number of flowers used.

INGREDIENTS

1 egg white, to coat
pinch of salt
a few drops of rose- or orange-flower water
perfect flowers (see left)
superfine sugar

1 Beat the egg white with the salt and rose- or orange-flower water until frothy. Let stand for a few minutes.

2 With a small, soft brush, paint the flower petals evenly

inside and out with the egg white. Generously sprinkle them with sugar, making sure that all surfaces are evenly covered.

3 Fill a baking sheet with a layer of sugar about ½ in (1cm) deep. Gently lay the sugared flowers on top and generously sprinkle with more sugar. Let dry in a warm, well-ventilated place for 1–2 days, or until the flowers are hard and dry to the touch. Store in an airtight container between layers of waxed paper.

☆ **Degree of difficulty**
Easy

Special equipment
Artist's small paint brush; airtight container

Shelf life
3 months

Serving suggestion
Use to decorate cakes and desserts

PRESERVING & DRYING GUIDE

MAKE THE MOST of seasonal fresh produce by referring to the chart below to find out which methods of preserving are best suited to individual fruit and vegetables. The chart also indicates the pectin content and acidity levels of fruit used to make jams, jellies, and other sweet preserves, as these factors directly affect the jelling ability of the finished product. If there is too little pectin and acid, a jell will not be achieved without the addition of commercially prepared pectin or a homemade pectin stock (see page 47 for recipe). Alternatively, you can mix pectin-rich fruit with fruit that has a low concentration, and then test the pectin level (see page 47) to ensure that it is high enough to achieve a jell.

OVEN-DRYING FRUIT AND HERBS

To dry fruit and herbs, preheat an oven to 225°F (110°C). Select unblemished fruit or herbs and prepare as described in the chart, right. Most fruit are dipped in acidulated or sweetened water (see page 61 for recipe) to help retain their color and prevent them from browning. Place on wire racks and dry for the time specified.

Preserving Fruit and Vegetables

KEY
H . . . . *High content*
M . . . . . . *Medium content*
L . . . . *Low content*
X . . . . . *Recipe given in book*
X* . *No recipe given, but can be preserved by this method*

	Apples	Apricots	Artichokes (Globe)	Beans	Beets	Blackberries	Black Currants	Blueberries	Cabbages	Carrots	Cauliflower	Celeriac	Celery	Cherries	Chilies	Clementines/Mandarins	Corn	Crab Apples	Cranberries	Cucumbers/Gherkins	Damsons	Eggplants	Figs	Garlic	Gooseberries	Grapefruit	Grapes	Greengages	Guavas
Pectin content	H	M	–	–	–	M	H	M	–	–	–	–	–	L	–	H	–	H	H	–	H	–	L	–	H	H	M	H	H
Acidity level	M	M	–	–	–	M	H	M	–	–	–	–	–	M	–	H	–	M	M	–	H	–	L	–	H	H	M	M	M
Pickling and spicing	X*	X*	X*	X	X	X*	–	X*	X	X	X	X	X	X*	X	X*	X	X*	X*	X	X*	X	X*	X	X	–	X	X*	–
Jams/jellies/marmalades	X	X	–	–	X*	X	X	X	–	X	–	–	–	X	X*	X*	–	X	X*	–	X*	X	X	X*	X*	X*	X	X	X
Curds/butters/cheeses	X	X*	–	–	–	X*	X*	X*	–	–	–	–	–	X*	–	–	–	–	X*	–	X*	–	X*	–	X*	X	–	X*	X*
Chutneys/relishes/sauces	X	X*	–	X*	–	X*	X*	–	X	X	X*	–	X*	X*	X	–	X	X*	X	X	X	X	X	X	X	X*	–	X*	–
Preserving in oil	–	–	X	X*	–	–	–	–	–	–	–	–	–	–	X	–	–	–	–	–	–	X	–	X*	–	–	–	–	–
Syrups/alcohol/vinegar	–	X*	–	–	–	X	X	X	–	–	–	–	X*	X*	X*	X	–	–	X*	X*	X*	–	X*	X	X	X*	X	X*	–

Oven-drying Fruit and Herbs

	PREPARATION	DIP	DRYING TIME
APPLES	Peeled, if desired, cut into ¼ in (5mm) rings	Acidulated water	6–8 hours, until no trace of moisture when cut
APRICOTS	Halved and pitted	Acidulated water	36–48 hours, until dry and leathery
BANANAS	Peeled and halved lengthwise	Acidulated water	10–16 hours
BERRIES	Left whole	Dip in boiling water for a few seconds	12–18 hours
CHERRIES	Pitted, if desired	Dip in boiling water for a few seconds	18–24 hours
CITRUS PEEL	Cut into long strips, all white pith removed	–	10–12 hours
HERBS	Tied in bunches or laid on racks	–	12–16 hours in the oven; 2–3 days in the sun
PEACHES	Peeled, halved, pitted; sliced, if desired	Acidulated water	Halved: 36–48 hours; sliced: 12–16 hours
PEARS	Peeled, if pitted, halved, and cored	Acidulated water	36–48 hours
PINEAPPLE	Peeled, if desired, cored, and sliced into ¼ in (5mm) rings	Honey	36–48 hours
PLUMS	Whole or halved and pitted	Dip in boiling water for a few seconds or prick all over	Whole: 36–48 hours; halved: 18–24 hours
STRAWBERRIES	Halved	Honey	12–18 hours, until dry and brittle

Jerusalem Artichokes	Kiwi Fruit	Kohlrabi	Kumquats	Lemons	Limes	Litchis	Mangoes	Melon	Mushrooms	Okra	Onions	Oranges	Parsnips	Passion Fruit	Peaches	Pears	Peppers	Pineapples	Plums	Pomegranates	Pomelos	Prickly Pears	Quinces	Radishes	Raspberries	Red Currants	Shallots	Strawberries	Summer Squash	Tomatoes	Turnips	White Currants	Winter Squash & Pumpkins	Zucchini
–	L	–	H	H	H	L	L	L	–	–	–	H	–	L	L	L	–	L	H	L	H	M	H	–	M	H	–	L	–	M	–	H	–	–
–	L	–	H	H	H	L	L	L	–	–	–	H	–	L/M	L	L	–	L	H	M/H	H	L	M	–	M	H	–	L	–	L/M	–	H	–	–
X*	X	X*	X*	X	X	–	–	X	X*	X	X	X	X*	–	X*	X	X	X*	X	–	–	–	X*	X*	–	–	X	–	X*	X	X	–	X*	X
–	X*	X*	X*	X*	X*	X	X*	X	–	–	X	X	X*	X*	X	X*	–	X	X	–	X*	X	X	–	X	X	X	X	X	X	X*	X	–	–
–	X	–	–	X	X*	X*	X	X	–	–	–	X*	–	X	X	X	–	X*	X*	–	X*	X*	X	–	X*	X*	–	X*	–	X	–	X*	X*	–
–	–	–	X	X*	X*	–	X	–	X	–	X	X	–	–	X	–	X	X	X	–	–	–	X	–	–	–	–	–	–	X	X	–	X	X*
–	–	–	–	X*	X*	–	–	–	X	–	–	–	–	–	–	–	–	X	–	–	–	–	–	–	–	–	–	–	–	X	–	–	–	–
–	–	–	X	X*	–	–	X*	–	–	X*	X	X	–	X*	X	X	–	X	X*	X	–	X*	X	–	X	X	X*	X	–	–	–	X*	–	–

TROUBLE-FREE PRESERVING

BECAUSE SO MANY FACTORS affect the preserving process, it is possible that the end product may not look, smell, or taste the way you expected. If this is so, you need to know what went wrong and, more importantly, whether the food is safe to eat. The most common problems that are encountered during preserving are listed below.

Pickles

The pickles are not crunchy.
• The vegetables were not salted for long enough beforehand.
• The vinegar or salt solution was not strong enough.

The pickles are hollow.
• The raw cucumbers were too mature or kept for too long before use.

The pickles are dark.
• Iodized (table) salt was used.
• Too many spices were added.
• Iron or copper utensils were used.
• A dark vinegar was added.
• The brine was made with hard water – try filtered or bottled water.

The pickles look pale or bleached.
• The jar was exposed to light during storage.

The pickles are soft and slimy.
• The salt or vinegar solution was not strong enough.
• The jar had a poor seal.
Discard the product immediately.

Garlic looks green.
• Fresh garlic may turn a harmless but unappetizing shade of green when steeped in vinegar; blanch in boiling water before using.

Jams & Sweet Preserves

The jam or jelly is not setting.
• There is too little pectin. Add pectin stock or commercial pectin and reboil until the setting point is reached (see page 47). Note: frozen fruit contains less pectin than fresh fruit.

• There was an incorrect balance between pectin and acid. Add lemon juice and reboil (see page 47).

The fruit looks too dark.
• The preserve was cooked for too long and the sugar started to caramelize. (The traditional advice is to warm the sugar before adding it to shorten the cooking time, but this makes little difference.)

Fruit has risen to the top of jam.
• The jam was not allowed to settle. Let stand until cold, fold in the fruit evenly, then ladle into sterilized jars and seal.
• The syrup is too thin. Drain it off and return to the pan with more sugar. Boil rapidly until the setting point is reached (see page 47).

The jam has crystallized.
• Too much sugar was added.
• The storage temperature was too cold. This is harmless and does not affect the flavor of the product.

Sweet & Savory Preserves

There is mold on the surface.
• A result of a fungus contamination. *Discard the product. Molds send out a network of invisible threads and produce spores that may be harmful.*

The preserve has fermented.
• If a sweet preserve ferments, too little sugar was added.
• For a pickle or chutney, the brine or vinegar solution was too weak.
• Storage conditions were too warm.
• Equipment or containers were not sterilized thoroughly.
• Cooking time was too short.

Discard the product immediately; this fermentation may produce harmful toxins. Note: Some pickles are fermented as part of a recipe.

Unpleasant odors have developed.
• *Any product that develops an off smell should be discarded immediately.*

Salami & Cured Meat

There is a white powdery mold on salamis or cured meat.
• This naturally occurring mold is encouraged by the right storage conditions. It is harmless and adds to the flavor of the product.

There is green or black mold on salamis or cured meat.
• The salt solution was too weak.
• The meat was not cured properly.
• The storage atmosphere was too damp and warm.
Discard the product immediately.

White salt burns appear on drying cured meat.
• The salt solution was too strong.

The dried cured meat has a powdery texture.
• Too much vinegar in the cure.

The curing liquid turns syrupy.
• Not enough salt was added.
• The temperature during storage was too high.
Discard the curing liquid and make up a new batch. Resterilize the container. Wash the meat well with cold running water, then rub all over with some vinegar. Dry the meat thoroughly with paper towels and immerse in the new cure.

INDEX

ACKNOWLEDGMENTS

Author's Appreciation
This book is the fulfilment of a life-long obsession with preserving, and would not have been possible without the help of hundreds of passionate picklers, recipe writers, recorders, housewives, grocers, farmers and taxi drivers, who shared with me their culinary secrets. Without good-quality raw ingredients pickling is impossible, and I would like to thank my local suppliers, especially Graham and David at Graham Butchers, Pedro at Pedro Fisheries, Green Health Food Store (Finchley), and Gary at Ellinghams, for their help and advice.

As always I would also like to thank Saul Radomsky for his patience and support, and the many friends who have helped, schlepped, tasted and commented: Trudy Barnham, Jon, Ann and Marjorie Bryent, the Blacher family, Iris and John Cole, the Hersch family, Jill Jago, Dalia Lamdani, Joy Peacock, Bob and Ann Tilley, Eric Treuille, Jo Wightman; and a special thanks to Rosie Kindersley who made this book possible.

Finally, many thanks to my assistant Alison Austin; photographer Ian O'Leary and his assistant Emma Brogi; Jane Bull, Jane Middleton, Kate Scott, and all at Dorling Kindersley, whose enthusiasm, help and expert eye made the writing of this book such a happy experience.

Dorling Kindersley would like to thank Carole Ash for initial design work; Lorna Damms and Anna McMurray for editorial work; Paul Wood and Harvey de Roemer for DTP design; Cynthia Hole for picture research; Tables Laid for props; Tate and Lyle for the supply of preserving sugar; Graham Brown at Meridian Foods for the supply of fruit concentrate; Cecil Gysin at the Natural Casing Co. Ltd for the supply of sausage casings.

Special thanks to Ian Taylor at Taylor Foodservice for the supply of a smoker; Barry Chevalier from Aspall Cyder for the supply of cider vinegar; and Maureen Smith at SIS Marketing Ltd for the supply of a food dehydrator.

Picture Credits: key to pictures: t= top; b= bottom
Ann Ronan, Image Select 9t; E.T. Archive 9b, 10t; Corbis-Bettmann 11t

OTHER RESOURCES

There are many variables in preserving, and it is always wise to consult a local expert before you start any new project; our explanations of techniques are intended only as general guidelines.

Your best resource on preserving information is the cooperative extension agent in your county. The United States Department of Agriculture's Cooperative Extension Service is the governing body for these invaluable authorities. You can find your agent by looking in the Blue Pages of your phone book, often under county government listings. Every state has a land-grant college, and these colleges run the extension services, so check under state college listings as well.

Your extension agent will be able to give you the most up-to-date information on canning and other forms of preserving.

The US Government Printing Office is a source of valuable publications. Ask at your library for the Consumer Information Catalog from the Consumer Information Center, Department EE, Pueblo, Colorado 81009.

Useful books include *Putting Food By*, written by Janet Greene, Ruth Hertzberg, and Beatrice Vaughan, published by Plume Books; *Keeping the Harvest*, by Nancy Chioffi and Gretchen Mead, published by Storey Publishing, Pownal, Vermont (800-441-5700); and *Ball Blue Book: The Guide to Home Canning and Freezing*, which is sold wherever Ball Jars are sold. *The Kerr Canning Cookbook* is also a reliable guide. (Or, for information on Ball and Kerr products, write to Alltrista Consumer Products, Consumer Affairs, 345 South High St., Muncie, Indiana 47305-2326; phone 800-240-3340.) Morton Salt offers *A Complete Guide to Home Meat Curing* (Order from Cumberland General Store, One Highway 68, Crossville, Tennessee 38555; phone 800-334-4640; the store also offers pickling salt and other Morton products). Many other makers of canning and preserving equipment also produce useful guides on home preserving.